ESSAYS ON POLITICAL EDUCATION

ESSAYS ON POLITICAL EDUCATION

**Bernard Crick
and Derek Heater**

 The Falmer Press

First published 1977

ISBN 0 905273 03 6 paper

ISBN 0 815273 04 4 cased

Printed by Billing & Sons Limited
Guildford, Surrey
for
THE FALMER PRESS
Broome House
26 Delves Close
Ringmer
BN8 5JW

Made in England

Contents

Preface

Concern for the frail condition of political education in Great Britain drew us together in the late 1960s to try to stimulate an urgent sense of responsibility among those professionally involved in this neglected field of the school curriculum. We were both active in the founding of the Politics Association (under the sponsorship of the Hansard Society for Parliamentary Government) as a forum for pedagogical debate for teachers in both secondary and further education. For we soon saw that the problem lay quite as much in the inertia of stale syllabuses and lack of new ideas among teachers as in the nervousness of some local education authorities and the total failure of some schools to attempt the teaching of politics in any form at all.

We used various methods to further the cause. We have both lectured, lectured and lectured at numerous schools, colleges, teachers' meetings and short-courses. At least there was, in the beginning, a healthy demand for lectures on 'Should Politics be Taught?', though we have been gratified to see that this has now changed to a demand for talks on 'How Should Politics be Taught?' At Easter 1976, for instance, both the National Association for Adult Education and the Community and Youth Service Association took political education as the theme for key-note addresses at their annual conferences. The media have also been helpful in giving 'the cause' publicity which has often focused on genuine public concern but which has never (as yet, touch wood) attacked the whole thing as improper. And we have sat across the table talking to many headteachers, local advisers, councillors and local and national inspectors. But we are both old-fashioned enough to believe that the printed word is still unsurpassed as a means of creating intellectual discussion. So we are grateful for the opportunity to gather together in one place, even though they have all appeared before in various journals (now not always easily accessible), the essays we have both written on the provision, the nature and the methods of political education. They were written individually, at different times and for different audiences, and some thoughts changed over the years; so we do not claim that this is a fully coherent or an especially comprehensive manual of

political education, but merely something useful to those who have
read most of it before, interesting to those to whom it is new.

The mounting interest in the subject shows, fortunately, that
we are far from alone in this work. For example, many people have
contributed to these developments, particularly through the pages
of *Teaching Politics*, now in its fifth year (originally published
by Longman, and now by Sage). The Politics Association and the
Hansard Society have jointly sponsored a Programme for Political
Education, a three-year programme of curriculum development and
research financed by the Nuffield Foundation with some supplementation from the Schools Council; and with that is associated the
Political Education Research Unit at the University of York,
headed by Professor Ian Lister. Both their final reports are
eagerly awaited. A BBC Radio 3 Study Series of eight programmes
appeared and was repeated, resulting in a most useful handbook,
Teaching Politics: Problems and Perspectives, edited by Tom
Brennan and Jonathan Brown (BBC Publications, 1975). The
Institute of Education of the University of London have just this
year established the first specialised lectureship in the subject
in the capable hands of Alex Porter, who was Curriculum
Development Officer to the Programme for Political Education. We
ourselves have edited a new A-level series for Longman called
Political Realities, and would draw the attention of the reader
who is new to these concerns to one book particularly, T. Brennan,
Political Studies: A Handbook for Teachers.

In collecting these essays together we have grouped them into
three sections. The first set covers the range of difficulties
that have inhibited the development of political education at the
school level, and ways in which these problems can be, and now in
many cases are being, overcome. In the second section, we re-
publish a series of articles which analyse the fundamental nature
of political education and set down suggested guidelines within
which syllabuses might be developed. The final section is devoted
to an examination of a number of contexts in which politics might
in practice be taught. The essays are not, it must be emphasized,
a coherently thought-through manual; rather they are offered as a
series of first thoughts about a crucial area of the school curriculum that has at last been jerked into chaotic life.

1.0
Challenge and Hesitation

1.1
The introducing of politics in schools

Bernard Crick

Since it cannot be avoided, it had better be faced. Since it should not be avoided, quite a lot of care and time should be given to it. And since it is an interesting subject, it should be taught in an interesting manner. Civilized life and organized society depend upon the existence of governments, and what governments should do and can do with their power and authority depends, in turn, on the political structure and beliefs of the subsidiary societies within the range of influence of these governments. To take a Greek or a Jacobin view of the matter may now appear to go too far: that a man is only properly a man when he can be a citizen and takes part in public life. But it remains true that a man is still regarded as less of a man than he can be if he has no 'public spirit', has no concern for and takes no part in all the jostlings of self-interest, group interests and ideals that constitute politics. Only a few would maintain that the good life consists in the avoidance of public concerns; but nearly all would recognize that our whole culture or style of life is less rich, that is less various and shapely, and is less strong, that is less adaptable to change and circumstances, if people of any age-group believe that they should not or cannot influence authority.

This may sound very abstract, but the implications for education are embarrassingly concrete. Any worthwhile education must include some explanation and, if necessary, justification of the natural-ness of politics: that men both do and should want different things that are only obtainable by means or by leave of the public power, and that they can both study and control, in varying degrees, the means by which they reconcile or manage conflicts of interests and ideals.

The point of departure is all-important. When we ask for

---

* First published as the introductory essay in HEATER, D.B. (Ed) (1969) *The Teaching of Politics*, London, Methuen Educational. This present version contains amendments beyond those already incorporated in my collection of essays, *Political Theory and Practice*, London, Allen Lane, 1973.

directions, there are occasions on which we should receive the
rustic reply, 'I would not start from here if I were you'. In
practical life, we have to start from where we are: perhaps as
an inhabitant of a state that conceives politics as either subver-
sive and divisive, or as the implementation of a single and
authoritative set of truths which are to be extolled, but not
questioned. But in education in a reasonably free society (and
education in its full sense can only exist in reasonably free
societies), we are reasonably free, despite practical limitations
of various kinds, to start from where we choose. So we should
start with politics itself. If we start from some other point,
and I will discuss some of these conventional and innocent-
sounding points of departure - such as 'the constitution' or
'good citizenship' or 'reform', we may risk either heading off
in the wrong direction entirely or creating a positive distaste
for the most positive and natural part of the journey. Faced with
the growing 'alienation of youth' or the 'conflict of the genera-
tions', public authorities are likely to insist that schools put
more time and effort into Civics. But this could prove a Greek
gift to teachers of politics, and it could easily make matters
worse if constitutional platitudes of the 'our glorious Parliament'
kind are thrust on an already sceptical youth, rather than something realistic, racy and down-to-earth which focuses on politics
as a lively contest between differing ideals and interests - not as
a conventional set of stuffed rules. If, indeed, one were to explore school studies intended to be preparatory to university, I
would have to admit to some scepticism as to their value. Even if
all existing A-level syllabuses in 'British Constitution' were
reformed, I would still not be unhappy for universities to have to
start from scratch in teaching all the social sciences - with the
sole and not very comforting exception of Geography. In my own
experience as a persistent first-year teacher both at London School
of Economics and Sheffield, where one could properly point to entrance standards which were among the highest in the country, it
was rarely any advantage for a student to have taken 'British
Constitution' at school, often the contrary. And this was not
simply because he thought that he knew it already, but because (as
I will argue later) his mind was often astonishingly full of irrelevant and picturesque detail about parliamentary procedure and
'constitutional institutions', so that he had none of that inquisitive turbulence about the manifold relationships of ideas to
institutions and to circumstances that is surely of the essence of
a political education. Better that he had done History, English
and either Mathematics or a foreign language, in our present
ludicrously over-specialized sixth forms, or, in some reformed
system, these and almost any other reputable subjects. An interest
in politics might more naturally spring from an old friend
'Current Affairs', which should, in any case, be a prominent part
of secondary education throughout. The tendency of the universities to try to get schools to do their work for them is deplorable. The social sciences should not enter into a competitive race

with other subjects for compulsory prerequisite subjects: for one
thing, this perverts the purposes of secondary education, and for
another, it is quite unnecessary - the social sciences are popular
enough already despite the absence of prerequisite requirements
and of offerings in the schools on like scale to the older,
established school subjects.

As a professor of political studies, I am interested in political education at the secondary level of education because it
should be there both in its own right and in the public interest,
not as a feeder to the university Moloch. GCE 'British
Constitution' or 'Politics' has its justification in allowing at
least a few to specialize as the climax of a good general education,
not as new and necessary preparation for university in a subject or
area of concern which should already have been experienced at many
points in the school timetable. At some stage all young people in
all kinds of secondary schools and in industrial day-release
courses should gain some awareness of what politics is about. In
some schools it may best occur in Liberal, General or Social
Studies hours actually labelled 'Political Education', but in
others it can best be explored where it may more naturally arise -
always in History, always in Social Studies, often in English when
certain books (like *Animal Farm* and *Lord of the Flies*) are studied,
and often in Geography with its growing concern with conservation,
environmental controls and local planning procedures and controversies. It is more important that all teenagers should learn to read
newspapers critically for their political content than that they
should have heard of Aristotle or know - may heaven forgive us
all - when the Speaker's Mace is or was over or under the table.
So the best age for a conscious political education to begin is the
age at which children begin to read the newspapers anyway - their
political puberty. And it should continue into people's careers.
That so much General Studies in further education is, in fact,
concerned with political and social problems, demonstrates the
neglect in so many schools.*

I do insist that we must all start from such a point, and argue
on its merits the case for helping children to understand what
political conflicts are all about and what purposes they serve, not
take refuge in some politically denatured 'British Constitution' or
'Good Citizenship' (by whatever name that genteel god goes).

There are three objections at least against beginning with 'the

* Looking back, I am now far less sceptical than I was seven years
  ago (one can continue to learn) that Politics can be taught much
  earlier in the school than people have often supposed, or at
  least skills and concepts (as in moral education) necessary for
  a later and fuller understanding of political conflicts.
  Certainly it is foolish to think that 'Politics', if at all, is
  only for the sixth form. What despair or cynicism towards 'all
  our nation's children'.

constitution', and these objections also apply to beginning with
'good citizenship': (a) there is no such thing which is not itself
a matter of intense political dispute; (b) it is usually just a
subterfuge to escape *nasty* politics and usually does the very
thing it seeks to avoid: insinuates partisan biases, none the less
real for being oblique; and (c) it makes an interesting and lively
subject dull, safe and factual.

Let us take the constitution first. Taught in a legalistic
manner, a study of politics is hardly worth having (although, it is
fair to add, it is hardly likely to have much effect either). The
analogy between the difficulties of teaching about political and
sexual behaviour is irresistible. Both are natural activities in
which it is as proper for the child to be curious as it is for the
school to take up the burden of teaching what is socially acceptable
and what is conventional morality. Some teachers and some parents
wish strongly to avoid both or either of these things, while others
conceive it their duty to be dogmatic - whether directly or indirectly; so the usual compromise or line of least resistance is to
teach these things in a purely structural, anatomical or 'constitutional' way. But in both spheres the proper role of education must
be to create an awareness of why it is that some people regard
these matters as either taboo or as dogma, and to offer some
practical protection to the child by instilling not a knowledge of
what is right or wrong (which is beyond most of us to presume to
teach), but a knowledge of what his society and the sub-groups in
which he may move regard as right or wrong. I think we often over-
estimate the difficulties of leaving some questions quite open and
explicitly quite open, without either shattering personal faith,
trust in the teacher, or encouraging a sort of educational hypocrisy. As a political theorist, I seem to spend half my teaching
life attempting to create a sense of the plausibility and practical
importance of ideas that I do not myself accept either morally or
as universally true empirically.

When I used to be asked by first year undergraduates, 'But what
are *your* opinions, Prof.,' I took a proper and political care,
first, to make a little sermon that this is no way to settle any
question; secondly, to be a little ironical at why my personal
opinions are interesting to the questioner, and to explain that
my skill which gives me some authority consists mainly in exposing
bad answers, but does not extend as far as being equally sure that
I can give true ones; and, thirdly, to give nevertheless an honest
and reasonably full answer - although its fullness will naturally
depend on the occasion and the context. I both can and should
speak more freely and fully on contentious matters to students in
a common room, a corridor, a cafeteria or in a bar than from the
podium - or else I am a very dull dog; but I am no teacher if I
use my classroom authority to be a preacher ('a hedge-priest for
some doubtful orthodoxy', as Michael Oakeshott once put). For a
teacher must explain why so many honest men worship the Devil,
whereas a preacher is bound only to blacken him - even if with that

condescending type of tolerance which is the sign of not taking
another person's views or behaviour seriously. We should encourage
the holding of opinions - strong and firm opinions - but in ways
that are open to argument and exposed to refutations. To have some
doubt about all things is not to believe in nothing; we are sceptics
because ideas are important, otherwise we would be mere cynics.

To teach 'the constitution' is like teaching elementary anatomy
or biology instead of the nature of sexuality. They may be necessary first steps, or collateral studies, but by themselves they
would either be an evasion, or quite simply something else. Much
'British Constitution' teaching in schools seems to me to be of
the same nature: either nervous of politics, or a curious dedication to a vocational training in local government law or, still
more odd, in parliamentary procedure - as if there was a massive
shortage of clerks of the House of Commons rather than of citizens.

There is no constitution in the sense the syllabuses usually
assume (it is a concept invented to be taught to others), or rather
there is only one in a highly abstract sense that is very difficult
to grasp. We learn games best, after all, by playing them - rarely
by reading the rules. We read about the rules or attempt to formulate them clearly only when we begin to play very much more
often, or want to play better or to play in different company.
The British Constitution is those rules, formal and informal, by
which we can practise the kind of politics that we have wish to
practise. The conventions of the constitution have no legal force
and cannot be reduced to precise formulations without intense
political dispute. And it is important to be able to explain why.
Let me digress slightly to give a concrete example. Most textbooks
state that it is a convention of the Constitution, arising from
Baldwin's selection as Prime Minister, that the Prime Minister
'shall come from' the House of Commons. Then there came the
metamorphosis of the Earl of Home into Sir Alec (so that for a few
days the Prime Minister was in neither House). Thus, at first
sight, the constitutional rule was either wrong or, more likely,
misformulated. So new editions hastily said that the convention
is that the Prime Minister 'should not be in' the Lords, not that
he must come from the Commons. This would make sense as a legal
rule, and can be learned - as we oddly say - by heart. But then
look what happened. Not only was Sir Alec defeated, as happened to
Baldwin twice, but, unlike Baldwin, he quickly lost the leadership
of his party - though a man personally popular and of great self-
lessness and sincerity. Why did he resign as leader? Fairly
obviously, because he could not control his powerful colleagues
in the House of Commons. Why could he not? Partly temperamental
factors, perhaps, but all these factors were subsumed in his lack
of experience of attempting to do so before or of seeing it done
at all recently as a House of Commons man. In other words, the
original formulation may still be best, if seen not as a quasi-
legal rule but as a maxim drawn from political experience:
leaders coming from the sheltered atmosphere of the House of Lords

are unlikely to have had the kind of experience which in modern
conditions would fit them to be able to control their followers in
the far more stormy House of Commons.

I simply give this as an example of political thinking, a concrete example of what even Sir Ivor Jennings meant by saying that
'conventions are obeyed because of the political difficulties
which follow if they are not'.[1] Is this really too difficult
or too contentious a point to get across to fourteen or fifteen-
year-olds? I would think the question an impertinence to ask of
school teachers, if I had not found it hard to get across to
twenty-year-olds and even to fifty-year-olds - so fixed in some
people's minds is the disjunction between 'the constitution' (good
and teachable) and politics (bad and amorphous).

Here is not the place to examine the reasons for dislike of
politics - whether by the unpolitical Conservative who may wish
himself to rise above it, the a-political Liberal who wishes to
protect from it everything he believes in, or those anti-political
or revolutionary Socialists who see politics as the mark of an
imperfectly unified society. But such mistaken sentiments assume
a peculiar importance in education. Small wonder that politicians
and educationalists eye each other so warily, each feeling that
the other should 'keep out of his business', and yet each wanting
something from the other very much - resources, on the one hand,
and respect on the other. Plainly, nearly all educational progress
makes people able to contribute more to the aggregate of social
wealth and skills, but it also makes them less easy to be led by
the nose, less respectful of authority - whether in politics or in
education - simply by invocation of its name. The danger in States
like ours is now, indeed, not lack of ability on the part of the
people to contribute, nor any great popular desire to hinder,
obstruct or radically change, but is simply indifference, incom-
prehension, alienation, the feeling of a huge gap between what we
are told and what we see, and above all between what we are told
we can do (the 'influence of public opinion' and every little vote
adding up, etc.) and what we can in fact do.

Teachers of politics must themselves develop and thus be able
to convey to others an intense sense that, as the good children
would say, there are 'faults on both sides'. This is as good a
fiction or framework as any and, in this basic problem of the relation between politics and education, it might be thought unreason-
able to deny that it happens to be true.

We need to be able to say at the same time, 'Look how they
govern!' and 'But look at how we educate about the business of good
government!' A growing disillusionment with the government tends
to increase either resistance to teaching politics at all, or,
where it is taught, the determination to keep it narrow and dull.
But disillusionment with governments - and I take for granted that
I am writing at a time when no sane man can find more than a
qualified enthusiasm for his party's performance or prospects - is

a general phenomenon and has three obvious aspects, none of which are to be ignored. People are disillusioned with actual governments and hence with politics, (a) because of what governments do; (b) because of the limitations in which governments operate; and (c) because they expect too much.

These factors are all far more important than being sure that people 'know the Constitution'. Someone has to point them out and explain them. The press does a good job on the record of governments, but can rarely create any awareness of the second or third factors (general factors are never topical on the crazy day-to-day basis which the press regards as essential to form 'news', and the frustration of unreal expectations is too abstract a point when 'news' also has to be 'hard' and 'personal' as well as instantaneously topical). Perhaps it is the behaviour of politicians and political journalists which makes the teaching of politics, one should candidly admit, as difficult as it is important. They should be the first to explain the limitations of resources, existing commitments and environment under which any Government must suffer. And politicians should be the first to warn against hoping for too much. But they are usually the last to do this. I am convinced that politicians talk down to people and that ordinary people are capable of understanding the basic facts about the economy - if they are simplified intelligently. At that point the professions of politics and education should meet, but rarely do. The politician is at fault for neglecting to adapt to modern educational standards his - as even Bagehot called it - 'educative function'; the disputes between the parties are commonly conducted by intelligent men in a deliberately stupid and stupefying manner; and the public, including adolescents, seem well aware of this, often seeing politicians as figures of fun, especially at election time. But teachers are at fault for not trying to raise the level from below: they commonly teach 'the Constitution', but one can search in vain the standard school books on the British Constitution for the simplest list of what have been the major policy disputes between the parties in recent years, or the simplest diagrams of national income and expenditure under different headings (which possibly suffer from the double handicap of being 'Economics').

If politicians will not be more candid, it is hard to blame teachers for being evasive, especially when they are thus starved of interesting, topical and realistic teaching materials. To this point we must return, but it suffices for the moment to suggest that sometimes dull and abstract books have to be used, which avoid the subject-matter of political disputes and expound and extol highly dubious constitutional and legal limitations on government, simply in default of others more realistic[2]. There is a dearth of simple, informative books of what one could call, by other names, 'contemporary history' or 'current affairs' (and here, of course, the university level textbook is completely unhelpful, even for the teacher, with its methodological rather than substantive or practical preoccupations).

The nature of politics demands that we should always teach and show the two sides of things: what we want the State to do for us, and what we wish it to be prevented from doing to us; or, quite simply, aspirations and limitations. For the one without the other is as misleading as it is useless. So it is not 'finding excuses' to talk more seriously than politicians commonly do of the nature of limitations. Indeed, to do so may protect children from that one great cause of radical disillusionment or alienation from politics which is simply a product of starting with quite unrealistic expectations. This can take a socialist form, of course, but can equally well take a liberal form, or what would be called in America 'a League of Women Voters', or here (once upon a time, at least) a 'Hansard Society' mentality. Even or particularly the idealist must remember that Pilgrim had to walk through both Vanity Fair and the Slough of Despond before he could attain the slopes of Mount Zion.

To give one more example. Rarely do the actual policies of parties figure much in teaching or classroom discussion - although any good journalist *could* give a reasonably objective and clear account of them. If policy is tackled at all, then a kind of half-way house of realism is gratefully found by reading and considering the party programmes. But to take programmes at their face value is positively to create disillusion. For we then measure the success or 'sincerity' of governments in terms of whether or not they have 'carried out their programme' - a kind of political football pools; and some actually denounce any trimming of the sails to changed winds as going against prior instructions or 'the mandate' (whatever that may be) and, therefore, as arbitrary and undemocratic. Certain things have to be said first about programmes and manifestos in general before there can be any meaningful discussion of their relationship with the actual policies pursued by a government. They were, for instance, originally almost exclusively a part of radical and reformist politics in the twentieth century; they were unknown in the nineteenth century except as socialist pipe-dreams; and the famous 'Tamworth Manifesto' of Peel was simply an unusually elaborate 'election cry': it entirely lacked the comprehensive character of a programme, and, in any case, one lark does not make even a false dawn. The Liberals did not offer a programme until Lloyd George's unofficial 'Yellow Books' of 1932, and Conservatives resisted having a comprehensive programme until as late as 1950 because, quite sensibly, they held that it was impossible to foretell the future and unwise to commit oneself to do things when circumstances might change - indeed this follows from their general view of politics as concerned basically with the management of existing interests, rather than with deliberately fermented change. Programmes are essentially a reformist and democratic device; but then even democracy has its limitations: it is no verbal quibble but a profound truth that government itself cannot be democratic, it can only be restrained or even strengthened by democratic devices. Another point to be made is that, in any

case, programmes commit parties but not governments. So the un-
moralistic lesson is surely to show that if programmes are seen as
promises, then it is odd, by analogy, to employ a man for a job
solely on what he promises to do without also considering his
record. If he appears to promise too much, one will not necessarily hold it against him; one may sagely take his words with a
pinch of salt, but only if his record is good. General elections,
in other words, are not likely to be decided and nor should they
be decided on programmes and promises alone, nor - in rapidly
changing societies - on record alone; the record must show that
someone is capable of adaptation and change. Again I put these
points forward simply as an example of political thinking, and as
realistic points that can be got across objectively and which are
far more important, both from the point of view of 'civic
morality' and of conveying correct information, than knowing weird
details of election law.

Again, is it too difficult to show that parties hold different
views not just about what should be done, but about the facts of
the case? In the above case, the radical believes that a general
election decides a programme to be carried out, but the Conservative
believes that a general election decides which group of men shall
be trusted with the complex and shifting business of government.
I do not think it a weak or evasive conclusion to state that it
would be an odd and bad world in which either conclusion were
pushed to extremes. For strong and definite words should then be
spoken of the folly of applying the right theory in the wrong
circumstances. There is no prejudice in trying to show, to fish
for a carefully matched pair of examples, that it was as politically unrealistic for the Conservatives to offer no real programme
in 1945 as it was for Mr. Wilson to saddle himself with over-
elaborate programmes in the economic circumstances of 1964,
1966, and 1974.

What I argue for is the need for a more realistic study of
whatever we call it, and I have no objection to a grand old name
like 'The British Constitution' (God bless it and preserve it from
all enemies!), so long as we tacitly translate this eighteenth-
century, Whiggish phrase as 'The British Political System' or
simply 'British Politics' (although the question does arise, to
which I will return, why just British?). A political education
should be realistic and should chasten the idealist. Ideas are
too important to be embalmed, they must be wrestled with and con-
fronted, but fairly and openly. There is no room for evasion:
as teachers we must openly argue with that kind of liberal who
thinks that children should be protected from knowledge of politics,
just as the grand old Constitution tries to protect us from party
politics; and should argue too with that sort of businessman who
thinks that we could do without it, that 'political factors' spoil
rational economic calculations, forgetting as he does that probably nine-tenths of the big decisions in industry are political in
the sense that they arise from distributions of personal power and

influence rather than the logic of cost-accountancy.

A political education, too, should inform the ignorant; but realistically. Politics is, after all, like sexual activity, undeniably fascinating. If we act as if it is not and offer instead largely irrelevant background or constitutional facts, then children either see through us or are suitably bored. But realism involves talking coolly about politics, not striking hot political attitudes. The teacher who goes on and on about the Mace, the stages of Public Bills and the difference between the powers of the House of Lords and of the House of Commons in the scrutiny of Statutory Instruments, is only slightly less of a menace than the few teachers (but their fame goes a long way) who treat 'British Constitution' as a chance to indoctrinate students in their view of THE TRUTH. If sinners are far fewer than local education authority committees and school managers sometimes imagine, the varieties of sin are probably greater. I meet quite as many first-year students who cite school-masters for the authority that 'Mr. Wilson has violated the Constitution' (to which I reply, 'first catch her'), as for the more famous view that 'THE WHOLE SYSTEM is grinding down the workers' ('especially', I allow myself the comment, 'the third of the working class who regularly vote Tory').

It is all too easy to exaggerate the difficulties of a reasonably objective teaching of politics, so that most institutional nervousnesses that studying politics means partisan debate are quite unnecessary. I say 'reasonably objective', however, because part of political morality, or the morality that tolerates real conflicts of opinion rather than seeks to stamp them out, consists in appreciating how much all our views of what we see in society are affected by what we want to see. This is no dark secret and nor should it make teachers worry that Politics is not as objective - may one sometimes say, 'cut and dried'? - as some other school subjects: the element of subjectivity in perception is the basis of literature and art as well as of politics. We do not insist that one way of doing things is true. On the contrary, rational argument in politics and therefore in the teaching of politics follows a method of trying to show that on such and such an issue different people, who ordinarily see things rather differently, are for once, in fact, agreed. The artful Communist quotes *The Times* to support him, and the shrewd Conservative the *Morning Star*.

The teacher's task is, at whatever level, primarily a conceptual one, not a matter of conveying an agreed corpus of factual information. He needs to build up and extend an elementary vocabulary of concepts through which we both perceive the world and use them to try to influence it. The teacher has, above all, to show the difference between talking about an opinion and holding it. And from this he or she can go on to show how and why political events are interpreted in different ways by equally honest people. Here,

to speak without undue irony, British popular newspapers furnish
excellent and readily available teaching materials. The teacher
must then be able to convey imaginatively an understanding of the
plausibility (or, as Laski used to say, 'the inwardness') of
different political doctrines, even using unusual and unpopular
ones as examples. He must illuminate differences, not seek to
show that 'we are all really agreed about fundamentals' - for we
are plainly not, unless we have lost the capacity or inclination
for thought. He is then in a position at least to avoid - even in
the teeth of most of the textbooks - the most crippling and common
of all errors in considering politics, the belief that institutions
and ideas can be considered apart from each other, sometimes expressed as the difference between theory and practice. The teacher
should show that all institutions serve certain purposes and must
be judged by how they fulfil them; and equally he should show
that ideas which do not seek some institutional realization are
not political ideas at all. It should be a part of the beginning
of political education, not the end which few then reach, to accus-
tom people to probe and to discover what are, in fact, the general
ideas of people who claim to hold no abstract ideas and to be
acting in a purely practical manner. Those who claim to 'have
no time for theory' commonly hold the most interesting, sometimes
arbitrary, often quite fantastic, general views on how things work
and should work. Think of all those who wondered what would happen
to 'sovereignty' if we went into Europe, just as Rousseau, Lord
North and Walter Bagehot once all thought that Federal solutions
were *impossible*. 'What do they really believe in' and 'what do
they really think they are doing?' are two questions that ordinary
people, 'the People', should be taught to carry into every aspect
of their dealings with authorities.

The teacher himself should not advocate one doctrine or another,
even our 'British Way and Purpose' that was the title of a famous
Army Education Corps manual during the Second World War. He simply
points out the kind of conditions which appear to go with certain
ideas and the kind of consequences which appear to go with holding
them. For children must surely be brought to see society, in however elementary a form, as a system or a pattern of relationships
(so that the Conservative will typically say, 'Don't meddle - the
unexpected repercussions will overwhelm you'; the revolutionary
socialist will say, 'All or nothing, partial reform is impossible';
and many others in pursuing limited objectives will try to reassure
themselves that the unintended repercussions of their particular
policies are either trivial or, with proper forethought, avoidable).

Naturally the teacher must begin by teaching what the received
political ideas of our own society are, and how they relate to
other social institutions. But he must avoid implying any finality
or superiority to our traditional but severely local arrangements;
and it is hard to see how such an implication can be avoided if, even
or particularly at the beginning, some other system or systems are
not also looked at, however superficially. I am not convinced

that school-children need to know *anything* about the intricacies
of parliamentary procedure; I am convinced that they should know
something, however superficially, about how Russia, the United
States, China and some countries of the 'Third World' and of Europe
are governed. The point is not to establish any hierarchy of
institutions, either in our favour or to chasten insular pride;
but simply to show that there are different sorts of relationships
and that in none of them can political ideas or institutions be
considered apart from their social or national setting. And it
is precisely this that 'the Constitution over-all' approach denies
- to make this point for the last time.

Perhaps, however, a qualification or explanation is needed before
proceeding. I would not suggest that some study of abstract models
(for such they necessarily are) of institutional structure and of
formalized customary rules does not have a place. But its place
must follow and not precede some knowledge of the issues and traditions of actual politics. If it is put first, either in emphasis
or in order of teaching, it is likely to distort understanding of
government and politics to a degree almost, I find, beyond repair.
For, after all and again, customary rules arise from political
activity and experience, not the other way round; and the machinery
of government is made and remade by men to serve their purposes, it
is not a natural impediment.

The best analogy may well be with modern methods of language
teaching. Grammar is discarded as the way in, but it is then
introduced at a later stage as a framework with which to consolid-
ate and extend our existing knowledge. Few would now believe that
'the direct method' alone suffices; some structure, whether called
grammar (the Constitution) or structural linguistics (categories
of political behaviour), must *follow*. But at the moment there is
little doubt that most horses find the cart firmly harnessed up in
front of them, and one can hardly go too far in possible exaggera-
tion to redress a balance already weighed down ponderously in
precisely the wrong direction.

Another common disguise or perversion of a study of politics is
'good citizenship': the use of Civics or Liberal Studies classes
to urge participation in this and that. Sometimes this may degenerate into a crude moralism, and a rather romantic and prissy one at
that - of 'the people versus the politicians' or 'I wouldn't let
my daughter marry a politician' kind. There is a type of Civics
which is straight, early-nineteenth-century Liberalism, teaching
or preaching that the individual should directly influence this
and that and make up his own mind in proud and independent isolation
(whether he is a humble citizen or elected representative); and
that he should avoid like the plague parties, pressure groups,
unions and all other 'organized interests' (as if disorganized ones
were better). This is simply unrealistic, individualistic in a
thoroughly antisocial and unsociological sense, and often highly

partisan: one must insist that Liberals, whether of ancient or modern ilk, must be no more immune that Tories or Socialists from some scepticism that their own account of what politics is all about is, taken by itself, fully adequate.

The less obvious danger of the 'be good boys and girls and participate' kind of teaching is the more insidious: the assumption that participation is both a good thing in itself and the best possible thing. Since personal participation in national politics other than by simply casting a vote is plainly impossible for most people in societies as large as we need to ensure the benefits we demand, it follows that the teaching of participation as an end in itself is only likely to create disillusionment in practice - if it does succeed in influencing local activities and does not simply sound so much cold pie in the classroom.

The virtues of participation are an important half-truth, but a lame half-truth if advanced alone. The other and complementary half is quite as important: that people must know, however vaguely, what decisions are made by governments, how they are made and what is happening. Informed and wide-ranging communications are as important for democratic politics as is direct participation - which, in practice, only involves a few, usually the few who preach it. Governing authorities of all kinds are more apt to urge participation, because they know that in a widespread manner it is impractical, than they are to study how to make themselves govern more openly and less secretively. Governments are fundamentally restrained and directed in societies such as ours not by the participant-representatives (who are mainly the recruiting ground for members of the government), but by their knowledge that nearly everything they do may become a matter of public knowledge. Governments can ordinarily depend on their parliamentary support but only to a far smaller degree on their electoral support. And by the same token the people's representatives can pass economic legislation and orders until they are red or blue in the face, but putting them into practice almost wholly depends on governments or other authorities being able to explain them and to obtain some response from the working population.

Knowledge of what is happening and how things happen is quite as important as theoretical opportunities for participation. Therefore, both in the light of the subject itself and for its practical consequences, I am rather sceptical of the American-style 'teaching of democracy' by way of fabricating democratic situations in the classroom games, debates, mock parliaments and class elections, etc. These may be fun, may teach some political manners, may develop some expressive skills and provide some alleviation of routine, but they can only supplement, not replace a realistic knowledge of how the real system works.* Governments are as much restrained by

---

* An American professor recently spoke to me with enthusiasm about 'the public high school itself as a model of democracy' - lucidly

knowing that their acts are publicized as by participant devices themselves. The absence of political censorship and the presence of an independent press are quite as important as free elections, and this should be said. When Aristotle talked about political justice he invoked two basic criteria: that we should rule or be ruled in turn - participation; and that the state should be no larger than that we can know the character of the other citizens or, as he otherwise put it, no larger than that the voice of the Stentor or herald could be heard from one boundary to another. Modern political ideas and theory have almost exclusively stressed the first criterion - as if abandoning the second as unrealistic, paradoxically at the very moment of time when mass communications have rendered it readily applicable to huge states, not just to small communities. Participation of persons and communication of knowledge must, in other words, go together.

Content must not be sacrificed for process. Even to play 'United Nations' is surely difficult if all the little countries or role-players have not some prior knowledge, however simple, of how their characters behave, both in New York and back home. Peanuts, perhaps, had it all: 'Charlie Brown, Charlie Brown, gee, you were dumb in school today.'
'I thought I did all right.'
'Nope, you were dumb, downright dumb. You got everything wrong.'
'Gee, I misunderstood. I thought one only had to be sincere.'

Ultimately that is the difficulty of all attempts to enliven the teaching of politics by remorselessly discussing nothing but 'how should things be reformed?' The question is meaningless, except to an anarchist revolutionary (not even to a genuine Marxist), unless it arises from a realistic knowledge of how things are actually done. The politically desirable can only be the sociologically possible (though not for one moment denying that we differ politically in our judgments about what is possible almost as much as in our judgments about what should be done.

It is quite plain that we in Great Britain can no longer take for granted, if ever we could, that people either here or elsewhere know or care much about our political institutions and ideas. The

summarising his many writings. He must think to this day that I was being rude or facetious, when I thought that I was being sad and a little wise to say: 'But don't build Vietnam, Watergate or Lockheed into the model'. Or perhaps he thought I was being anti-American? I would cheerfully have given less famous but still significant British examples. More profoundly, the point is that a school cannot as a school be democratic. It can be more democratic or, for the worse, less democratic. But there is teaching as well as learning to be done if we are to progress and not regress. A school needs authority, but all authority (as I will argue later) is not authoritarian.

knowledge of ordinary people and school pupils about politics is
abysmal. We were once famed for our political abilities and knowledge. We now worry that our own younger generation is becoming
actively alienated or sullenly indifferent to our political institutions; and internationally we have grown noticeably more
silent about being an Athens of example now that we are no longer
a Rome of power. It is almost as if we now have to begin all over
again, like the seventeenth-century Commonwealth men and the
eighteen- and nineteenth-century radicals, rediscovering our
nature and rethinking our possibilities. This can hardly begin
too early, and it will surely fail or prove irrelevant if it is
not done in a manner both stimulating and realistic. And this depends almost entirely on the schools. To give children the 'low-
down' on how political institutions work and what political
conflicts are about, rather than the dry bones of parliamentary
procedure or the elevated abstractions of 'the Constitution', will
not be to feed disillusion or to encourage cynicism, quite the
contrary: it will encourage ordinary young citizens (and I speak
technically, not rhetorically, as the voting age moves closer to
the classroom), their teachers and their politicians to think in
terms of common problems to be solved, and to talk about them in a
common language, not to build up protective walls of mutual incom-
prehension. It will encourage to think morally, *what should be
done*; but to think realistically as well as morally: what should
be done that is possible, *what should be done* in the context of
other people's opinions of contradictions, difficulties and traditions.

Says the teenager, 'We are being got at again'; says the head-
master or chairman of the governors or of the examining body,
'This is dangerous ground, be *very* careful, stick to clear *facts*,
cleave to the Constitution ... politics is not a real subject in
educational tradition' (at which the ghosts of Aristotle and our
great English Hobbes, Locke, Burke and Mill should arise to haunt
them nastily and rebuke them for their ignorance); and says the
politician, 'People do not understand what we are trying to do for
them in very difficult circumstances, and blame us for mirroring
their own divisions, doubts and uncertainties.'

The task of re-establishing a popular tradition of political
discourse both critical and aspirant must begin in the schools and
with teachers. And it will plainly have to precede a suitable
literature. It is not my task or competence to review the literature on politics for schools - if it can be called such, for it is
mostly about the structure of government and the rules and conventions of the Constitution, the dull and heavy statues of Prometheus
waiting for a divine touch of humanity. Nearly all such books that
I know to be commonly used lack the two essentials of a political
education: realistic accounts of how governments and parties work
and critical discussions of political ideas, or of what should be
done and how - the moral assumptions and preconceptions that people
carry, necessarily but usually unrecognized, into practical

activities. For instance, if teachers follow the arguments of
Colour and Citizenship: A Report on Race Relations (E.J.B. Rose and
associates, Oxford University Press, 1969) and lay stress on a
tolerant perception of social differences rather than an assimila-
tionist stress on common moral factors, they may soon find that
there are better and more down-to-earth books being produced about
the minority groups than about the English majority. But supply,
being partly at least and often pleasantly venal, will inevitably
follow demand - if the demand comes first, as indeed there are many
signs, like the volume in which this essay first appeared
(although this is certainly not for the children), that it is beginning to do. We all should love our subjects, or else, like
benevolent autocrats, we are misplaced or due to be replaced. But
the teacher of Politics can have some justification and pride in
claiming that his subject has a peculiar combination of difficulty,
importance and fascination.

NOTES

1. Quoted by Geoffrey Marshall and Graeme C. Moodie in their admirable *Some Problems of the Constitution*, 4th edn. (Hutchinson,
1967), p.34, from Jenning's *Law and the Constitution*. They add
that 'conventions describe the way that certain legal powers are to
be exercised if the powers are to be tolerated by those affected.

2. Professor F. F. Ridley had some interesting and trenchant things
to say on textbooks in his review article, 'Introductions to
British Government', *Parliamentary Affairs*, Spring 1968, pp.178-81.

1.2
Political studies in the school: some problems

Derek Heater

English children receive little political education at school.
British Constitution and Civics are comparatively unpopular subjects in CSE and GCE; Current Affairs and Civics lessons tend to
be accorded the low priority of 'minority time' work; while in some
schools even this concession is denied and political education has
to be mediated through the better-established subjects, particularly
History. The whole problem is, indeed, fraught with difficulties
and needs much more careful investigation than it has hitherto
received in this country. In this article I should like to confine
myself to the discussion of three issues, though they are, I believe, of central significance. These three issues concern the
degree of maturity necessary for the study of politics; the problem
of bias; and the relative importance of formal class learning and
school organisation and activity.

Politics, it is sometimes argued, is an adult activity and study:
it is meaningless to children because political activity is outside
their experience; it is beyond their comprehension as a discipline
because it is so complex and dependent on abstract concepts.
Professor J.D.B. Miller (1965) expresses this view when he writes:

> A man who has seen a few elections go by, who has tested the
> promises of political parties against their performance ... is
> better equipped to see politics whole than an ex-schoolboy who
> may know nothing but what his teachers have told him about the
> need to serve his country (or not to serve it, depending on the
> teacher). [1]

In very recent years, however, a more optimistic note has been
struck by British official reports and American psychological research. The Schools Council Working Paper No. 2 (1965) strikes
indeed a remarkably bold note by urging the study by non-academic
pupils of such 'seminal ideas' as 'the rule of law, a sense of
justice ... government by consent, respect for minority views,

* First published in *Education and Social Science*, July 1969.

freedoms of speech and action'[2]. The main reason for believing
that the Schools Council are not over-ambitious in conceiving work
for 15 and 16-year olds in these terms lies in motivation. Political debate is part of adult life and adolescents are anxious to
be considered adult. Even so, it need scarcely be added, such
material needs very skilful handling.

But if the subject might have an appeal to adolescents precisely
because they are on the threshold of adult life, does this mean
it is unsuitable fare for children below this age? Politics is
concerned with choosing between alternative courses of activity;
choice is determined by attitudes; and attitudes crystallize at an
early age.

Little research has, in fact, been done in this country on this
subject. The work of Jahoda (1963) on the acquisition of concepts
and attitudes in terms of national identification and of Morrison
(1967) in terms of international relations is the most relevant.
Both discovered variations dependent on socio-economic status; but
found also that basic ideas are comprehended and basic attitudes
are formulated before 11 years of age and without the assistance
of formal teaching. In summing up research in this area, Morrison
has written that 'by the time pupils enter the secondary school,
quite complex, if conventional, structures of evaluations and
beliefs may exist.'[3]

Much more research has been undertaken in the USA, where the
work of Greenstein (1965) has been particularly valuable.
Greenstein's research was conducted with children in the age range
9-13. At this level he recognizes that influences such as the
home and mass media may well be more important than the school.
However, although many of the children had little equipment in the
way of political *knowledge*, political *attitudes* rapidly develop
at this age. For example, the children were asked what changes
they would make in the world, and by the sixth grade (i.e. 11 years
of age) a majority of the responses were political. The political
statements were rarely partisan, much less ideological; most common
by far (perhaps stimulated by recent summit conferences) was simply
the wish for peace[4]. The overall picture is, in fact, of early
absorption of political attitudes. This situation has important
implications for political education in later years, not least
because early-acquired orientations are those most firmly embedded
in the individual's mind.

In considering the age factor as a relevant argument in the
debate over the teaching of political subjects in schools, there is
one final point to be touched upon. Schools, this argument runs,
are responsible institutions and teachers, by and large, are responsible people. They are responsible not only because they are
committed to a (albeit unwritten) professional code; but they are
uncommitted as a body to a sectional political interest as some
newspapers, political parties and trade unions are. And it is
these latter influences that will determine the individual's

political responses, either by direct impact or indirectly through
parents, if the schools abdicate this responsibility. Moreover, if
the schools do not participate in this work they do not leave the
child's mind empty, but rather receptive to less impartial purveyors
of ideas and opinions. Sir Richard Acland (1966) for example, has
been particularly eloquent in arguing for the positive exercise of
this responsibility[5].

Yet it is not sufficient to make an assertion of this kind. One
must ask what meaning can be attached to the word 'responsible' in
this context. Does it mean 'impartial'? Indeed, can it mean
'impartial'? This is a most important question, because it is the
fear of introducing propaganda into the schools perhaps more than
any other factor that has inhibited the development of political
studies by teachers at this level.

As with the question of age, so the issue of controversy in the
subject-matter of Politics derives from the links between the
theoretical and the practical. As Dr. R.F. Atkinson (1965) has
argued, the problem of indoctrination is a difficulty in the sphere
of 'moral truths' (which includes political evaluation) rather than
of 'scientific truths' precisely because the former have such close
connections with conduct. Moreover, because absolute truths cannot
be determined in moral as they can in scientific investigation,
there are bound to be areas of wild disagreement. But if a person
feels strongly committed to a policy or a point of view, as
Bertrand Russell (1932) has pointed out, he will seek allies to
support him and will use emotional appeals to secure that support.
Furthermore, if the point of view is undermined by rational criticism, the adherent will tend to fall back on emotional defences.
It is this emotional potential which teachers most fear. It is
true that some teachers feel that they are not morally justified in
introducing controversial political issues into the classroom - that
this would lead to their indoctrination of their pupils and therefore an abuse of their position *vis-à-vis* the developing minds of
their class. But, others are restrained by fear - fear of how
pupils will respond, fear of how the parents will respond, fear of
how the governors and head-teachers will respond. For emotion
breeds emotion.

Yet there is a powerful contrary case. In the first place, if
controversial subjects like Politics are omitted from the curriculum the school is failing in its duty to prepare young people for
life in the world beyond the school. To be an effective citizen
in a democratic society a person must develop judgment, 'sales
resistance' to political propaganda, and the ability to enter into
cool discussion. Furthermore, if this position is accepted, it
follows that it is dishonest to use comparatively uncontroversial
issues as material for this kind of teaching, both because it is
precisely in the most disputed topics that the training in dispassionate judgment is needed, and also because the teacher's
silence on a controversial issue may be taken to mean acceptance of

the 'Establishment' point of view (see Wilson, 1964).

And yet the teacher's uneasiness is justified. There is a distinction between legitimate teaching and illegitimate indoctrination, and the borderline between them is not easily distinguishable. This problem has, in fact, received a certain amount of attention from philosophers of education in the past few years (for example, see Snook, 1972).

One may attempt a clarification of the teacher's duty in this problem. In the first place, he must know himself - be honest enough with himself to be aware quite clearly what his position is on the controversial issues he is going to teach. Secondly, he must have enough professional integrity to refrain from the conscious indoctrination of his pupils. Thirdly, his examination must be thorough enough to prevent him from indulging in unconscious indoctrination. In the fourth place, he must have sufficient skill and humility to open his pupil's eyes to all points of view and encourage them to think out their own attitudes. And finally, he must have a relationship with his class that is free enough for them to *want* to think and not be swayed by the teacher's personal opinion. But, above all, the teacher of political subjects must have skill in handling complex and difficult material.

The problems of bias and indoctrination focus our attention on the formal classroom teaching situation. But this is only one way in which the school can influence the political socialization of the young person. A wide range of activities have been tried in schools to develop political interests, with particular regard to the fostering of democratic and international attitudes. Special days, such as United Nations Day, might be observed; charities like Oxfam are supported; visits to the Palace of Westminster or the local Town Hall are sometimes arranged; and many schools hold mock elections, especially at the time of national elections. Yet some teachers feel that even these activities have but a negligible effect on children's minds: only by living in a democratic or international school, so they argue, can a true understanding be gained of the political problems raised by democratic government or international affairs. Thus, efforts have been made in some schools to establish a school parliament through which the children themselves wield important authority in the running of the school. Also, special schools have been founded to prepare their pupils for world or at least regional citizenship - the Atlantic College, for example.

Experiments in 'school democracy' have provoked much discussion. Dr. Entwistle (1964 and 1971) now of Concordia University has given thought to this question and is highly critical of mock elections. He starts from the assumption that the essence of democracy lies in participation in voluntary associations. It follows that one of the main functions of a school is to prepare young people for this activity. But for this purpose mock elections are not suitable - 'They divorce the machinery of government from its responsible use'[6]. Nor are school parliaments, since in the last analysis authority must rest in adult hands. The answer, he believes, lies rather in making available a number of situations, particularly in school clubs, where limited but real and effective decision-making can be exercised.

Whatever form Political Studies take in school at the moment or may take in the future (and I believe reform in the curriculum is urgent in this sphere), it is clear that the effectiveness of the teaching will be influenced by the measure to which the three factors I have discussed are taken into account. The nettle of bias must be firmly grasped and syllabuses must be taught in the full realization that a wide range of home and school influences, some impinging at an early age, will affect the young person's responses to his lessons.

NOTES

1. J.D.B. Miller (1965) page 286.

2. See Schools Council (1965) paragraph 68.

3. See A. Morrison (1967) page 197.

4. See F.I. Greenstein (1965) page 69.

5. R. Acland (1966) page 98.

6. H. Entwistle (1964).

REFERENCES

ACLAND, R. (1966) *Curriculum or Life?* London, Gollanz.

ATKINSON, R.F. (1965) 'Instruction and indoctrination' in R.D. Archambault (Ed) *Philosophical Analysis and Education* London, Routledge and Kegan Paul.

ENTWISTLE, H. (1964) Mock elections in schools, *The Times Educational Supplement*, 11 September.

ENTWISTLE, H. (1971) *Political Education in a Democracy*, London, Routledge and Kegan Paul.

GREENSTEIN, F.I. (1965) *Children and Politics* Newhaven, Yale University Press.

JAHODA, G. (1963) The development of children's ideas about country and nationality *British Journal of Educational Psychology*, 33, Parts 1 and 2.

MILLER, J.D.B. (1965) *The Nature of Politics* Harmondsworth, Penguin Books.

MORRISON, A. (1967) Attitudes of children towards international affairs *Educational Research*, 9(3).

RUSSELL, B. (1932) *Education and the Social Order*, London, Allen and Unwin.

SCHOOLS COUNCIL (1965) *Working Paper No. 2: Raising the School Leaving Age*, London, HMSO.

SNOOK, I.E. (Ed) (1972) *Concepts of Indoctrination: Philosophical Essays*, London, Routledge and Kegan Paul.

WILSON, J. (1964) 'Education and indoctrination' in T.H.B. Hollins *Aims in Education*, Manchester, Manchester University Press.

1.3
Political education in schools: the official attitude

Derek Heater

There are occasions when, slumped in the gloom of professional depression, I believe that a Rip van Winkle who had dozed off while teaching in 1945 could resume his work a quarter-century later with no more effort than it takes to yawn and to stretch the limbs. Such depressing visions are occasioned by the apparent failure of some teachers to revise the content and method of their lessons. Chalk and talk are the vehicles that transport the received wisdom of the dust-laden teacher's notes to the note-books of the pupils (without, as the saying goes, passing through the mind of either).

Now if there is one subject where change should have occurred over the past quarter of a century it is Politics teaching. Attitudes towards secondary education and adolescence, the political condition of the country and the academic standing of Politics as a discipline have all been transformed since the Second World War. Since the 1944 Education Act we have entered upon the era of secondary education for all, with two stabs at raising the school-leaving age (one still recent it is true, and the implications only just being worked out), comprehensivisation and concern for the curricula of the lower-ability groups. Additionally, the Latey Report recognized the earlier maturation of young people, so that, with the lowering of the age of franchise, one can simultaneously be *in statu pupillari et civitatis*. Meanwhile, Britain has moved from being a bulwark of democracy against Communism to a de-imperialised off-shore island of Europe. Finally, we must note the proliferation, especially during the 1960s, of university departments of Politics, firmly establishing the subject in the academic life of the country.

It would be unrealistic to expect such a range of events to leave political education untouched. This is not, of course, the place to write a history of the subject[1]. I wish rather to survey one aspect which has an intrinsic educational and political interest of its own - namely the officially expressed attitudes of central bodies like the Ministry of Education and the Schools

* First published in *Teaching Politics* May, 1972.

Council. For although England enjoys wider freedom than most countries from central direction of her schools' curricula, official
pronouncements at one and the same time reflect practice and help
to guide those teachers who are slow to follow trends.

Citizens Growing Up

The pamphlet *Citizens Growing Up* was published by the Ministry
of Education in 1949. It discusses, in three separate parts: The
Meaning of Citizenship; The Study and Practice of Citizenship in
the Schools; and The Study and Practice of Citizenship in After
Life. And when I read the following I get my Rip Van Winkle feeling, because it could almost have been written yesterday:

> It can certainly not yet be said that the requirements of our
> modern society, and particularly of our modern democracy, in
> respect of education for citizenship have been digested within
> the body of our educational system. Too widely, political and
> social studies of this kind are regarded as 'extras'. The need
> is granted and a lesson is duly devoted to 'current affairs' or
> to 'civics' or to 'citizenship'. But is this enough? Is it
> even the right approach?(2)

The answers to these questions, as might be expected, were in the
negative. However, when we review the prescription we realize just
what a different educational world we now inhabit. For, it is declared quite roundly, 'citizenship is a matter of character'(3):

> ... there are forward-looking minds in every section of the
> teaching profession ready to reinterpret the old and simple vir-
> tues of humility, service, restraint and respect for personality.
> If the schools can encourage qualities of this kind in their
> pupils, we may fulfil the conditions of a healthy democratic
> society.(4)

The key-note is a grudging admission that Politics could be taught,
in some places was being taught; but its advocates were misguided
since they miss out the essential core of the whole process, namely
service to others(5). We struggle today with out consciences and
our local authorities about value-laden Politics. There was certainly no nonsense about that in the late 1940s: the teacher's job
was to inculcate the worthiness of doing good in the Baden-Powell
tradition. The teacher's responsibility was to prepare his pupils
to be citizens with duties rather than with rights.

Politics via history

One of the most worn of pedagogical clichés is that all teachers
are teachers of English. *Citizens Growing Up* wished to establish
the view that all teachers are teachers of Citizenship. However,

even if the moralising climate of those times had not been changed,
it is unlikely that this policy could have been sustained. It was
too amorphous. Even the Social Studies programmes that were popular
at the time, tied to specific syllabuses as they were, were too
invertebrate to survive. The official attitude that dominated the
1950s and 60s was therefore to refurbish the doctrine of Politics
through History - a well-established tradition dating back to the
nineteenth century. This treatment of the problem is enshrined in
two ministry pamphlets, namely *Teaching History* (1952) and *Towards
World History* (1967).

The emphasis in these pamphlets, inevitably, is on the relationship that can be built into a History syllabus between the traditional aspects of the subject and political (including international)
education. The assumption that underlies these pamphlets, and
which we may take leave to question, is that 'most (History)
teachers tend to stress the preliminary training which the subject
provides in responsible citizenship'(6). We may note parenthetically the retention, as late as 1967, of the phrase 'responsible
citizenship'. However, the main justification for using History
as a vehicle for political education is its interest potential.
The authors of *Teaching History* are worried by the boredom induced
by Civics lessons: 'And if the procedure at Westminster is tackled,
at best, with resignation, can we expect more zest if we place
before them the committees and procedures of the United Nations?'
'We must simplify,' they urge, 'and dramatise, presenting issues
in terms of the individual decisions of responsible men'(7). One
also has a feeling that the authors of these pamphlets are not only
staking a claim for History and justifying its use because of its
positive interest potential, but also because the existence of
European and World History will prevent political education conducted in this context from becoming too insular in content.

In some moods the ministry spokesmen suggest that the relationship between History and political education is a matter of rounding
off the History syllabus chronologically or giving it a political
slant(8). At other times they go the whole hog and suggest that the
two subjects are identical: thus, 'it will be as well to give (the
next generation) as good a political education as may be, which
means giving it an education in history'(9).

The Crowther and Newsom Reports

By the late 1950s the post-war secondary system of education - of
grammar and secondary modern schools - was well established. It was
time for its operation to be investigated. The Central Advisory
Council for Education set up two committees, one to report on the
education of senior secondary pupils (the Crowther committee)(10),
the other on the education of the average and below average pupils
(the Newsom committee)(11). Neither provides a very full discussion
of political education.

That, indeed, is an understatement for the Crowther Report virtually ignores the subject. Paragraphs 168-173 of the report are
devoted to 'The Adolescent's Needs': not a word about political
education. Paragraphs 402-10 are devoted to Sixth Form General
Studies: not a word about political education. Like an oasis in
this desert stands paragraph 175, which declares:

> The fact that politics are controversial - that honest men dis-
> agree - makes preparation for citizenship a difficult matter for
> schools. But it ought to be tackled, and not least for the
> ordinary boys and girls who now leave school at 15 and often do
> not find it easy to see any argument except in personal terms.

But the desert is so vast, we may be forgiven for wondering whether
the oasis is not a mirage.

The Newsom Report is more positive. It even contains the now
well-known categorical assertion that:

> A man who is ignorant of the society in which he lives, who
> knows nothing of its place in the world and who has not thought
> about his place in it, is not a free man even though he has a
> vote.(12)

Nevertheless, it is still severely limited in its horizon of political education. References to the subject are scattered and lacking
in depth of consideration. And, despite the rallying optimism of
paragraph 500 (' ... other schools can tell a different story ...
Optimism is possible'), the reader is reminded on three separate
occasions (paras. 213, 321 and 499) that the general picture is
pretty gloomy. Where there is positive encouragement and advice
the message comes through with most conviction where the authors
urge the teaching of *world* affairs. The word 'world' echoes and
re-echoes throughout the report (see paras. 79, 117, 501-505,
511-512). Like the History pamphlets already referred to, world
consciousness and citizenship is the ideal towards which pupils
should be striving. Now I say this in no spirit of criticism: the
teaching of world affairs is of crucial importance. But national
issues and the place of the child's own community in the wider world
also demand careful treatment.

The Schools Council

The Schools Council was established in 1964 to engage in research
and development work in the whole field of school-level education,
and although it is technically an independent body, drawing its
personnel from all sectors of education, it has come to speak with
the authority of an Establishment voice. Passing references to
political education may be found in their *Working Paper No. 11:
Society and the Young School Leaver* (1967), *Working Paper No. 12:
The Educational Implications of Social and Economic Change* (1967),

and *Enquiry 1: Young School Leavers* (1968). Their message is that
the job is being done badly and that more attention should be paid
to doing it better, especially in the field of world affairs. The
message, however, is muted. A more strident note is struck by
Working Paper No. 2: Raising the School Leaving Age (1965).

Much of what is said in the Newsom Report is reiterated in
Working Paper No. 2. The vital necessity of political education
is cogently and economically expressed: 'When every man is King how
does he become enough of a philosopher to wield power wisely?'(13)
'Everyone more plainly than before must bear some of the world's
weight'(14). The failure of present programmes is also again de-
plored: 'Nothing is more distressing than the fact that very many
pupils who leave our schools at 16 (or before) have very little
good to say for what they have learnt in those subjects which are
concerned with the understanding of human nature and institutions'(15). And the global perspective is once again emphasised(16).
But it is gratifying that the working paper goes further than the
report. Comparatively speaking the working paper places more emphasis on political education than do the mere passing references
of the Newsom Report. Paragraphs 67-71 are largely concerned with
such matters. What is perhaps even more encouraging is the cour-
ageous optimism and adventurousness of the working paper's remarks,
especially in paragraphs 68 and 71 where the teaching of political
abstractions are advocated - even for the less able pupils. 'It
is large ideas which are seminal,' the authors declare, 'not the
details'(17). Ideas which are listed as desirable to teach to
'members of a civilised society' include the rule of law, government by consent, respect for minority views, freedoms of speech
and action. Many teachers would have strong reservations about
entering these realms with such pupils. And while these teachers'
hesitations must be respected we must recognize the bolder view
of the working paper and express the hope that the challenge can
be met. 'It is often said that these pupils are not interested
in ideas ... they are only interested in people and concrete situations. It is just these assumptions which the raising of the school
leaving age gives all in the sphere of secondary education the
opportunity to challenge. For the more able pupils, now staying on
voluntarily in increasing numbers, the fifth year has revealed
powers which many did not suspect'(18). It is the realization of
these powers that is the great test and opportunity and no one is
more directly challenged than the teacher of political studies.

Conclusions

Incredible as it may seem to those who are submerged beneath the
plethora of pamphlets that emanate from the DES and the Schools
Council, no complete statement has been published since 1949 by
any official body on the subject of political education. And what
has been produced has largely been in the nature of unsatisfactory
snippets. 'The Newsom Report's treatment of education for

democracy,' writes Professor Robson (1967), 'is pedestrian, narrow and unimaginative. It makes no mention of trying to make boys and girls understand the place of the individual in society, the duties and responsibilities of a citizen, the probable or possible directions in which society is evolving, the basic problems of international relations. None of these topics is beyond the understanding of a normally intelligent boy or girl aged 14 or above.' From an authority of Professor Robson's standing that is pretty damning; and yet, as we have seen, in many ways the Newsom Report has more to say than many other documents that have recently been published.

Working Paper No. 2 is tantalising in the brief suggestions that it makes. What is needed for the morale of the teachers of Politics and the standing of the subject is a full exposition of these (and other) ideas. For example, the Schools Council *Working Paper No. 39: Social Studies 8-13* is a substantial document. But there are only fleeting references to Politics; indeed, one would not expect more for this age level. What is needed is a comparable work for the 13-18 age group where full emphasis would be accorded to Politics as one of the constituent Social Science disciplines vital for this level. Such a document would take a long time to prepare. In the meantime, is it too much to ask the DES to up-date *Citizens Growing Up*?

NOTES

1. This has been done, but is not available in English. See K. Schleicher (1969), *Politische Bildung in England 1939-1965* (Quelle & Meyer, Heidelberg). A brief survey is available in English in M.E. Bryant, 'Education for citizenship in England' in *Paedagogische Studiën: Maanblad Voor Onderwijs en Opvoeding*. Jaargang, 42 (1965).

2. Ministry of Education (1949) page 14.

3. Ministry of Education (1949) page 21.

4. Ministry of Education (1949) page 41.

5. Ministry of Education (1949) pages 41 and 54.

6. DES (1967) page 2.

7. Ministry of Education (1952) page 53.

8. See for example Ministry of Education (1952) page 31.

9. Ministry of Education (1952) page 2.

10. *15 to 18* (The Crowther Report) (1959).

11. *Half Our Future* (The Newsom Report) (1963).

12. The Newsom Report (1963) paragraph 499.

13. Schools Council (1965) paragraph 48.
14. Schools Council (1965) paragraph 67.
15. Schools Council (1965) paragraph 62.
16. Schools Council (1965) paragraph 70.
17. Schools Council (1965) paragraph 68.
18. Schools Council (1965) paragraph 40.

REFERENCES

C.A.C.E. (1959) *15 to 18* (The Crowther Report) London: HMSO.

C.A.C.E. (1963) *Half Our Future* (The Newsom Report) London: HMSO.

DES (1967) *Towards World History* (Pamphlet No. 52) London: HMSO.

MINISTRY OF EDUCATION (1949) *Citizens Growing Up* (Pamphlet No. 16) London: HMSO.

MINISTRY OF EDUCATION (1952) *Teaching History* (Pamphlet No. 23) London: HMSO.

ROBSON, W.A. (1967) *Politics and Government at Home and Abroad* London: Allen and Unwin.

SCHOOLS COUNCIL (1965) *Working Paper No. 2: Raising the School Leaving Age* London: HMSO.

SCHOOLS COUNCIL (1967) *Working Paper No. 11: Society and the Young School Leaver* London: HMSO.

SCHOOLS COUNCIL (1967) *Working Paper No. 12: The Educational Implications of Social and Economic Change* London: HMSO.

SCHOOLS COUNCIL (1968) *Enquiry 1: Young School Leavers* London: HMSO.

SCHOOLS COUNCIL (1971) *Working Paper No. 39: Social Studies 8-13* London: Evans/Methuen Educational.

1.4
On bias

Bernard Crick

Many councillors, officials and parents would believe in principle that politics should be 'taught in schools' because it is 'so important to us all', but in practice oppose or obstruct because they also believe that it cannot be taught without bias. This poses an important and interesting problem that is both practical and philosophical. The answer is not easy. For to reply that it *can* be taught factually and objectively is then to denature the subject into the kind of irrelevant dullness against which I complained in the first essay, and even then is to give no lasting guarantee that a teacher will not *pronounce* the facts with a sneer or with ecstatic benevolence. And scepticism about whether total objectivity is possible in politics might spread into what should be (but oddly seldom is) equally suspect history. Were I a parent living in Ireland (North or South) I might well be, for instance, in favour of disallowing any history teaching in schools; and if I were living in Hungary, Poland or Czechoslovakia, for instance, I might not, as a matter of personal pride and principle, believe a word that I was taught - though I could do well in the examination, giving 'em back what they want, as may Mrs. Jones' Willie even.

The problem may, rather, be to distinguish between inevitable and human bias, when people can see where we stand, but can see that we are giving a truthful and recognizable account of something; and gross bias, where people may be puzzled where we stand and uncertain (or sure) that we are lying or, at least, grossly distorting. To distinguish between mundane and gross political bias, we have to go back to what we mean by 'politics' at all.

Politics is the creative conciliation of differing interests,

---

* This essay arose from an address given as President of the Politics Association to their annual conference in 1971 and on discussions afterwards. It was printed in *Teaching Politics* May 1972, but this present version has been amended and a postscript is added which is a review of two important books on indoctrination published about the same time as my article.

whether interests are seen as primarily material or moral. In
practice they are usually a blend of both. In all societies known
to history some differences of interests exist, even in the simplest tribal societies with minimal government and even in the
most complex and oppressive totalitarian regimes. But only if it is
accepted that it is natural for men to differ about interests and
ideals does politics cease to be something furtive and residual,
usually scorned and persecuted in autocracies however much practised, and become - in rare and favoured historical circumstances
- something public, tolerated, perhaps even honoured. Sometimes
politics is even the organizing principle of a society, as when
there are actual political institutions, representative assem-
blies and parliaments, which represent the attempt to maintain
order and justice (the primary business of government) amid diversity (the primary condition of liberty) and also amid an increasing well-being for every inhabitant (a specifically modern
condition of stability).

It is necessary to begin so abstractly, to try to see what is
basic or prior to our particular form of parliamentary institutions, precisely in order to make a very concrete point. If
politics is the recognition and tolerance of diversity, so must
be a political or civic education. No wonder the young, in a
growing complicated society, sometimes rebel against, but are more
often cynical about, teaching which simply asserts *the* values of
our society, *the* consensus, *the* parliamentary system and *the*
Constitution. In fact, we live in a society which represents considerable diversity of values. Consider only the major religions
and branches of Christianity, true that they have much in common,
but we cannot take their adherents seriously if we ignore their
great differences. There is always a case for toleration, for
understanding something of which one disapproves so that one knows
how not to overreact to it, how to practise forbearance, how to
persuade but not to proscribe or persecute: but there is seldom a
real case for an ecumenicity which obliterates all distinctions
of doctrine. And the argument is similar for secular and political
moralities, for they too are not one but many. To stress deliberately 'what we have in common' and to underplay differences is
both a false account of politics and a cripplingly dull basis for
a political education.

'The consensus' can be imposed and, if it is imposed, it is,
indeed, oppressive[1]; but if it is imposed, it is imposed for the
sake of particular political doctrines, not for the sake of the
maintenance of order as such: only in a minimal sense of adherence
to rules of procedure is 'consensus' a necessary condition of order.
In the maximal sense of distinct moral systems, there have been
plenty of political systems, both free and unfree, which have
survived for long periods of time amid the most vivid diversity of
moral codes (our own, for example, but even the Roman, the Hapsburg
and the Ottoman Empires). There are outer limits, of course, and
what these are is a difficult, interesting but different question.

It is simply not true, however, that the greater the consensus,
the more stable and just is the state. There is much evidence
that points in the other direction, that the more such a consensus
is imposed, the more oppressive and brittle the state becomes
(by 'brittle' is meant something strong if used in a fixed and controlled position, but fragile if exposed to unexpected pressures).
'Consensus' is not something to be invoked like spiritual cement
to stick something together that would otherwise be broken apart;
it is, on the contrary, a quality which arises to ease the continued co-existence of those who have already been living together.
It is not prior to the experience of a political community; it is
a product of that experience, and therefore cannot meaningfully be
taught until a person understands, however generally and simply,
the actual political problems and controversies of his community.

Certainly 'the parliamentary system' and 'the Constitution'
are values, but they must not be treated as if they are primary
values - like justice, equality, freedom, love, truth, welfare,
fraternity, compassion, and responsibility: they are secondary
values or procedural conventions, valuable in so far as they help
enhance and realize primary values in many different forms and
circumstances. If all that is taught is the need to respect the
secondary or procedural values of 'parliament' or 'the Constitution' as if they were primary values, then naturally any people of
any individual or civic spirit will suspect, as the socialist rev-
olutionaries put it, that these concepts are masking hidden values
- and because hidden, oppressive and bad.

I have found it difficult to convince some students that the
concealed values which they seek to unmask can, in fact, often
be innocuous, sometimes even good values; and that the appearance
of deliberate indoctrination, that can easily be created by going
on and on about the rules and procedures of Parliament and the
Constitution, is as often bad teaching as it is covert politics.

I find the case for teaching politics in schools, as part of
a general and a liberal education, an obvious one. But is must
be taught realistically, otherwise it can create either more cynicism or more disillusion than would have been created by its
absence. By 'realistically' I mean teaching which will encourage
a growing and more detailed awareness that 'the Constitution'
and the particular form of a parliament are devices for conciliat-
ing, sometimes resolving but as often merely containing, basic
conflicts of interest. To say 'differences of opinion' is, I think,
too weak an expression. 'Conflict' does not necessarily imply
violence, not by any means, it is perhaps more often a matter of
persuasion and of ballot; but conflicts of economic and social
interest can easily turn violent, if political will and skill fail.
This is precisely why a political education is so important, and
why it must inform the pupil, in an increasingly complex manner up
through the age groups and ability levels, what the basic conflicts in our society are. Only then can the pupil grow to

understand the importance of mere procedural rules. He is indeed a fool if he takes it for granted that the Constitution is a good thing. He will want to know - if he is the kind of person whom free societies need as citizens, not simply subjects - how it actually works and which problems it resolves, stifles or ignores. The difficulty about civic education is that it must be aimed at creating citizens. If we want a passive population, leave well alone.

There are some who are tempted to argue that we face disaster and a breakdown of the parliamentary system unless we do something urgently about civic education! Personally, I am not, thank God, one who can, in Great Britain, beat these alarm drums with much conviction. 'Breakdown' is a stirring melody, but someone at the other end of the drum can also beat in perfect harmony a revolutionary theme: that the system will break down, without any help in this direction, so hurry down to the pot cellars and wait. In some ways I wish I could beat the drum, it might stimulate some energy somewhere. But I notice that people who do beat the drum at whichever end, do not seem to act accordingly. The leaders of the Festival of Light and the editors of *Oz* were each as theatrical as the other. What I think is far more likely than breakdown is a gradual decay of civic spirit in this country; I do not fear a growth in the following of extremists of either Left or Right so much as a retreat into the immediate home and the materialistic self, a growing selfishness, seediness, secondrateness, lack of energy, indifference and a growth of 'permissiveness' in its true sense. A sense that should affront any radical as much as any author of a Black Paper on education, that of simply not caring to draw any moral distinctions any more, a kind of liberalism gone soft, as if it is as wrong to persuade as to coerce; a care only for external excitements, no interest in caring for others. Such permissiveness is, of course, not really a socialist or a radical ethic, but an aristocratic one, not even anarchist in logical outcome but nihilistic; and it is propagated far more effectively by ad-men, trying to break down the remnants of a sensible middle class and puritan prejudice against extravagance than it is by the underground press or by, as some profess to believe, aberrant teachers. The opposite to an oppressive society is not a permissive society, but a tolerant society, not the absence of values, but a plurality of values[2]. It is in this context that a genuine civic education is needed. In any case, if it were true that we are faced with an impending breakdown of society, schools would be unequipped to arrest it: solutions could only lie in the sphere of public action by political parties and governments. It is as dangerous to expect too much from civic education, indeed from education generally, as it is to expect too little. But if the real fear is decay, decline and purposelessness, then an enhanced civic education, both more of it and with heightened standards among its teachers, has a crucial role to play.

The case for political education is obvious: to learn about politics

as one should learn about anything important; to equip an individual better to protect and extend his rights; to give to society as
a whole that greater strength and flexibility that comes from
voluntary participation rather than from coerced or bribed com-
pliance; and to create or convey that experience of respectful
disapproval of other viewpoints which is the basis of toleration
which is, in turn, the condition of freedom.

How then, in general, should we teach? I have already argued
for a greater realism and for beginning with a tale drawn from
current affairs and contemporary history. The subjects of political dispute must first be identified rather than constitutional
rules and parliamentary procedure. The horse really must precede
the cart if we are to get anywhere. Any politician knows this; it
makes sense. But any politician will doubt the objectivity of
any teacher. Your objectives are fine, he may say, but are they in
fact possible? Does not the teaching of issues degenerate into
attempted indoctrination? If faced with a choice simply between
the old constitutional approach or else open indoctrination, might
not the alternative be neither? We have doubts about churches
relying on schools for the teaching of religion, and so do churches.
Could not political parties and the media look after civic education better than the school?

Of course, there is a problem. It should not be denied. And
some of us at all levels of education could at times brush up our
professional standards. Certainly I will defend that certain
Lecturer's right to his own political opinions (although certainly
not to the death): but I would seek to persuade him not to be so
self-indulgent; and I probably would not promote him for he sounds
to me like a thoroughly bad teacher. It is all very well 'etc.' of
him to go on about the dangers of authority in general; but it
would help if he realized that no society can flourish without
some authority, that the question is not one of authority as such,
but of the use and abuse of authority. The abuse of authority
occurs precisely when a person or institution goes beyond his or
her competence in fulfilling the function for which he or she
should be given attention or obedience, as the case may be, into
laying down the law about irrelevant things - however important.
I myself, for instance, claim or gracefully acknowledge, considerable authority as a teacher of politics. I notice that people turn
up voluntarily when I come to speak and treat me, if not always
with perfect respect, at least with substantial lack of open
interruption. I am reasonably expert as a *political theorist* in
conveying the plausibility of different political doctrines or
policies, in identifying basic problems, and in analysing what price
has to be paid for pursuing one policy rather than another, and when
'contradictions' are practical rather than formal. Opinions of
other authorities may differ, but I notice a fair number of us who
are treated as authorities nonetheless. I can go further than
that: I have a more modest and tentative authority as a *political
philosopher* in analysing what kind of principles, rules or standards

can be sensibly invoked in debate about political differences
(which has nothing to do with the differences themselves). But I
have no kind of authority whatever in propagating *political
doctrines*, that is, to say what should be done. I may say so, I
do frequently say so; but in doing so either abuse my authority
in speaking thus on formal or academic occasions, or more often,
my authority is simply not relevant and is, I hope, ignored.

Three obvious types of flagrant bias exist. The socialists of
57 varieties (or 58 counting myself) who go on and on teaching
that 'it's all a racket' and 'what should be done about it' are
only the most famous case, and somewhat unfairly so, for there is
also the Tory who avoids all discussion of political problems,
sticks to the Constitution but builds into its alleged rules all
his own prejudices about the virtues of traditional order and the
dangers of change. Similarly, there is the Liberal who teaches
that institutional and electoral reform alone will solve all
things, and in the name of civics creates a unique and deadly brew
of disillusionment with the past coupled with a guarantee of per-
petual frustration in the future. And, of course, we all mean so
well. I do not, in fact, believe that flagrant bias is very
common: but the indulgent or unselfcritical few discredit the
sensible many.

Among those who admit that there is a problem of flagrant bias,
two kinds of response have been the most usual. The first I call
the Swinburnian or the exhortatory school. Like Swinburne they
take the view that if one needs must sin, and one needs must, then
sin openly, grandly and 'honestly'. Bias cannot be avoided (or
a few hardy souls are simply sure that they are right and others
are wrong); in which case, air it openly! To be openly and im-
passionately 'Somethingistic' will stimulate one's hearers into
taking the subject seriously, into forming their own views or
counter-attack. This is how Harold Laski used to teach. And it
was wonderful to hear him: such a completely dedicated, biased but
tolerant man. He took great delight in occasionally being contra-
dicted even during a lecture; even in those far off disciplined
days before the invention of Mr. Wedgwood Benn and participation.
He needed to, for excited interventions alone could vindicate this
alleged method. Few students were, in fact, stirred to an equally
passionate and informed opposition; those who did not like it,
simply switched off, were more sceptical about authority than ever.
For to them *he* became authority and its typical abuse; and they
turned in the expected answers in the exams. (There was parrot
Laski at the London School of Economics just as there was to be
parrot Oakeshott.) If university students did not respond by
'creative antagonism' to this one-way dialectic, how much less
likely that school pupils will? They will either accept or reject
not just it, but the whole problem or subject. And a good job too.
I admire the natural, protective scepticism of secondary school
children which limits the damage that exhortatory teaching can do
in any field of practical morals. The trouble is, however, that

this scepticism is negative, it prevents disaster (much like our
present state of parliamentary politics), but it seems to inhibit
the making of real decisions and commitments by the individuals
in politics.

The other common response is the constitutional approach, sometimes supplemented by catalogues of pure facts about administration and local government. When I argued against the adequacy
of 'teaching the constitution' as a starting point, I did not deny
that there are in a clear sense important constitutional rules.
But if they should not mean anything to the wise except as a
response to the basic political problems of our recent and past
history, then how can they be meaningfully and interestingly taught
in schools in advance of a knowledge of what our main political
problems are and have been? And the particular deadly badge of the
constitutional-factual approach is 'the comprehensive text-book'.
For once the bit is riveted to the teeth, anything can be tackled
and reduced to the same apolitical flatness and oppressive dullness. 'What have been the main proposals for parliamentary reform?'
asks an A-level board, which is then tackled in exactly the same
prepacked spirit as 'What are the duties of the Speaker of the
House of Commons?' 'Why did demands for Parliamentary reform arise
in the 1960s?' is a much more interesting and political question,
whereas a full answer to the former could only and should only
be given by the Clerk to the Select Committee on Procedure.

In reducing politics to quasi-legal fact, or in avoiding it
altogether in schools and colleges, who knows whether bad teaching,
bad syllabuses or ultra-caution is most to blame? But if there
are local politicians who are nervous of schools and colleges
'teaching politics', surely their sense of realism could lead them
to see that probably more harm is done by the constitutional-factual
school in boring pupils and making them believe that the real
problems are being withheld from them, than can be done even by
the excesses of the 'open and honest bias school'. I do not favour
that school. I think it is a mistaken theory of education, frequently an irresponsible self-indulgence on the part of the teacher
or lecturer, or sometimes just plain incompetence to convey the
inwardness of other doctrines. I only speculate that it does at
least keep alive a sense of citizenship, and an interest in politics, whereas the former however well-meant makes politicians
seem both dull and evasive (which is a type they certainly are not,
being more often quirky individualists willing to talk very freely,
if asked).

How then, specifically, should politics be taught? The constitutional and the exhortatory-bias schools have the most spokesmen,
but they do not exclude other possibilities. There is an alternative. What I want now very briefly to argue (and to spend some
years working out its implications) is not so much novel, as seldom
expressed: it is probably the commonsense of the average good
teacher.

Start from the premise that in politics and in morals there is
no way of proving what is best. But that there are ways of arguing reasonably, which at least exclude some possibilities. Everything that is possible is not therefore equally desirable. At
the end of the day, however, people will differ; but it is likely
that they will differ less violently the more they know about the
lives, motives and beliefs of those they differ from. Prejudice
does not vanish with greater knowledge, but it is usually dimin-
ished and made more containable; and I personally do believe that
there are genuine differences of values, not simply of prejudices.

While it is not possible to say objectively 'what should be
done', it is easily possible to be reasonably objective and truthful in our use of evidence in political and moral argument, even
to reach broad agreement among antagonists as to what counts as
evidence relevant to a dispute. Political education is not unlike
a judicial process in the Common Law tradition. Evidence is
presented not by a judge or officials but by advocates. But it
has to be of a kind that would convince a neutral judge or jury.
The advocate has no business being on his feet if he has not a
case; but he is incompetent to present his case if he cannot handle
evidence objectively. The analogy is not exact. It is relevant
to the relationship between bias and objectivity rather than to
the structure of authority in courts or schools. I am not saying
that the teacher should simply be neutral, judging and conducting
teaching always or often by debate. Even if he were to try this,
he would have to teach the young the reasonable cases that provide
justifications for their prejudices. The teacher has, certainly in
the early stages, to be judge, prosecution and defence rolled into
one. But just as he has to show what is evidence, he also has
to show how it can reasonably be interpreted differently - and in
typical patterns, that are often conservative, liberal or socialist. And not just the concepts they hold, but how they use them.
His own view (for I think it likely that he will have one, or else
he will be a very dull teacher), will be relevant at the end of
the process, if his pupils ask. It would be an evasion not to
answer truthfully, especially if silence fortified the myth of
objectivity about values. But it is impertinent and irrelevant to
put the question too soon. After showing how the same facts get
interpreted in typically different ways, then 'my view' as teacher
falls much more into place, can do less direct harm than others may
fear or less direct good than I may rashly hope. But they may be
thinking for themselves a little bit more and with a better knowledge of consequences.

Where to start? As a political theorist, I can only offer some
amateur but commonsense suggestions, for educationalists in this
country, unlike Germany and America, for instance, have given the
subject little thought. It seems to me that there is a strong case
for starting with the issues of the moment (of course, one keeps
on coming back to them at every level), and of giving an accurate
and simplified account of what they are. At the next stage,

ability level or class year, set these problems and disputes in
their historical context (the dead-ground of recent history, ignored by most of the books). One must start somewhere. 'What was
the effect of the war on British politics?' 'What did Labour do
after it and why?' 'How did the Conservatives come back and what
changes did they bring about?' This may worry the historian (too
near) and disappoint some of the more lively teachers of politics
(too far). But I cannot see how one can create any understanding
both of the objectives and the limitations of British politics (for
it is always necessary to trim between the disinterest that comes
from there being no objectives and the disillusion that comes from
those objectives being unrealistic) unless topical problems are
set in a fairly broad historical context, however thin the detail
has to be. (We are talking, please, of political education for
all, not of A-level as pre-university exams.)

Then at the next stage, there is a double need. By then there
should be enough general knowledge of political issues and problems to see how the institutions of government, parliament and
party deal with them - which leads one into some of the more important conventions of the constitution. At the same time one must
attempt to formalise how and why the parties have differed through
the events of the first two stages, that is to elaborate an understanding of them as bodies of doctrine which involve not merely
different objectives but also different ways of perceiving political problems, sometimes even different views as to what are problems. This dual task sounds a tall order, especially if one were
talking of a one-year rather than a two-year process. But I would
argue that it is so important to relate institutions to ideas, to
show that the one necessarily involves the other, and that the two
final stages in a political education must be taken together, however big a sacrifice is needed of content. It is so much more
important that children learn to think politically than that they
can define the powers of the District Auditor or name all the
parliamentary regimes of the world.

I would also argue that underlying each level the teacher should
have clearly worked out some short *catalogue raisonne* of the basic
political concepts, such as 'power', 'authority' and 'liberty', etc.
whose usage his examples should illustrate. I do not think that
they can usefully be taught and discussed directly and explicitly
except at a really advanced level. Always start with problems, but
use them to illustrate concepts; otherwise realism is wholly
directionless and impressionistic. I am not quite saying, as do
some educationalists, that every subject can be reduced to a limited vocabulary of concepts. There are special difficulties in
politics as in other moral subjects and problems. But I think some
simplifications are possible and better almost any framework for
the teacher or the school than none, or the pretence that there is
none which merely means that the concepts are implicit, unconscious,
and 'masked'.

At every level, however, the main task is to create empathy[3].
To create an understanding of the plausibility of the differing
viewpoints that the student is likely to encounter in his life,
and how these viewpoints do not merely define objectives, but define problems too. That 'willing suspension of disbelief' of
which Coleridge spoke as constituting poetic faith is called for
every day in politics and in political education. Political
thought does not call on us to love an adversary, or anything
as extreme or as way out as that, but simply that we understand
him; perhaps in order to oppose him more effectively. Political
thinking may create more mutual respect, but it will not obliter-
ate differences. It is lack of this empathy that often worries
me about university students and some teachers. I may lay claim
to some strong views; but although a socialist, I am obsessed with
the plausibility, for instance, of conservatism. I teach that
conservatism is a doctrine of government: it says that those who
govern best are those who are most experienced, thus the rise and
fall of societies is to be explained by the character of the
governing class. And it is a doctrine of change: that gradual
change is always best, to respond flexibly to events (of which so
much cannot be controlled anyway), rather than to try to shape
them. Hence the importance of tradition. Many other versions
could be advanced, but I think my account would be regarded as
fair in the sense that many Conservatives would accept it. And I
'teach it' not just as a doctrine to be described but as a highly
plausible theory of history and politics to be used. Certainly
Conservatives have succeeded in governing this country more often
than not since the great Reform Bill of 1867, and certainly most
situations are to be understood in terms of historical antecedents,
rather than as acts of deliberate will. The Liberal would say that
societies rise, fall, prosper or decay because of individual invention and initiative: he sees politics in terms of the rights
and capabilities of individuals. The Socialist sees the basis of
society as the relationship of man-as-worker to methods of production; individuals are defined and limited by their position in
social groups, and ultimately groups formed by cooperation will
prove more strong and productive than groups formed by economic
competition.

Now, of course, that is a foolishly over-simplified model. There
are many sub-categories; and there are even political doctrines
which cut across such party ideologies - such as nationalism and
faith in technicians. I only report that I have found this simple
triad reasonably fruitful to use, and think that it can be used at
any level. Perhaps at the very simplest level one can say that
the Conservative thinks that the distribution of power and goods
would not be as it is without good reason; the Liberal thinks that
distribution could and should be more fair in relation to ability;
and the Socialist thinks that distribution could and should be made
radically more equal. But I also report a lack even in some first-
year university students of any ability to express the plausibility

of other persuasions than their own, either as doctrines of action
or theories of society. Something of this nature both could and
should be done earlier. At present there is more need to stimulate knowledge and empathy rather than mere self-expression. That
is the challenge to teachers. And it can be assessed.

Thus I would reject both the 'value-free' and the 'honest bias'
approach to political education. Quite simply, it is impossible
to be value-free and attempts to achieve this blissful state of
moral suspension involve high degrees of either boredom or hypocrisy. At the end of the day, after - *but only after* - a sense of
empathy has been stimulated for the beliefs, motivations and circumstances of the plurality of political doctrines and moral codes
that coexist in our society, the recognition of bias can even be
helpful in stimulating a concern for active citizenship. Biased
opinions by themselves do no harm: what matters is *how* we hold
our opinions, whether tolerantly, reasonably, with respect for
those of others, and with some knowledge of the consequences together with regard for contrary evidence.

Simple bias, then, is all but unavoidable and is no more harm-
ful than tastes for this or that food or drink - when not pressed
to excess at the expense of reasonable judgment about everything
else, like a child calling foods that it simply does not like,
'horrid' and 'nasty'. What is excess? When one's taste or part-
isanship for something or somebody leads one not merely to run
down everything else but invariably to give almost wholly unrecog-
nisable accounts of what they are. Simple bias is when one's
prejudices are clear but one's judgment is reasonable; and gross
bias is when one's perceptions of what one is prejudiced against
are so distorted as to be useless in dealing with those problems or
people in a political manner. Gross bias, in other words, destroys
one's perceptions.

The proof of the pudding is ever in the eating. Assessment,
that is examination, of the style of teaching politics which we are
advocating will tell one far more than the memory tests of 'the
powers of the Prime Minister' and 'the stages of a Public Bill'.
I would have examinations assess whether students can argue a
case for *and* against a proposal, whether they could identify what
party adheres to which of some stated policies, and how *different*
political adherents would react to a stated problem. The practical
answer to fears of bias is for the objects of the course to be
clearly assessable: will it have increased their knowledge of what
political issues there are and of other people's reactions?

After informative and empathetic teaching can come commitment,
for the pupil, or the 'unmasking' of the teacher; but only after,
not before. The temporal order is crucial. Syllabuses need
changing and making more realistic to ensure this, but professional
standards may need tightening as well. Political teaching should
at least be open. The 'honest bias' school are right in this, at

least. The teacher is one man, just as is the party member of the
local education committee. In civilised states we are used to
playing different roles at different times, but rarely, only in the
most special cases, does one role utterly exclude another. Some
bias and some confusion of roles cannot be avoided, so to go to
drastic extremes to avoid them is usually to create a cure far
worse than a mild disease. We may sometimes need more self-
restraint, but seldom sterilising. If there is flagrant bias, it
would matter far less if the syllabuses were more realistic and
the teaching more knowledgeably empathetic. Good Politics teaching
is not entirely a matter of honesty and dedication: it is also a
matter of a greater professionalism. Colleges and Institutes of
Education should give up their economic or nervous habit of treat-
ing Politics as, at best, a subsidiary part of another discipline;
far more specialist appointments are needed, and creative work on
curriculum development. But, of course, in the end it does all
depend on the teacher. And if teachers cannot be trusted to teach
Politics, however professionally, they ultimately should not be trusted to teach geometry - for one man who taught me, I remember well,
taught geometry as a proof that God designed the universe and another saw it as a self-evident demonstration of the truth of
materialism. Both were good teachers.

Postscript

Two important books on indoctrination appeared at about the same
time as I wrote and published the first version of this article 'On
Bias'. Since the subjects are closely related, I add here a review
of them that I wrote at the time.*

As the general editor of the International Library of the
Philosophy of Education says - of which series Dr. Snook's anthology is part: 'there is a growing interest in the philosophy of
education among students of philosophy as well as amongst those
who are more specifically and practically concerned with educational
problems.' Professor Richard Peters may seem, with some excuse,
to be blowing his own trumpet - which I have always thought much
more modest than inducing others to do it for one. Philosophers
in the analytical tradition are not necessarily becoming more concerned with ethics, education and politics, but they are showing
welcome signs of boredom with the world of purely invented examples.
They are taking the trouble to inform themselves a little about

---

* *Concepts of Indoctrination: Philosophical Essays* Edited by
  I.A. Snook (Routledge and Kegan Paul, 1972, 210pp.)
  Indoctrination and Education Edited by I.A. Snook (Routledge and
  Kegan Paul, 1972, 118pp.)
  This review originally appeared in *Teaching Politics* May, 1974.

some other disciplines or problem-areas which raise interesting, part philosophical and part factual, questions.

'Indoctrination' is one of the most interesting and important of these. Nowadays there is a widespread suspicion that if anyone talks about religious, moral or political education, some form of indoctrination is being suggested and that indoctrination is bad. But not so long ago it was taken for granted that indoctrination *should* take place in these areas: the main debate was whether it should be done directly or indirectly. Have our attitudes changed or has there been a shift of meaning in the concept? I think it fairly clear that our attitudes have changed. We do think it wrong that religious or political belief should be imposed on children. And also our beliefs have changed: most social scientists are now very sceptical that general adherence to a clearly defined moral doctrine is necessary for the preservation of social order. This was once regarded as axiomatic. We are aware that politically organized societies can and commonly do contain a plurality of value-systems within them. If 'consensus' has any meaning - and I for one am very sceptical of its use as an explanation of how order is maintained, especially as it is then so often treated, in the next breath, as a consequence of order rather than a cause; if consensus has any meaning, it is plainly at a level of abstraction concerned with norms, rules and procedures, not with the substantive content of moral and political doctrines.

We now all seem suspiciously unanimous against indoctrination. The traditionalist fears that any political education will necessarily involve indoctrination; and the revolutionary generously hints that the whole educational system is indoctrinatory. So perhaps the usage and meaning has also shifted as well as our attitudes to it, if all feel against it: 'you are a hack teacher, he indoctrinates, I am ideologically correct.'

The two books under review cover much the same ground, even reach much the same qualified, tentative but clear enough conclusions, but they are at different levels of complexity. The symposium gathers in all the most important articles on the problem of recent years, except for two, constantly referred to, which were not available because of copyright difficulties: John Wilson's 'Education and Indoctrination' and R.M. Hare's 'Adolescents into Adults', both of which can be found in T.H.B. Hollins (ed.) *Aims in Education: the philosophical approach* (Manchester University Press, 1964). The controversy about the actual meaning or the most useful meaning of the concept centres on *method, content* and *intentions*. Some hold that any beliefs can be indoctrinated, others argue that 'indoctrination' can only properly be used of false or doubtful beliefs, and others that only beliefs in the elaborated form that it is sensible to call 'doctrines' can be indoctrinated (i.e. it refers to something both systematic and important). Difficulties abound. If *method* is the key, must it work? Suppose my sample is deliberately biased, and yet nonetheless I reach a true result; or is all unmethodical teaching (as the sociology of education crew would suggest) indoctrinatory - in the sense of uncritically relaying accepted social values? If *contents* is the key, then falsehood should reign, yet surely very often precisely what we mean by indoctrination is when the truth is thrust on us. And the content could be false, expertly indoctrinated and yet somehow not believed: the effort proves counter-productive. Suppose a man teaches a false scientific belief, say that the earth is flat or that the universe is finite. If contrary evidence is not available, it would be foolish to call such teaching of received truths 'indoctrination'. The evidence may be available in principle, but it is necessary to remember whom we are considering: a school teacher is not a scientist. Strictly speaking he cannot be held responsible for whether such things are true or false, only responsible for whether the sources he uses can reasonably be regarded as authoritative. All authorities - to anticipate - must be questioned, none must be above explaining why they may be treated as authoritative; but the teacher himself cannot replace authorities.

The twelve essays are nearly all of a high standard and very stretching. I find the contributions by Antony Flew, R.F. Atkinson and John Wilson particularly interesting. But it is fair to warn that they are more likely to interest philosophers in some aspects of education than to be readily grasped by any but the most able B.Ed. students in the colleges of education. So a most excellent idea to bring out at the same time in the justly famed 'Students Library of Education' a short and truly elementary book covering the same ground. Snook's own book should be read and pondered by every teacher of politics. And it has an excellent bibliography.

He lucidly expounds the distinctions he made in his own important essay in the anthology. 1. *Cases of clear indoctrination*: (a) teaching an ideology as if it were the only possible one with a claim to rationality; (b) teaching, as if they are certain, propositions the teacher knows to be uncertain; and (c) teaching propositions which are false and known by the teacher to be false. 2. *Cases which seem like indoctrination, but which are not since they are unavoidable in any possible society*: (a) teaching young children what is conventionally regarded as correct behaviour (i.e. there will always be some conventions, and not indoctrination if taught as conventions and not as truths); (b) teaching facts by rote (e.g. the tables - whichever way round); and (c) unconsciously influencing the child in certain directions (although once you realise that you are having such and such a side effect, it could be indoctrinatory not to attempt to reduce or change the effect). 3. *Problematic cases*: (a) inculcating doctrines believed by the teacher to be certain but which are substantially disputed (i.e. problematic because one doesn't know whether the textbook writer is just a lazy old dog or a deliberate reactionary refusing to present newer, alternative explanations); and (b) teaching *any* subject, he concludes, 'e.g. chemistry, without due concern for understanding'.

To Snook understanding, rationality and evidence are the divides between education and indoctrination. In the small book he sums up his contentions:

> I have argued that the indoctrinator intends the pupil to be-
> lieve P 'regardless of the evidence'. In full blown cases of
> intention, this captures very well the difference between the
> indoctrinator and the educator. For the educator, the beliefs
> are always secondary to the evidence: he wants his students
> to end up with whatever beliefs the evidence demands. He is
> concerned with methods of assessing data, standards of accuracy,
> and validity of reasoning. The answers are subsidiary to the
> methods of gaining answers. The indoctrinator, however, is
> typically more concerned with the imparting of beliefs ... it
> is the evidence that is of subsidiary importance.

Thus, Snook argues convincingly that indoctrination is teaching something in such a manner that it is believed regardless of evidence. Evidence is, of course, not scorned; Snook points out that the real doctrinaire may rehearse his classes in the most elaborate 'proofs' by rote; but my sole criticism of Snook's exposition is that he does not really explore procedures for discriminating between such proofs and those probabilities which carry with them 'the inner worm of doubt', true civilised scepticism and tolerance. Here I find John Wilson's work in moral education very helpful. I would want to put to Snook that in moral and political education there is usually a fairly limited stock of recognized alternative viewpoints and explanations: the pupil must be made aware of these, indeed if he is lacking in empathy for them, if he cannot understand how a sensible person can possibly be a conservative or a socialist or whatever, then he must be worked upon by the teacher - with techniques perhaps very much like those of the indoctrinator, except that the object is tolerance and understanding and not belief.

A further question at a deeper level raises itself in both books. Can indoctrination ever be justified? Surely the democratisation of Germany after the war? or what about aversion therapy? Should we not indoctrinate democracy?

Oddly, this question is never quite met head on. The readings lack a political philosopher, and Snook, like John Wilson and Jacob Bruner, despite many a glancing side-reference to politics, somehow avoids the most difficult and important field of applied ethics (at least to Aristotle and the whole speculative tradition of reason and nature that followed from him), politics. I think the formal answer is fairly simple. To indoctrinate democracy is a contradiction in terms if 'democracy' is really democratic. This is a different question from whether constraint is needed or not to introduce political education (of a new kind) into German schools, or more generally to keep children in school (an assumption that some mystical-technocrats would now challenge). But a democratic political process, a genuine political education and a scientific method that attempts to falsify its own hypotheses as its only view of truth (and which can, nonetheless, proceeding through doubt and scepticism yet generalise with such astounding accuracy), have, after all - why do we so often hesitate to say? - much in common.

I find it odd to reflect that in the fields where people are most worried about indoctrination, that is religious and political education, there is already a plurality of viewpoints which should actually make the task of the teacher easier - once he sees that the task is not to avoid any discussion of beliefs, but is to explain and understand the differences between the beliefs that there are. It is much more difficult to avoid indoctrination, believing that one is teaching the truth and nothing but the truth, in fields some of whose occupants give themselves such (pseudo) scientific airs, like Psychology and Economics. But full-blown indoctrination is probably a more rare thing than most suppose - simple bias is the more common and difficult problem.

NOTES

1. 'The consensus can be imposed, and, if it is imposed, it is, indeed, oppressive.' Let me allow myself an indulgent commentary on my own text since so many young teachers, particularly of socialist persuasions, not necessarily 'extremists' by any means, are plainly worried, morally worried, that to teach the consensus is oppressive. 'Oppression' carries both physical and psychological connotations. Young radicals who are always contrasting 'oppression' and 'liberation' often confuse these senses. They do not really mean that school civics is oppressive in the sense that behind the facade of the school is the reality of the capitalist system etc. and its instruments of violence, the army and the police, etc. They mean that school is 'oppressive' much in the sense that I can remember using the word in a suburban adolescence for the special quality of compulsory religious instruction and for Sunday evenings at home when the whole family, who did not get on at all well together, felt they had to sit together: oppression meant the inevitable, the tedious and the restrictive. One longed to be out or away, or doing something on one's own: that would be 'liberation' enough.

It is melodramatic to pass automatically from this psychological sense to the physical sense - as does the superficial radical. There is no necessary connection. But it is equally silly of bad teachers by dismissing out of hand the 'physical oppression' charge to think that thereby they have answered the psychological one. They have not. The radicals raise the right questions but give fan-

tastic answers. But in refuting the answer, one has not removed
or answered the question. Dull, formalistic and evasive political
teaching *is* oppressive - very oppressive: not dramatically restrictive and destructive like physical coercion, but deadening, ener-
vating, and productive of cynicism. If much civics teaching is
thus 'oppressive', it does not threaten the structure of our society, nor does it do much to preserve it; but it debilitates it
and renders the quality shoddy and unconsciously it helps to keep
inhabitants down to the level of subjects, rather than to help them
to raise themselves up to be citizens.

2. I have expanded this distinction in a popular way in my
'Toleration and Permissiveness' in a symposium *Towards An Open
Society* (Pemberton Books, 1971), and more academically in
'Toleration and Tolerance in Theory and Practice', *Government and
Opposition*, Spring 1971.

3. Empathy is an ability and a value which needs encouraging far
more than personality. I am tempted to say that there is too much
encouragement of personality, bringing hot coals to a burning
Newcastle in many cases; and there is too little attempt to instil
that kind of knowledge of other people's beliefs, motivations, and
circumstances which is a necessary condition of empathy and toleration. It is foolish to praise and encourage mere opinionating and
expression, unless it is based on some knowledge. 'Role playing'
exercises and 'mock-parliaments' are pretty useless if the actors
have no knowledge of their parts. We are in danger of swinging
too far from teaching to learning. Good political behaviour cannot
be learned or imposed by traditional instruction, but equally all
learning, even in 'self directed learning' needs direction, direction needs a sense of tradition, a sense of the point of departure;
and early learning particularly needs good teachers. Certainly
they should not learn by rote; they should extend, explore, em-
broider and speculate (even about the organization of and the
patterns of authority in the school - why not? homely example);
but from some shared, sure and secure basis. It is unlikely that
this basis will not need,in some quite old-fashioned sense, to be
taught. It is not part of the experience of a child; and the discovery of what are untutored perceptions of politics may have its
social scientific interest, but it has little educational value.
The humanistic tradition of education sees knowledge as part of
the growth of a person. The cult of personality is ultimately the
enemy of knowledge, and thus of humanistic and humane values. The
two together, never the one without the other. And ideas are always
to be understood in contexts and circumstances, but they are never
mere inhuman and unfree products of circumstances.

1.5
Politics as a university discipline and political education in schools

Derek Heater

The development of politics as a university discipline

Forty years ago Ernest Barker in his inaugural lecture at Cambridge described Political Science as 'certainly nebulous, probably dubious and possibly disputatious'[1]. The struggle by political scientists to give their subject both clearer definition and greater respectability has met with considerable success in recent years. The consequent blossoming of university departments of Political Science (or Politics or Government) has been a notable academic achievement. Vagueness, doubt and dispute still restrain the subject, though one cannot question that the break-through has now been achieved. Even as late as 1954, Professor Robson stated that Oxford, London and Manchester were the only universities with flourishing courses[2]. A variety of evidence reveals how the position has been transformed in the 1960s. One indicator is the number of senior university appointments in the fields of Politics and International Relations. The number of Chairs in English and Welsh universities in 1948 was 10; there were still only 16 in 1960; while in 1966 the number had risen to 38[3]. The availability of courses was revealed by a survey conducted by Dr. Nettl (1964) based on questionnaires completed by 27 U.K. universities. He calculated that:

> roughly 26 per cent (7 of the 27 universities) offered a politics special Honours degree, 37 per cent (10 of the 27) a combined Honours degree only, and 37 per cent (10 of the 27) offered politics specialisation within a social science or economics degree.[4]

Nettl was able to conclude that 'Certainly politics has become institutionalised as one of the major social science subjects in Britain.' But even since Nettl's survey the subject has further expanded. In the session 1966-67 special degree courses were

---

* First published in *Political Quarterly* July-September 1969.

available at 19 universities in England and Wales and the subject
appeared in the combined courses of a further 10[5]. Because of
the increasing popularity of combined degree courses it is difficult to acquire accurate figures of students pursuing and graduating
in the subject. But from figures that are available it is possible
further to corroborate this expansionist trend. For example, the
Heyworth Report (1965) revealed almost a doubling (from 107 to
202)of the number of Honours graduates in Politics from the academic year 1955-56 to 1962-63[6].

If we turn to the content of undergraduate courses, Nettl's
survey again can provide interesting data. For convenience, let us
use a four-fold classification of Political Theory, Political
Institutions, Political Sociology and International Relations. It
then becomes clear that as late as the end of 1964 the study of
Political Institutions was still the most important aspect of the
subject despite the widespread complaints about the sterility of
this kind of work. Out of a total of eighty-six entries in Nettl's
tabulation of this information, more than half (forty-five) belong
to this category - they include British Government, British and
Commonwealth Government, Modern Foreign Government, Public Administration, US Government, USSR Government, Local Government and
Constitutional History. Only four entries (for Edinburgh,
Leicester, Sheffield, Keele) are for compulsory courses in
Political Sociology, though one may add the nine additional entries
under Political Science, a category not clearly explained. Nevertheless, Political Sociology is steadily gaining ground and increasingly colouring the nature of Politics as an academic discipline, emancipating it from its former position of subordination to
History, Philosophy or Law. And the trend will probably not be
reversed despite the reservations voiced by some university
teachers[7].

The problem of teacher-education in political studies[8]

Institutions of teacher-education (the University and Polytechnic Departments and the Colleges of Higher Education) are placed in
a peculiarly ambivalent position in their relationships with other
educational institutions. On the one hand, they look to the university subject departments to provide the yard-sticks of academic rig-
our in these subjects; on the other, they must reorientate their
students to think in terms of material and attitudes suitable for
the given age-range of children they are being trained to teach.
When students are being prepared to teach a subject that has an established tradition in the schools, the task is a fairly straightforward one. But Politics has no such tradition; nor indeed is there
yet any consensus about the most desirable way of structuring the
teaching of this kind of material. One may discern, in fact, some half-
dozen kinds of work in this field. The first is called variously
Citizenship, Civics, Public Affairs, British Constitution, and is

concerned principally with contemporary local and national affairs
particularly as viewed through institutions. An allied subject is
Social Studies, though this is often little more than a loose
amalgam of Geography and History with a certain emphasis on the
environment. In the third place, one may mention Current Affairs,
distinguished from the other kinds of teaching by its lack of formal
syllabus since topics of interest are dealt with as they occur in
the news. Fourthly, there is teaching for International Understanding, which is often no more than an emphasis given to subjects like
Geography or History rather than a definition of a subject in its
own right. The fifth approach is Contemporary History: the history
of the world in the twentieth century is studied the better to
understand the world of the present. Finally, many teachers of
History, and to a certain extent Georgraphy, would claim that the
best approach to Political Education is through the medium of
their own discipline.

There is an expanding pool of potential specialist Politics
teachers entering the teacher-training courses from the sixth forms
and the University Departments of Education from undergraduate
courses. They are precisely the people who might be thinking
through the problems raised by this confusion. But there are
virtually no opportunities for them to undertake the task. There
are scarcely any specialist courses in Politics in teacher-training
institutions, though a few are getting under way and a few are now
starting to mount courses in Social Studies (or Sciences) with some
attention to Politics[9]. Scarcely no leadership is coming from the
very institutions whose task it should be to help resolve the confusion in the schools in this field, except the London Institute of
Education.

The influence on schools of politics teachers

The situation sketched in so far raises the interesting speculative issue, namely, what the distinctive contribution of the
specialist Politics teacher would be to the content or approach
to the syllabus of Political Education (however articulated) compared with the non-specialist teacher (e.g. historian). Having
posed the question, it is by no means presupposed that the specialist teacher would directly translate his undergraduate or college
syllabus material into the school classroom; the wisdom of teaching
in this way could clearly be challenged.

We may first of all ask what the general influence of a specialist teacher is likely to be. If the school curriculum contained
direct Political Studies in any form, *viz.*, British Constitution,
civics, current political affairs, then clearly the specialist
will have a surer grasp of the material than his non-specialist
colleague. He will be able to teach more deftly: reveal relationships more expertly, draw on a wider stock of knowledge and make
more illuminating generalizations than his colleague. But this is
a comparatively simple situation. The problem is more difficult if

the curriculum contains only indirect political subjects. What differences are likely to be evident in the teaching, for example, of a course of Contemporary History by the Political Scientist teacher on the one hand and the historian on the other? The person who is, or thinks of himself as, primarily a history teacher is likely to organize his material with greater regard to chronology than the more analytically minded Political Scientist. Also, of course, the historian will concern himself with economic, social and cultural matters rather than confine himself to the specifically political. The history teacher is concerned mainly with the narration and explanation of individual events; the teacher of Politics might well, in contrast, be more concerned with the categorisation of the material.

The contribution of political sociology

An example may help to clarify these general remarks about the approach that might be expected from the specialist Politics teacher. And let us use as the example the topic of Political Sociology. How would a teacher's approach to Political Education be coloured by having pursued a course of study in Political Sociology?

Of all branches of Politics as an academic discipline, Political Sociology would seem the most fruitful for posing our question, for both academic and pedagogical reasons. Academically, Political Sociology typifies Politics as a modern academic discipline more than any other branch. The pedagogical justification for using Political Sociology as the example is two-fold. First, in so far as a teacher organizes his teaching material in a way that reveals the stamp of the Social Scientist, it will probably be the Political Sociology element in his own studies more than any other that will have provided this perspective. Secondly, Political Sociology will make the teacher aware of the importance and complexity of the political socialisation process and will consequently lead him to encourage his pupils in class and club participation as valuable formative activities.

We are now in a position to assess how this transfer from university or college lecture-room to school classroom is likely to be effected. First, we must define rather more closely what the academic equipment of a teacher who has studied Political Sociology is likely to be. A useful summary is provided by Dr. Dowse (1967) in the symposium *Political Science*, edited by Professor Wiseman. Dowse identifies three contributions that Political Sociology makes to a course of study in Politics. First, it makes the student conscious of the social context within which political institutions operate and political activity is entered into. In terms specifically of the individual operating as a political being, Political Sociology is concerned with the establishment and expression of political attitudes, with the individual's political role (as activist or mere voter) and with the efficacy of the individual's political activity. In the second place, Political Sociology makes the student keenly aware of the variety of ways that different societies have devised for institutionalising power and authority. The study of this branch of Politics has thus freed the discipline from the narrow study of the Westminster parliamentary model. And finally, as a Political Scientist, the Political Sociologist places great emphasis on the methods by which he collects and validates his data. His concern for scientific objectivity thus leads to almost as much emphasis being placed on methodology as on any conclusions that might be drawn from an investigation.

It is now possible to turn finally to the core of this discussion, namely, the relevance of Political Sociology as our exemplar branch of Politics to the school class-room situation. We must now ask, not 'How will the teacher trained in Political Sociology translate this knowledge into school syllabus terms?' but rather 'How will a training in Political Sociology influence a teacher in handling a programme of Political Education however articulated?' Five areas of relevance may be discerned.

In the first place, if the teacher gives greater emphasis to the study of political behaviour than to the more traditional description of institutions, the teaching material is likely to be more interesting for the bulk of pupils. The material will, after all, be concerned with people - of higher interest value than institutions. There is greater reality for the pupil, also, in discovering how ordinary people act and are acted upon politically in contexts which he might not have realized are effectively political, for example, his parents' selection of a daily newspaper or the local authority's plans for comprehensive education. In short, by emphasizing the social context of politics and the political perspective of ordinary people's beliefs and actions, the study of Politics is brought down to earth where the ordinary pupil can understand its operation and see its relevance to his own life.

This leads on to the second point. Political behaviour is essentially a study of adult activity; but the teacher versed in Political Sociology will be well aware that the political socialisation process starts well before the age of enfranchisement. Discussion of political behaviour can be made even more relevant to the pupil by relating such questions as attitude formation and feelings of efficacy to the pupils themselves. This encouragement of self-awareness by the teacher would be valuable in itself apart from its value in stimulating interest in the subject. An understanding of the ways in which people, including children, develop political stances and are led to involvement in political debate and activity will inevitably bring both teacher and class to a realization of the complexity of the socialization process - the third point for discussion. The school will be seen as a micro-political unit that will help to shape the pupil's political attitudes and provide opportunities for political participation in far more diverse ways than the formal lessons in political affairs. The authority structure of the school, the personal relationships between pupils and staff, the opportunities for pupil-run clubs will all have an influence on the general political socialization of the children. The teacher who has studied Political Sociology will be conscious of these forces and opportunities and will make use of them and relate his class teaching to them far more effectively than a colleague who lacks this dimension in his own studies.

The fourth point can be dealt with very briefly: this concerns the probable tendency of the Political Sociologist to be less insular in his choice of teaching material than a colleague with a more traditional academic background. He is perhaps more likely, for example, to think that contemporary China provides a more interesting contrast to Britain than the USA. Finally, we come to the emphasis on methodology. By introducing this element into the classroom the teacher will shift the emphasis from 'This is what we know', to 'This is how we find out'. This change of focus has important educational implications and can help to ease two difficulties facing the teacher of Politics. One of the problems is the question of bias and indoctrination. If the teacher places the emphasis on the problems of discovering *why* people adopt different attitudes rather than a discussion of *what* these attitudes are, there is less likelihood of his being embarrassed by having to reveal his own commitment to an ideological position: his teaching can be more clinical. It can also lead a teacher to place the pupil in an inquiry position instead of a position in which he passively receives information from the teacher. The teacher will require the class to collect data, assess it critically and draw conclusions. And by concentrating on the development of skills rather than the accumulation of large quantities of information, the lessons might well have a more permanent impact on the pupils.

Conclusion

In this short paper it is not possible to draw firm conclusions. For one thing, so many issues have been sidestepped - for example, the age and ability level at which any of this work is possible; whether macro-political lessons can be drawn from school micro-political experience. It is possible, therefore, only to draw the discussion to a conclusion by stating that Politics has now come of age as a university discipline; school work in parallel fields is in immature confusion; and opportunities for fruitful development would seem to offer themselves in this vital area of the educational process.

NOTES

1. See E. Barker 'The study of political science and its relation to cognate study' in W.A. Robson *The University Teaching of Social Science: Political Science*, Paris: UNESCO (1954) page 16.

2. See W.A. Robson (1954) page 25.

3. *The World of Learning*, London: Europa Publications, see 1948, 1960 and 1966/67 editions.

4. See J.P. Nettl (1964) page 2.

5. *Which University?* 1966.

6. DES (1965) Table 1, page 9.

7. See, for example, D.G. MacRae, Foundations for the Sociology of Politics , *The Political Quarterly*, Vol. 37, No. 3, July-September 1966; R.E. Jones and R.K. Alderman, Politics: some problems of the discipline , *Political Studies*, Vol. XIII, No. 3.

8. For a more detailed discussion of this aspect, see the present author's contribution to D.B. Heater (1969).

9. For a description of what was probably the best developed of College of Education courses at the time, see T. Brennan (1968).

REFERENCES

BARKER, E. (1954) 'The study of political science and its relation to cognate study' in W.A. Robson *The University Teaching of Social Science:Political Science*, Paris: UNESCO.

BRENNAN, T. (1968) Political studies in a college of education, *Bulletin of the General Studies Association*, No. 12, Winter.

DES (1965) *Report of the Committee on Social Studies* (The Heyworth Report) Cmnd. 2660, London: HMSO.

DOWSE, R.E. (1967) 'Political behaviour: parties, groups and elections', in H.V. Wiseman (Ed) *Political Science* London: Routledge and Kegan Paul.

HEATER, D.B. (1969) *The Teaching of Politics* London: Methuen Educational.

NETTL, J.P. (1964) *Political Studies in Universities in Great Britain*, unpublished report of a conference at Leeds University, December 1964.

ROBSON, W.A. (1954) *The University Teaching of Social Science: Political Science* Paris: UNESCO.

Which University? 1966, London: Cornmarket Press, 1965.

1.6
A burgeoning of interest: political education in Britain

Derek Heater

Introduction

It is a complacent, perhaps even a self-satisfied society that
ignores the political education of its growing generation of young
citizens. Those countries, like the USA, that strive for social
cohesion; those, like the Federal German Republic, that need to
construct a new political consciousness; and those, like the
Soviet Union, that are built upon an ideology which must be sustained - all such recognize the weighty significance of political
education. If one could locate countries along a spectrum of
activity in civic education, Great Britain a mere decade ago would
undoubtedly have been placed on the far edge of neglect. Today,
although there is still an immense amount of work to be undertaken,
the position has shifted quite markedly. This essay is an attempt
to describe and explain this remarkable change.

The privately-funded so-called Public Schools in the nineteenth
and through into the twentieth century consciously prepared the
ruling-class youth for government - at home and in the Empire.
But the civic education of the masses remained virtually confined
to the annual flag-waving ritual of Empire Day. Even the success-
ive extensions of the franchise failed to generate any significant
widespread concern: Robert Lowe's oft-cited comment about educating
our masters at the time of the 1867 Reform Bill related only to
basic literacy, not socialization to an emerging democracy. True,
the rise to terrible power of the totalitarian regimes of the
1930s and 1940s shook the country's complacent pride in its happy
political traditions of freedom and toleration: perhaps, after all,
these traditions could not just be taken for granted; perhaps
they had to be constantly reaffirmed and protected. The mid-1930s
saw the establishment of the Association for Education in Citizenship - a professional organization led by a galaxy of eminent

* This article was originally written for the *International
 Journal of Political Education* which will be published in Autumn
 1977.

scholars and public figures[1]. And in 1949 the Ministry of
Education was sufficiently roused to publish a pamphlet on the
matter, entitled *Citizens Growing Up*. But the commitment to
the task - by politicians, government officials, scholars and teachers alike - was short-lived. By the early 1950s the impetus had
died, no evident threat or crisis looming to sustain what now seems
in retrospect merely a reaction of fear rather than a deeply-seated
positive belief in the value of political education for its own
sake. As already explained, the main burden of this essay is the
remarkable progress that has been made since the late 1960s.
However, in order to appreciate these achievements it is first
necessary to take stock of the situation as it was in the middle
of the decade.

The situation in the mid-1960s

The faintness of the government impulse to civic education circa
1965 is readily shown by the casual references to the matter in
recent official publications[2]. Three sets of publications are
relevant. First, there is the pamphlet issued by the Department
of Education and Science (DES, 1967) on the teaching of History,
relevant because that subject has traditionally been thought to be
the most appropriate vehicle for political education in Britain.
This was published as recently as 1967, yet two very old-fashioned
notes are struck: the view that political education can safely be
left as an incidental spin-off from History lessons and that the
sole purpose of political education is the inculcation of 'responsible citizenship'. Concern about the changing nature and needs of
secondary education led to the production of two very important
reports, known by the names of the chairmen of the committees that
wrote them: The Crowther Report (1959) and The Newsom Report (1963).
These furnish our second category. It is incredible, but true, that
the quite bulky Crowther Report on the education of 15-18 year olds
contains only two bland, almost indifferent sentences on the subject of political education. The Newsom Report on the average and
below-average secondary-school pupil has more to say, but the
thought behind the scattered comments is very superficial. The
failure of the Newsom Report is all the more serious in the light
of its massive influence upon educational thinking and practice
at the secondary level in England in the 1960s.

Thirdly, the semi-official Schools Council, set up in 1964 to
promote curriculum development, has published some working papers
that should be germane to our topic of political education. Titles
like *Society and the Young School Leaver*, (1967), *Social Studies
8-13*, (1971) raise one's expectations; but there is little encouragement or advice in their pages. A rallying cry is, however, to
be heard from the slender pamphlet on *Raising the School Leaving
Age* (1965). The urgent challenge to teachers is clearly sounded:
'When every man is King how does he become enough of a philosopher

to wield power wisely?'[3] Scything through the luxuriant growth
of officially promoted educational literature of recent years, one
reaps a pitifully lean harvest of references to political educa-
ion. Perhaps most symptomatic of this official neglect is the
failure of the DES to publish in its official pamphlet series a
new statement to replace the quaintly obsolete *Citizens Growing Up*
produced in the shadow of the Second World War.

But, of course, official publications are not the only professional support and stimulus for the teacher. Were there any
other signs of professional activity in the field of political
education a decade ago? Truth to tell, the scene is one of pervas-
ive stagnation. In the field of publications, no book specifically
on political education had been written since pre-war days; nor did
any professional journal exist - indeed, articles on political
education in any educational journals during the two post-war decades could probably be counted on the fingers of one hand. Even
the buoyant school-book trade merely sailed through the well-
charted waters of 'British Constitution', not daring to venture beyond the 'safe' descriptions of central and local government institutions. Nor should this bleak and uninspiring scene occasion
surprise when placed in the context of the complete absence of any
professional association for teachers of political subjects, (the
Association for Education in Citizenship finally spluttered out of
existence, having been moribund for some time, in 1957); the
failure of any academic body or individual to undertake any research or development projects; and the lack of even any proper
teacher-training facilities in any of the colleges or university
departments of Education[4].

Was there *any* political education in British schools in the
1960s? It is difficult to generalize about the medley of inchoate
Civics and Current Affairs lessons. But some indication of the
more formally structured teaching may be gleaned from the condition of 'British Constitution' in the General Certificate of
Education examinations in schools (and colleges of further education) in England. (Scotland has a separate school and examinations
system and the situation there will be described later.) The GCE
examinations, organized by eight different boards, are taken by
the more academically-inclined pupils at two levels - Ordinary
(O-level) at about 16 and Advanced (A-level) at 18, the latter
acting also as a criterion for entrance into higher education, including universities. The comments that follow immediately relate
to A-level only. This is for two reasons: official statistics are
not available for O-level and the main point that is being emphasized is the *academic* standing of political studies. The development of syllabuses at a more modest level will be dealt with below.
In 1965 political studies syllabuses were entirely confined to
institutional studies, entitled for the most part 'British
Constitution'. Topics such as political theory, party policies,
voting behaviour, comparative government were outside the purview

of the syllabuses and thus the experience of the students. Furthermore, and in some measure perhaps because of this limited
range of subject-matter, the courses had the reputation of being
academically less demanding than most other cognate subjects like
History and Geography; whilst the number of candidates entering
for the subject compared with the more traditional disciplines was
very limited. Let us dwell a little on each of these two indica-
tors of the standing of the subject.

First, the subject-matter. In making offers to applicants of
a place at a university, it is common practice for entrance requirements to be specified in the form of the number, range and
grade of A-level subjects. It was quite common for university subject departments not to accept British Constitution or to count it
as 'half a subject'. Even departments of Politics had reservations
about the value of the course as a preparation for undergraduate
study. Bernard Crick damned these syllabuses roundly:

> In my own experience as a persistent first-year teacher both at
> the London School of Economics and Sheffield, where one may
> properly point to entrance standards among the highest in the
> country, it is rarely an advantage for a student to have taken
> 'British Constitution' at school, often the contrary .... Better
> that he had done almost any other *reputable subject*.(5)

A former chief examiner for London University A-level, Col. F.W.G.
Benemy (1970), has tried to refute the argument that British
Constitution has been an easy option by asserting the qualities
sought for in answers and by comparing results with results in
History(6). But he admits that the numbers and kinds of candidates
are so different that comparisons are very hazardous. This brings
us on to the question of numbers. An examination of the figures
for all the A-level boards reveals the following situation(7):

	British Constitution	History
Summer 1961	2,459	10,205
Summer 1973	13,660	36,271

Clearly British Constitution developed in popularity considerably,
though still substantially lagging behind the more traditional subject, History. However, two important factors need to be thrown
into the balance, both seemingly confirming that the intellectual
demands of the subject have been somewhat modest. First, it has
been very common (much more common than in History, for example)
for candidates to sit the examination after one rather than the
usual two years course of study. And secondly, trends in the mid-
1970s show a *decline* in the popularity of the subject - trends that
have coincided with the revision of syllabuses to make the examinations intellectually more demanding (see Leng, 1975).

The reasons for this situation

The picture is a dismal one. What explanations can we provide for this almost total neglect of a vital area of education? Four main factors can be identified: lack of tradition; lack of teachers professionally committed to this field of work; a belief that the study of politics can only be an adult activity; and fear of indoctrination.

Although organizations like the Association for Education in Citizenship and the Hansard Society for Parliamentary Government flourished in the 1940s, these were unusual times: the need to defend democratic systems and ideals against totalitarianism was so evident to the whole nation. The decline to the condition of neglect in the mid-1960s described above must not be interpreted as the decay of an established tradition of civic education, for no such tradition existed. True, one of the main functions of the Victorian Public School was to prepare personnel for government service. But the civic needs of the masses for all intents and purposes went unheeded.

Since schools were not encouraged to engage in political education, no cadre of teachers devoted to the task was recruited. This lack of a professionally committed group of teachers to press the claims of the subject and to develop syllabuses, teaching methods and aids must not be underrated. For example, it was generally held that if any work in Civics or Current Affairs was to be undertaken in a school at all, then it was the function of the English or, more frequently, the History teacher. But, of course, however committed and skilled they might have been at this work (and many were certainly neither), their own professional advancement lay in work in their traditional disciplines. The situation became something of a vicious circle. No strong body of teachers was built up because potential teachers in the field could not find posts; and posts were not created in schools because there was no professional pressure to create them. This is not to argue that teachers of History and English, for instance, cannot undertake vitally important activities in their own ways, but rather to explain the lack of professional dynamism and leadership until very recent years. Related to this lack of professional underpinning for schools work generally is the fact that until the 1960s Politics was barely established as a University discipline. For example, there were only sixteen Chairs of Politics and International Relations in England and Wales in 1960. If so few students were preparing to read Politics at the undergraduate level, there was little incentive for schools to develop the subject in the sixth form.

In any situation of neglect, one must ask whether the condition is the result of inertia and apathy or a positively thought-through policy. The evidence so far suggests perhaps the former - no real objection to political education, but at the same time no energetic thrust to promote it. Yet running parallel with this attitude was a belief that political education really is not very suitable for school children. The only reference to the matter in the Education Act of 1944, which set the scene for the postwar development of English education, is a recommendation that County Colleges should fulfil this function. (These Colleges were to have provided continuing education for school-leavers, though they were not, in fact, established.) Also, scholars of the calibre and influence of Sir Ernest Barker (1938) and Sir Richard Livingstone (1945) were firmly convinced that political education was otiose without practical experience of life - and consequently by definition quite inappropriate for the school level. And since this is a point of view expressed by no less an authority than Aristotle (in *Nichomachean Ethics I.3*), it is an opinion that cannot be lightly dismissed.

However, stronger by far than the argument of inappropriateness was the nagging fear that political education is a positive danger. It was this attitude of mind to which Michael Oakeshott alluded in the oft-quoted passage from his inaugural lecture in 1951: 'The expression "political education" has fallen on evil days,' he declared; 'in the wilful and disingenuous corruption of language which is characteristic of our time it has acquired a sinister meaning.'[8] He was referring, of course, to the totalitarian mobilisation and manipulation of malleable young minds through the Hitler Youth and Komsomol organizations. State encouragement could carry the seeds of state control. And even if individual teachers were to undertake the task, parents, head teachers and authorities feared the perils of personal indoctrination: what would happen to young minds if teachers loosed off their prejudices in the classroom?- particularly teachers with passionate Left-wing convictions, for that was the bogy of the 1950s and 1960s. Indeed, the logical conclusion was drawn by many, namely, that political education like the equally sensitive sex education is a domestic matter for the family to handle and no business of the teacher's at all. This belief, naturally, reinforced the practice of 'safe' teaching about institutions - the Civics and British Constitution approach to the subject: scarcely an encouragement to lively teaching and inquisitive learning. Indeed, the motto of the time might well have been, 'If the subject-matter is safe, it is dull; if it is interesting, it is dangerous.'

Developments since 1969

Since the end of the last decade the pattern has changed with remarkable swiftness. Our purpose now is to chronicle these changes and then to try to explain this sudden change of heart and interest.

First, it is necessary to record the establishment and achievements of the Politics Association because so many other important

developments have stemmed from the existence of this organization.
On 14th April 1967 a letter was published in the correspondence
columns of the daily newspaper, *The Guardian*, over the signature
of the present writer, deploring the state of political education
in Britain and recommending four courses of action to improve the
situation, including 'The establishment of a professional association to provide the service for political studies that the
Historical Association, for example, has provided for history.'
The result was a surprising number of letters saying, in various
ways, 'Do it!' The problem was to secure the help of people with
financial and administrative resources. A number of approaches
were made without success. The break-through eventually occurred
when Bernard Crick, then Professor at Sheffield University, recognized the importance of the projected organization. In turn, he
stimulated the waning powers of the Hansard Society for Parliamentary Government to arrange a conference of interested teachers at
University College London in the autumn of 1969. For all intents
and purposes the Politics Association came into existence at that
conference, though formally a year later - with Professor Crick
as President and the present writer as Chairman.

From the start it was evident that the new Association had
assumed a daunting task: there was so much to do over such a
wide spectrum of teaching, with so few dedicated volunteers and
with so little money. The major tasks and functions were identified as follows: to hold an annual conference, to publish a
journal, to publish books and other teaching aids, to engage in
syllabus evaluation and development and to create local branches
for grass-roots activity. It is the opinion of the present writer,
admittedly heavily *parti pris*, that the Politics Association has
been a success despite the considerable difficulties. These
difficulties have been mainly of two kinds. Especially in the
initial stages, the Association had a number of critics:

> Do the Politics Association have any care for the three quarters
> of the population who will ... never make the sixth form? ...
> Do they not see that with invention and experiment, working
> empirically, some teachers could even in these more difficult
> times present politics to any child from 13 upwards and make
> it pulsate like Pop? There is nothing that has come out of
> the Association for the past year which makes one think they
> do see.'(9)

Thus wrote Kathleen Gibberd, an experienced teacher in the field
and a leading educational journalist. Lord Arran attacked the
Association as a 'socialist conspiracy'; while Roland Meighan
(1972) of the University of Birmingham described the establishment
of the Association 'possibly as much a matter for regret as it is
for congratulation. The fragmentation of teachers of the social
sciences is now almost complete.'(10) The other difficulty was
the failure of the Association to achieve 'take-off' in numerical

terms. It aimed at 1,000 members; it achieved only about 400; and in 1977 still has only 600. The failure to recruit substantial numbers was more inhibiting than the criticism. Small numbers have meant low income and a severe limit to the range of people who could be called upon to undertake the tasks listed above. For example, at the time of writing, the two biggest gaps in the Association's activities have been the frailty of the local branches and the failure to launch published teaching materials for the less-able pupils, the very group whose needs are most urgent.

By 1973, however, the Politics Association (sometimes in company with its godmother, the Hansard Society) had become accepted as the normal body to handle matters relating to political education. The kind of criticisms quoted above ceased because they were partially or wholly unfair (Lord Arran's accusation could hardly have been further from the truth since the Association is, of course, utterly non-ideological in its aims, methods and membership). The break-through came in January 1973. A furore burst out over the arrangement of sixth-form conferences by the Conservative Party. The situation was potentially quite dangerous. The Conservative Party was accused by Labour Party spokesmen of trying to indoctrinate school pupils. The continuation of the conferences in these circumstances was clearly unwise. Yet, of course, the principle of sixth-form conferences on political issues had to be encouraged; and, more importantly, the value of political education in general had to be defended in a situation which seemed to revive all the old doubts and fears. The danger was most skilfully averted by Bernard Crick, acting as the President of the Politics Association, drafting a series of 'ground rules', which all three major parties agreed to for their future involvement in school work.* The quarrel stimulated considerable interest in the national quality press and provided the Association and the cause of political education with some welcome publicity among the lay public as well as within the teaching profession. 'It all makes a sensible compromise,' wrote the Political Editor of *The Times* on 1 February 1973. 'Conservative party managers, at once regretting Liberal community politics but admitting that all political parties need to make closer contact with the voters, especially the new voters of 18 years, had stolen a march on the other two parties at Westminster.' *The Times Educational Supplement* in its issue on 19 January 1973, took up the issue as its lead story and concluded 'Quite obviously this nonsense has to stop. Professor Bernard Crick and Mr. Derek Heater of the Politics Association have moved in with suggestions of talks with both parties which should lead to sensible guidelines and the tea-cup storm will be over.'

Since this *cause célèbre* broke, the work of the Politics Association has been recognized by the award of a three-year devel-

---

* The text of the 'ground rules' is included as an appendix at the end of this essay.

opment grant by the DES and been acclaimed in an address by a
Secretary of State for Education. Moreover, either as an organization or through the activities of leading individual members, it
has played important roles in a development project funded by the
Nuffield Foundation and in a series of radio broadcasts; and its
journal, *Teaching Politics*, is established as the foremost vehicle
for the publication and exchange of ideas about political education
in Britain. To each of these points we shall return at the appropriate place in this section - under the headings of the DES publications and broadcasts, developments in examination syllabuses, and
research and development.

Throughout the 1950s and 1960s - after the publication of the
pamphlet *Citizens Growing Up* in 1949, in fact - the Ministry of
Education and its successor, the DES, for all intents and purposes
ignored the topic of political education. More recently, interest
has revived, albeit in a tentative way. On occasions the DES
provide grants to organizations devoted to educational work. In
the spring of 1974, the Department eventually responded to an
application made some time before by the Politics Association. The
grant was of £1,400 per annum for three years in order to expand
and develop its activities: in short, to place it upon a more
secure footing. In the autumn of the same year, Mr. Reg Prentice,
at that time Secretary of State for Education and Science, accepted
an invitation to address the annual conference of the Association,
during which he applauded its activities. Finally, it is notable
that the DES has appointed a member of H.M. Inspectorate to act
as an official observer on the working party of the Nuffield-
funded Programme for Political Education (this project will be
described below).

More impressive than this hesitant though welcome official
support, both as an index of and a stimulus to theoretical and
practical pedagogical developments, has been the efflorescence of
writing, and to a lesser extent broadcasting, on the subject. 1969
saw the sublication by Methuen Educational of the first book on
the subject for a generation - a collection of essays edited by
the present writer, entitled *The Teaching of Politics*. It was
important in assisting the breakthrough to greater activity and
thought; indeed, its very primitiveness and obsolescence from the
perspective of 1977 is a tribute to the progress that has been made
since its publication. During 1971-75 three further books were
published. F.W.G. Benemy's (1974) *Teaching British Government* is a
highly personal essay by an experienced teacher, examiner and
author of text-books in the very limited field of British
Constitution. *Political Studies: A Handbook for Teachers* has been
compiled by Tom Brennan (1975) of Bingley College of Education very
much as a practical guide for teachers of all levels, abilities and
contexts. Very different in style is *Political Education in a
Democracy* by Harold Entwistle (1971), now teaching in a Canadian
university but most of whose teaching career has been spent in
England. Basing his argument on findings in the field of child

psychology, he strongly urges that political education should be
undertaken through practical experience by using the school, for
example, as a micro-political entity. Finally, to provide background for a series of radio broadcasts, Tom Brennan and Jonathan
Brown (1975) edited a booklet entitled *Teaching Politics: Problems
and Perspectives*. In its short compass it provides a valuable
indication of the state of political education in Britain in the
mid-1970s.

Just as books discussing political education flowered after the
barren 1950s and 1960s, so articles, both journalistic rhetoric
and academic analysis, flowed from fertile pens from the late
1960s onwards. Material has been published in a variety of journals, though the most important organs, not surprisingly, have been
Teaching Politics for the substantial articles and *The Times
Educational Supplement* for the more ephemeral pieces. *Teaching
Politics* started life as the domestically produced Newsletter of
the Politics Association. In 1972 it was completely reshaped and
took on its present title when Longman undertook to publish it
commercially. In 1976 with volume 5 it has been transformed again
as its publication has been placed in the hands of Sage Publications.

The medium of print has its limitations in spreading the word:
broadcasting can sometimes be more effective. Unfortunately, it
has not been possible to utilise radio and still less television
very much in Britain. There has been some use made of local
radio; one or two radio interviews about the Politics Association;
and one of a series of eleven television programmes entitled
Politics Now screened in the early weeks of 1976 was devoted
to political education. The only really detailed coverage has been
a series of eight radio programmes organized by Jonathan Brown of
Newcastle University and broadcast twice - in 1975 and 1976 - a
very clearly devised series of discussions on every important
facet of the subject.

If so much discussion has been going on over the past seven or
eight years, how much practical influence, one might well ask,
has it had in the development and reform of syllabuses? The earlier discussion of syllabuses was focused upon the A-level examinations, so let us start with these here. The criticisms discussed
above have been taken very much to heart and changes are being
introduced: syllabuses are tending to broaden out from the narrowly
British Constitution to include actual politics - even the formerly
shunned word is being introduced into the titles of papers!
Changes along these lines were pioneered by Professor F.F. Ridley,
chief examiner of the Joint Matriculation Board (a consortium of
universities in the North of England). Some boards, rather more
hesitantly, are introducing options on the political systems of
other countries and political theory. Other boards, however, even
now seem reluctant to effect changes; but the movement for reform
is well under way. At the more modest O-level less change is

discernible. And below this level again in intellectual demand
is the Certificate of Secondary Education, introduced in 1963 and
managed by regional boards. The variation in syllabuses across
the fourteen boards is enormous, thus rendering generalization very
difficult. Suffice it to say that some very imaginative work is
being undertaken in various parts of the country in CSE courses.
One of the reasons why generalization about CSE syllabuses is
difficult is that many are not 'pure' politics syllabuses, but
broader social studies courses. A similar problem faces us when
we turn to Scotland. The examination system there provides for
a school certificate at two grades - Ordinary and Higher. Modern
Studies examinations containing elements of politics were introduced at these grades in 1962 and 1968 respectively and they have
steadily increased in popularity, there being, for example, 340
candidates for O-grade in 1962 and 4,857 in 1971, though the status
of traditional subjects like Geography and History remain higher.

   The development of the Modern Studies courses in Scotland has
stimulated considerable enthusiasm and interest. It is notable that
a significant proportion of the tiny amount of research in political education undertaken in recent years in Britain has been
conducted in Scotland in the context of Modern Studies teaching.
Morrison and French (1972) produced a report to the Social Science
Research Council, while Geoffrey Mercer (1971) wrote a substantial
study in the form of a Ph.D. thesis - in fact, this latter is the
only substantial piece of research in the field of political education undertaken in Britain in recent times. Indeed, during the
period of the 1960s and early 1970s only two other theses germane
to our study were written - Guy Whitmarsh's study (1972) of the
A.E.C. already referred to and Bob Holcombe's (1973) evaluation
of text-books. However, two pieces of institutional research are
being conducted, incomplete at the time of writing. Both are
being administered by the Hansard Society for Parliamentary
Government. One, financed by the Leverhulme Trust, is an investigation into the condition of political awareness and ignorance
in the country; the other, funded by the Nuffield Foundation, is
entitled the Programme for Political Education. The latter is a
more ambitious scheme to provide a theoretical framework for
political education, to develop syllabus ideas for realizing this
theory in various classroom contexts and to identify schools
where interesting work is already being undertaken. Sadly, inflation has eroded the original scope of the project; nevertheless,
the experience and information accumulated will undoubtedly be of
considerable value since this field of research and development
is so barren[11].

   A patchy pattern of progress, yet progress nonetheless compared
with the bleak picture of the mid-1960s. Little to boast about
compared with the strides made in some other countries and in
Britain in some other subjects. Yet again, for all the reservations, given the limited time and resources at the disposal of

the enthusiasts engaged in this area of work, something worthwhile
has surely been accomplished in the half-dozen years from 1969 to
1975?

Reasons for the developments

Attempts at explaining developments such as those described
here are hazardous undertakings, especially when one is so close
to the events. Should one properly emphasize the initiative and
energy of individuals or the force of social pressures? The
explanatory framework favoured here is rather the virtually for-
tuitous confluence of mutually reinforcing but distinct factors.

On the level of individual effort, it is highly unlikely that
so much could have happened in so short a time if the Politics
Association had not been created; and its creation and continuation
in being in face of adverse circumstances has been due to the faith
and selfless work of its most active members. As has already been
shown, the Association has undertaken work of considerable importance; yet these specific activities are of less significance than
just the bare existence of the Association. The existence of such
an organization has meant that teachers and educationists interested in this area of activity, who would otherwise in all probab-
ility never have heard of each other, have now come together and
are helping each other to refine their thoughts and improve their
practical skills. A team has been created that is far stronger
than its component members; for how many of the individual members
would have taken the trouble or had the opportunity to undertake
in isolation what they are now achieving in concert? The Association has thus been both a forum and a catalyst. It is interesting
to note that at the time of its formation both the Speaker of the
House of Commons [12] and *The Guardian* leader-writer (8 September
1969) wished the Association well - the former because of its aim
of 'encouraging teachers to come together and discuss problems of
government in order that our children may get to know more about
their precious heritage of freedom'; and the latter because 'the
provision for teachers and teaching (of politics) is still in many
ways far from adequate'. They both recognized the need for a
context and a stimulus if the situation was to be improved.

Nevertheless, it would be wrong to focus on the Politics
Association in isolation. It was established at an opportune time.
It was, as I have already argued earlier in this collection of
essays, in the 1960s that Politics was rapidly emerging as an
accepted discipline in universities and polytechnics and graduates
were therefore becoming available in appreciable numbers to teach
in schools and colleges of further education with more specific
expertise in and commitment to political studies than heretofore.
It was also a time when curriculum development was generally
accepted as a basic necessity in the educational system of the
country. The Schools Council and the Nuffield Foundation had

already set up projects that had renovated the teaching of some disciplines such as Mathematics and French and other subjects were being reformed by appropriate professional bodies, notably English. The aim of rejuvenating civic education in this atmosphere did not therefore appear a particularly strange objective. Even more favourable was the current emphasis in the 1960s on the educational needs of the average school-leaver. For all the deficiencies of the Newsom Report (1963), as noted above, in handling the issue of civic education, it does contain the now classic warning that:

> A man who is ignorant of the society in which he lives, who knows nothing of his place in the world and who has not thought about his place in it, is not a free man even though he has a vote.(13)

What is more, in 1972-73 the statutory school-leaving age was raised to 16. Far too little preparation was given to the needs of the schools, teachers and pupils affected by this change, but the cause of political education was enhanced by the widespread recognition that the social dimension of education should be particularly emphasized. It is surely no coincidence that the fullest commitment to the concept of political education in any recent official document was in the Schools Council (1965) *Working Paper No. 2: Raising the School-Leaving Age*.

At the same time as the school-leaving age was being raised, the legal age of majority was lowered - as from 1st January 1970. The fact that from that date on young people of 18 could exercise many rights, including the right to vote, hitherto confined to those aged 21 drew more people's attention to the problems of political awareness and education than any other recent event. To take just one example: one issue of the colour magazine published with the popular tabloid newspaper, *The Daily Mirror*, on 25 April 1970, featured on its front cover the caption, 'Who's Afraid of the Virgin Vote?' The accompanying picture showed an 18-year old bikini-clad 'baby' in a pram being fondled by a parliamentary candidate whose leer suggested that he would enjoy depriving her of her political maidenhood. Inside, readers were informed through a kaleidoscopic mixing of metaphors that:

> Two and a half million untried troops are being unleashed on the battlefields of Britain this year. They are the new idols of party politics ... the 18-to-21-year-olds.

Lowering the age of enfranchisement by three years was dramatic enough to enhance the country's consciousness about political education. But taken together with an increasing tendency to stay on at school to 18 and the raising of the minimum school-leaving age, the case against political education built upon the argument of immaturity was utterly demolished. It was now perfectly possible for school pupils to vote in elections; and even those young

people who left school at the first opportunity would be eligible
to vote only two years after leaving the classroom. Perhaps when
children left school at 15 and had six years to mature before
casting a vote - perhaps in those conditions the argument that
political education was inappropriate in schools could just be
sustained. In these new circumstances, however, the argument evap-
orated before the urgent need to prepare school-leavers for their
imminent responsibilities of citizenship.

Meanwhile, the case against involving young people in political
studies at too tender an age was being further weakened by research
in the field of political socialization. The findings of American
scholars were being made known in Britain in the 1960s, even though
no indigenous research on a comparable scale was being carried out.
This is not the place to debate the validity of this work. The
point here is, rather, the quite simple one that young people,
assuredly those in their teens, were shown to be possessed of a
certain basic political awareness, that elementary political material is not beyond their comprehension.

That young people could be politically conscious, particularly
when operating in environments they understood, was vividly dis-
played at the student level in the university and college demon-
strations of the late 1960s, rising in a crescendo to the events
of 1968. Demands for a greater say in the government of their
own affairs were even to be heard at the school level with the
creation of the National Union of School Students. Yet, the participatory movement was not confined to demands for perceived
rights; there was abroad, too, a heightened sense of social responsibility. The need for political understanding for the smooth
operation of voluntary bodies involved in social work and activism
was discerned, for example, by the National Association of Youth
Clubs, who sponsored a two-day 'consultation' in September 1971
to discuss the problems that were arising. Announcing the event,
they declared:

> The emergence in recent years of socially - and politically -
> orientated organizations which depend on the involvement of
> young people has in itself created problems. The youngsters
> concerned encounter difficulties in their dealings with local
> authorities and older established voluntary bodies.[14]

The 'problems' have frequently arisen because of increasing
disenchantment with the machinery and policies of the established
system. The results of this tension have been frustration among
the younger generation; and among those who feel there is sufficient worth in the system to preserve it - or at least, that any
radical alternative would be worse - grave concern about the
corrosive effects of apathy and alienation. The concern to battle
against these dangers is a motif that echoes through the debates
in recent years. On the occasion of the founding of the Politics
Association *The Guardian* on 8 September 1969 carried a report

beneath the bold headline, 'Politics teachers link up to fight
18-plus apathy', emphasizing 'the almost wholly negative attitude
to politics held by some young people.' On the sixth-form conference controversy on 14 January 1973, *The Sunday Times*, which exposed the Conservative 'plot', described the purpose of the man who
organized them, Mr. John Selwyn Gummer, M.P., in the following
way:

> Young people were not being given enough chances to argue the
> basics of democracy ... What was needed, he told one M.P. bet-
> ween sessions in the House of Commons, was to make the pupils
> aware of the problems with which British democracy had to deal.

A year later, Bernard Crick worried about the poor image of British
politicians particularly in the light of certain questionable
business deals wrote, in *The Observer* on 5 May 1974: 'Perhaps,
however, the main political education of a nation will always come
from the example of the top politicians themselves. Their conduct
is creating a crisis of public confidence in the system.' In the
autumn of 1974, just before the second general election of that
year, Mr. Reg Prentice, M.P. also expressed concern: 'On the
eve of this election,' he said, 'we should ask why so many of our
fellow citizens are saying: "A plague on all your houses". Why is
there so much cynicism and disbelief?'(15) He concluded by exhort-
ing politicians, teachers and citizens alike to rally to the
defence of parliamentary democracy.

Political education has thus become, in the opinion of a number
of observers, a political necessity. We have come full circle.
We argued at the start of this essay that the British neglect of
the matter in the 1950s and 1960s was the result of complacency.
The new interest in political education has been sustained with
some vigour because complacency has given way to nervous uncertainty concerning the toughness of the nation's political fabric to
withstand the wear and tear of current sharply contending forces.

APPENDIX

THE CONDUCT OF POLITICAL SIXTH-FORM CONFERENCES

The following is the text that was agreed by the three main
political parties on the politics in schools controversy in 1973
and circulated by the Hansard Society to local education authorities.

Preface

(a) On the initiative of the Politics Association (which is a

professional association of teachers in Secondary and Further
Education concerned with political and civic education) a meeting
was held with representatives of the three main political parties
on the premises of the Hansard Society. (Professor Bernard Crick
took the chair on behalf of the Politics Association and the
Chairman, Mr. Derek Heater, also attended; Mr. John Selwyn Gummer,
MP, represented the Conservative Party, Mr. Frank Underhill, the
national agent, represented the Labour Party and Mr. John Pardoe,
MP, the Liberal Party; Mr. Richard Tames attended as observer for
the Hansard Society, being their Research and Development Officer).

This following statement is simply a letter of advice prepared
by the Politics Association to be sent to its members and L.E.A.S.
which attempts to establish conventions and voluntary rules by
which schools may invite politicians to visit during school time
to talk about public affairs of any kind likely to prove controversial even if not directly partisan, or by which schools may
release pupils to attend such meetings in school time.

Following discussion, the representatives of the parties wish
to associate themselves with the following recommendations.

The representatives of the political parties also agreed that
they would hold further discussions with the Politics Association
to explore an experimental programme in the schools with a view
to improving and developing the role of the parties in civic education.

(b) The problem of the school-leaver, especially at the sixth-form
age, is particularly sensitive because, of course, of the vote at
18. Parties will now be seeking more than ever before to inform
and influence incipient young voters. The Politics Association
considers that this is wholly proper and should form part of a
civic education, provided that schools retain fundamental control
of the process and that certain conventions are observed. We
fear that the result of the recent controversy could be to make
some L.E.A.S. and head teachers even more restrictive than a few
already are - practices appear to vary widely - about visits from
and to politicians. We wish to avert this, indeed to try to get
more visits rather than less, but in an educationally meaningful
way.

(c) Civic education, whether in CSE, O or A-level syllabuses as
'British Constitution' or 'Government and Politics', or in sixth-
form General, Liberal or Social Studies time, is both a highly
important and a difficult, hence sometimes neglected area. It
needs expansion and more thought both for its educational value and
as a deliberate attempt to make young people aware of their responsibilities as citizens, which obviously must include the possibility of supporting and even joining political parties and pressure
groups. We deeply fear the social consequences if over-direct
approaches to schools by the parties make this whole area too
controversial for schools to handle. The suppression of political

controversy can lead to the rejection of politics, sometimes in
forms more worrying than mere apathy.

(d) Suspicion that civic education is partisan would tend to
drive out the good with the bad. Obviously the political parties
will seek to play a more direct role in civic education with votes
at eighteen, but obviously if schools are not to close down the
shutters the parties must themselves help to observe some such
rules of prudence or conventions as the following. Therefore we
suggest:

Recommendations

(1) That politicians talking to pupils on controversial matters
in school time should only do so in circumstances where they fit
into a systematic programme organized by the school or group of
schools and when there has been preparation by the teachers.
Isolated visits tend, we suggest, to be a waste of everyone's time,
and schools should not think that their responsibilities for civic
education are met simply by talks from the parties: they must be
prepared for and followed up afterwards by the schools.

(2) That there is a place both for the balanced panel discussion
and for a talk by one or more speakers from one party. But if the
latter, then in commonsense and prudence, we suggest that no
invitation should be given or accepted without it being announced
at the same time that a similar invitation has been given to or
accepted from one of the other main parties; and that in the long
run there should be balance-over-time between the parties. In
all circumstances ample time must be guaranteed for questions; and
if a panel, then schools should realize that fairly large numbers
are needed to justify the presence of leading local (let along
national) spokesmen of the parties together. Pedagogically, we
have some sympathy with the view that panel discussions can be
overdone, encourage mere debate and often leave little time for
questions and discussion from the audience; but obviously there
is a place for both, and we see no reason why speakers from one
party should not meet pupils on their own so long as balance-over-
time is observed (and the relevant time is the school year).

(3) That so long as balance within a meeting or balance-over-time
is observed, we see no issue of principle whether meetings are
within a school or held outside, but if held within a school for
that school alone, then balance-over-time must be interpreted
school by school and not district by district. Meetings organized
by heads or assistant teachers immediately after school hours on
school premises should, we think, follow the same rules of prudence
and public interest about balance. Where there are sixth-form
political or public affairs clubs, run by the pupils on school
premises, the question is somewhat different, although schools
should be well aware that the public do not always find the

distinction easy to draw, and balance should also be striven for
in this context.

(4) That it is clearly the responsibility of school heads and
L.E.A.S. to ensure that meetings, whosoever they are organized
by, which pupils attend in or from schools are either genuinely
non-partisan, multi-party or fit into a programme which is balanced
between the parties over the school year. We are firmly of the
opinion that meetings organized by single parties, on whatever subject, will inevitably be regarded as partisan.

(5) That the kind of meetings envisaged in this document should,
we believe, ordinarily be held on the initiative or by the permission of individual head teachers or groups of head teachers.
The role of the chief education officer or the education committee
is best limited to ensuring that balance is maintained over time
by retrospective scrutiny, not by prior permission for every invitation of a politician to a school or groups of schools. We
are aware that present practices vary widely in this respect.

(6) That the local constituency MP is in a special position.
Nowhere more than in schools does he ordinarily remember that he
is representative of all the people in his constituency. We simply
hope that the local MP will remember the danger to civic education
as such of engendering controversy about 'politics in schools'.
Also in a special position are individual invitations to acknow-
ledged authorities on the machinery of government, the organization
of the parties and the procedures of Parliament, even though they
are politicians.

(7) That, despite the recent controversies, we note continual
difficulties of schoolteachers to get party spokesmen to talk in
schools and that this sometimes affects balance. There is some
lack of realism in teachers asking the same individuals too often,
and there is also some lack of knowledge about how to approach the
parties as organizations, particularly in the regions. But the
parties could do more to inform schools about the availability of
speakers, or simply to acknowledge a responsibility to find local
spokesmen when asked.

(8) That non-partisan outside bodies could play a greater role in
organizing sixth-form conferences in public affairs and on controversial matters. The Council for Education in World Citizenship
(affiliated to the United Nations Association) already does much
excellent work for schools in the field of international understanding. But we think that issues of domestic politics can also
be handled in this way, and both the Hansard Society for Parliamentary Government and the Politics Association have considerable
experience in organizing sixth-form conferences (although these
have been mainly limited, for lack of funds and personnel, to the
London area). We also remind schools that on such occasions university and polytechnic teachers and journalists have often made
useful contributions in addition to politicians. All three bodies

stand ready to advise, organize or sponsor future meetings, within the limits of their resources, and already enjoy good informal contacts with the parties.

(9) That there is a similar problem with the minority groups and pressure groups that is partly met by the same considerations of balance-over-time, but also could be partly met if the practice were more widespread of having sixth-form noticeboards. These could be used to display circulars, relating to meetings outside school hours, couched in reasonable terms and issued by outside bodies - whether parties or pressure groups. This is, we know, a small but sensitive matter of head teachers' discretion but with votes at 18 and the increased activity of local pressure groups, we would suggest that a non-official notice board is less nuisance than continual leafleting by outside bodies at school gates.

NOTES

1. For a study of this organization and invaluable information on the early development of political education in Britain, see G. Whitmarsh (1972), *Society and the School Curriculum: The Association for Education in Citizenship 1934-57* (M.Ed. thesis, University of Birmingham).

2. For an analysis of these documents, see Derek Heater, 'Political education in schools - the official attitude', as reproduced earlier in this book.

3. Schools Council (1965) paragraph 48.

4. See D. Heater (1969) 'Teacher training' in D.B. Heater (Ed) *The Teaching of Politics* London: Methuen Educational.

5. See B. Crick (1969) page 3. Emphasis added.

6. Newsletter of the Politics Association, No. 2, Summer 1970.

7. Ministry of Education, *Statistics of Education, 1961: Part 2* (London: HMSO, 1962) and Department of Education and Science, *Statistics of Education, 1973: Vol. 2* (London: HMSO, 1975).

8. M. Oakeshott, Political Education reprinted in *Rationalism in Politics and Other Essays* (London: Methuen, 1962), p.112.

9. K. Gibberd, 'Politics Alive', *The Times Educational Supplement*, 11 September, 1970.

10. Letter to *The Times Educational Supplement*, 10 November, 1972.

11. For more information about the Programme for Political Education, see T. Brennan and J. Brown (1973).

12. Dr. Horace King, *Newsletter of the Politics Association*, No. 1, Spring 1970, p.3.

13. CACE (1963) paragraph 499.

14. *Towards the 80s: The Young in Politics*, mimeo.

15. 'Civic Education', *Teaching Politics*, Vol. 4, No. 1, January 1975, p.6.

REFERENCES

BARKER, E (1938) *The Citizen's Choice* Cambridge: Cambridge University Press.

BENEMY, F.W.G. (1974) *Teaching British Government*, London: Dent.

BRENNAN, T. (1975) *Political Studies: A Handbook for Teachers*, London: Longman.

BRENNAN, T. and BROWN, J. (1973) *Teaching Politics: Problems and Perspectives*, London: BBC Publications.

C.A.C.E. (1959) *15 to 18* (The Crowther Report), London: HMSO.

C.A.C.E. (1963) *Half Our Future* (The Newsom Report), London: HMSO.

CRICK, B. (1969) 'The introducing of politics' in D.B. Heater (Ed) *The Teaching of Politics*, London: Methuen Educational.

DES (1967) *Towards World History*,(Pamphlet No. 52), London: HMSO.

ENTWISTLE, H. (1971) *Political Education in a Democracy*, London: Routledge and Kegan Paul.

HEATER, D.B. (1969) *The Teaching of Politics*, London: Methuen Educational.

HOLCOMBE, R. (1973) *Education and Political Socialization in England and Wales with a comparative analysis of teaching texts for British and American Children age 11-16*, M.A. thesis, University of Exeter.

LENG, P. (1975) in *Grass Roots*, No. 9, October.

LIVINGSTONE, R. (1945) *The Future in Education*, Cambridge: Cambridge University Press.

MERCER, G. (1971) *Political Learning and Political Education: the development of political orientations among secondary school children in Scotland, with special reference to the teaching of Modern Studies*, (Ph.D. thesis, University of Strathclyde).

MINISTRY OF EDUCATION (1949) *Citizens Growing Up* (Pamphlet No. 16), London: HMSO.

MORRISON, A. and FRENCH, K. (1972) *The Teaching of International Affairs in Secondary Schools in Scotland* (mimeo).

SCHOOLS COUNCIL (1965) *Working Paper No. 2: Raising the School*

Leaving Age, London: HMSO.

SCHOOLS COUNCIL (1967) *Working Paper No. 11: Society and the Young School Leaver*, London: HMSO.

SCHOOLS COUNCIL (1971) *Working Paper No. 39: Social Studies 8-13*, London: Evans/Methuen Educational.

WHITMARSH, G. (1972) *Society and the School Curriculum: The Association for Education for Citizenship 1934-57*, M.Ed. thesis, University of Birmingham.

2.0
Theoretical Frameworks

2.1
Basic political concepts
and curriculum development

Bernard Crick

The concept of concept

Not quite thinking out loud (for which talk not print is the place), but far less than a conclusion, here is rather a speculative statement of first principles and policy (that is things to be abandoned next year if nobody likes them). I want to extend my general argument for teaching politics in a realistic manner, and the further argument that bias becomes less important when the teaching is empathetic about values rather than value-free, into a consideration of what should be taught. What minimally should be taught and what, anyway, does 'realism' mean?

I will argue for a conceptual approach, that is I believe that all education, whether in school or out of school, consists of increasing understanding of language and increasing ability to use it to adjust to external relationships and events, to extend one's range of choice within them, and finally to influence them. At all times we have some general image of the world in which we live, some understanding however tentative, primitive or even false, and the slightest degree of education consists in forming explanations of these images or offering generalizations, however simple, about alternative images or modifications of early ones, with some argument or some appeal to external evidence. The images are composed of concepts. Willy-nilly, we begin with concepts and we try to sharpen them, to extend their meanings to see links between them, and then to go on to invent or accept special sets of concepts for new problems.

Thus there is not really a choice about beginning with concepts. The real choice is between beginning with the concepts of a theoretical discipline and simplifying them - as Derek Heater (1973) seems to suggest following Bruner[1], or beginning with the usage of those whom one is trying to teach or who are supposed to be

---

* This essay was first published in *Teaching Politics*, January 1974.

learning under/with one (although one thing we do know from political socialization research, is that the influence of the school
on political attitudes is the least important among identifiable
factors)(2).

'People do not first make generalizations and embody them in
concepts,' writes Peter Winch (1958), 'it is only by virtue of
their possession of concepts that they are able to make generalizations at all'(3). One of the most interesting contemporary
political philosophers, Sheldon Wolin (1961) writes:

> The concepts and categories that make up our political understan-
> ding help us to draw connections between political phenomena;
> they impart some order to what otherwise might appear to be a
> hopeless chaos of activities; they mediate between us and the
> political world and the political world we seek to render intell-
> igible; they create an area of determinate awareness, and thus
> help to separate the relevant phenomena from the irrelevant(4).

But a warning, and from a powerful source: 'One should never
quarrel about words ...' argues Sir Karl Popper, 'one should always
keep away from discussing concepts. What we are really interested
in, our real problems, are factual problems, or in other words,
problems of theories and their truth'(5). Certainly this is a
proper warning against a sterile linguistic approach, as if ultimately a dictionary could settle disputes, or as panelists, say
'Well, personally I define democracy as everyone getting on with
their own thing'(6). But theories are built out of concepts.
Concepts are our primary perceptions of a field of cognate problems. 'Problems first', is Popper's proper exhortation to the
scientist; but to the teacher, who must be concerned with establishing usage and usages before he can consider generalization,
evidence and truth, this advice is dangerous; to the teacher of
politics, almost fatal - unless he can first establish objective
procedures for selecting what problems to introduce. But the
point taken: the object of the journey is not to learn to speak
proper, but to understand and explain general relationships; and
also to understand the probable consequences of following inferences drawn from one set of values rather than another. Ernest
Gellner (1973) reproves Peter Winch for his Wittgensteinian
belief (arrogance?) that to understand the concepts of a society
is to understand institutions of that society:

> Concepts and beliefs are themselves, in a sense, institutions
> amongst others; for they provide a fairly permanent frame, as
> do other institutions, independent of any one individual, within
> which individual conduct takes place. In another sense, they
> are correlates of *all* the institutions of a society: and to
> understand the *working* of the concepts of a society is to
> understand its institutions(7).

Gellner stresses that it is the working of concepts through which one understands a society; thus we need to start (as I will argue) with explicating meanings of 'power' and 'authority', *inter alia*, not to show the true meaning, but the role the terms play in, for instance, different political doctrines (conservative, liberal and socialists theories of each) and in different kinds of social or professional groups. Ian Lister puts the matter moderately but forcefully: 'although a command of the vocabulary of political education is not the same thing as a political education, it is part of it. In the beginning was the thing, but we cannot analyse the thing without concepts'[8].

Stephen Toulmin (1972) says in his monumental *Human Understanding*: 'What are the skills or traditions, the activities, procedures or instruments of Man's intellectual life and imagination - in a word the *concepts* - through which that human understanding is achieved and expressed?' And he coins the epigram: *'each of us thinks his own thoughts; our concepts we share with our fellowmen'*[9]. Certainly a private concept, unintelligible to others, would be no use as a concept. Concepts are not true or false, they are simply public and useful.

All right, but which concepts, by what method and at what level?

What sort of concepts?

We go wrong at the beginning of complicated enterprises. Any learned fool can elaborate. It needs a certain reckless simplicity to begin. My main prejudice is to begin at the beginning, that is to build a political education relevant to all the school population from concepts that children actually hold. I am under no illusions at all that such a set of concepts, however elaborated, refined and criticized, would be likely to remain adequate for an understanding of the real political world unless supplemented by concepts imposed, suggested, introduced or taught (what you will) from elsewhere. And I am under no illusion, alas, that apart from the commonsense and common experience of teachers, there is any great knowledge of these primary concepts anywhere. So much of political socialization research turns out simply to be over-structured investigations of the attitudes of school children to adult political concepts: there is nothing on the political 'lanuage and lore of school children', no political Piaget[10]. More research is needed in this area - if only to be able to check our commonsense about what terms mean to the children when we start teaching. Half the battle in education is knowing the preconceptions of the pupils[11].

A political education must assume that the teacher will prescribe and stipulate some body of concepts that he thinks fruitful. If there were 101 varieties, it would be better than now if at least the teacher were conscious of them and explicit in their use. But these concepts should in part be derived from what he knows of the existing political and moral concepts of the children - in as large a part as possible, only not possible when the concepts are so vague (perhaps even false - such as that Queen Elizabeth is boss) as to be incapable of modification for the next stage which must already be in the teacher's mind. It must necessarily be a kind of dialectic between what one finds and what one can offer.

Certainly at some stage it is perfectly proper for some, certainly the sixth form (but who else?), to be introduced to the conceptual language of the academic discipline. But what academic discipline? Does it not lie in the nature of politics that there are several quite different versions of political science? Only several - though this would be a digression: the range is not infinite. Clearly the J.M.B. A-level syllabus inclines towards a main-stream or 'political realism' view of the discipline, as does the A.E.B.; the Joint Oxford and Cambridge syllabus is close to the good muddle of university political studies, 'Ideas' *and* 'Institutions' - both at a high level, but never the twain shall meet. Essex and Strathclyde lack a relevant A-level - unless it be Mathematics and Economics; and the University of London A-level is now a stranded relic, seemingly impervious to criticisms or control, of a style of long dead university teaching of politics.*

Such can be perfectly proper. There may well be a difference between the conceptual language of politics needed for understanding and participation (citizenship) and for generalization and explanation (political science). The teacher must to some extent know both and mediate between them. But it is a dialectic which should not hope to reach a synthesis. I am sceptical that Bruner's famous pronouncement, that 'any subject can be taught effectively in some intellectually honest form to any child at any stage of development', has as much relevance to political education as my good friend Derek Heater suggests in his 'Political concepts and the construction of a syllabus'. Rather build up from concepts as primitive perceptions than build down from concepts as the categories of a discipline. Heater's 'six primary concepts' are: 'Ideas, Administration, Leadership and Decision-Making, the Role of the Individual, Techniques of Change, and Conflict'. He is surely right to say that all political material can be incorporated in these concepts, and his charts of related concepts show the fruitfulness of this in constructing a comprehensive, advanced syllabus. But to me none of these terms are primary concepts at all. They

---

* I now leave these words to my own shame, or rather I eat them and apologise. For now three years later I am joint chief examiner for the London A-level and a new syllabus is about to be taught, reflecting some of these ideas. Someone said to me on reading the original passage, 'That's unfair, but if you really believe it, don't just say so; try to do something about it.' A terrible sacrifice for one's principles.

are highly sophisticated and theoretically derived concepts which
form part of a language of explanation of political phenomena, with
a few clues embedded in them (in the extended charts) about what
is morally significant and relevant. Who perceives the world in
these terms? Answer, a political scientist of the kind of methodological persuasion (may I hasten to add) that I, too, would stand
up and be counted among as the students advance. Perhaps I am
not really criticizing Derek Heater, simply asking another question.
But I think it is the primary question, both in the sense that it
has to be asked first and that it involves more people, although
I admit that it is not a question about political science. I find
Bruner's theories extremely important and they have helped me to
see that abstractions, if set in concrete examples and kept close
to the pupil's experience (or imaginative extensions from it) can
be tackled much earlier than is commonly supposed. (Most A-level
teachers are sceptical about meaningful political education much
below 15+). But it is perhaps significant that Bruner has never
discussed political science and political studies (despite some
urgent entreaties for him to do so): for it is not like disciplines
of the kind that were tackled in 'Nuffield Science', for which
Bruner provides, knowingly or not, the philosophical underpinning.
If so he would realize that working down from any model of one of
the three or four main schools of political science would at some
stage involve a contradiction with what would happen if one worked
up, drawing out early perceptions of politics, mediating them from
the traditional language of political speculation and political
activity.

Indeed the very word 'syllabus' seems (a) to presume a discipline of the kind that can be defined as a construction of agreed
basic elements; and (b) a larger and more systematic share of the
timetable than is realistic to hope for, or possibly even desirable. The broad aims of political literacy for all will be
better reached by suggesting a flexible and minimal component for
many of the other timetable slots, or simply by making some political education part of all teacher training. (Certainly if I were
king for a day I would rather see that all teachers got some
political education themselves, rather than set up Politics like
History and Geography.)

This is why, following Graeme Moodie and Ian Lister, I prefer
to define the object of political education in schools as the increase of 'political literacy' rather than as knowledge of the
discipline[12]. By talking of 'literacy', one stresses right away
the right and proper holy trinity of all departments of education;
knowledge, skills and attitudes. Derek Heater is the last person
to wish to put undue stress on 'knowledge' alone; but this, I fear,
would be an unintended consequence of confusing the basic concepts of the 'discipline' of Politics with the basic concepts of
the practical language of politics.

Indeed to separate out 'ideas' as one of the six basic concepts

might perpetuate that division which we all wish to heal, the worst
curse of the good old 'ideas and institutions' school of Political
Science (in which one used fatuously to debate whether one should
start with 'ideas' or with 'institutions', with 'Plato to Marx', in
other words, or with 'Modern British Government'). Concepts are
ideas and all patterns of ideas are institutions. Ideas - such as
justice, rights, equality - are perceptions before ever they become
elaborated theories (that something is the case). Heater notes
that the Schools Council (1965) working paper on the raising of
the school leaving age urges the teaching of ideas, 'the rule of
law, a sense of justice, a willingness to accept responsibility ...
government by consent, respect for minority views, freedoms of
speech and action.... It is the large ideas which are seminal, not
the details'(13). I would cavil at some of their formulations (for
I can only teach several senses of justice, I know not 'a sense of
justice'), applaud his irony at their 'remarkable optimism' coupled
with their total neglect to do anything about it, and yet nonetheless feel that they are a bit more on the right lines for civic
education than his concepts-as-classificatory-categories-of-a-
discipline.

Start again. But what concepts? Ian Lister, for instance, set
out to test knowledge of political concepts of some English sixth-
formers, even, and the results were pretty bleak. The concepts he
tested were (with the percentage of 'workable' or roughly acceptable answers in brackets): feudal (29%), contemporary (34%),
monarchy (63%), democracy (69%), oligarchy (40%), capitalism (17%),
liberalism (15%), communism (12%), civil service (47%), state (28%),
constitution (60%), imperialism (32%), federalism (40%), the rule of
law (29%), nation (22%), nationalisation (68%), reform (81%),
diplomacy (21%) and treaty (78%) (14). Ian Lister let a panel of
pupils choose the actual concepts. Such a procedure is open to
objection. But for his broad conclusion it is enough that they
were all fairly widely used words. Obviously they are not all cats
that can fit in the same bag nor yet be skinned with the same
knife. But most of them are a bit more like the concepts used in
political life than those derived from political science.

What basic concepts? We should work from the bottom up, and I
have argued that we need to know much more about what we would find
if we did. When do children begin to have any perception of what
could be defined for the purpose of testing (albeit defined in
different ways) as 'the political'? and what concepts do they use
in anything analogous to political situations, resolving a dispute,
protesting at a grievance, or selecting a captain or a representative. One concept, for instance, is widely reported as rife in
primary schools - our old friend 'fair', usually in negative contexts of 'it ain't fair, Miss'. Now 'fair', in fact, is the concept most used by John Rawls (1972) and W.G. Runciman (1966) in
their truly seminal analyses of, respectively, 'justice' and
'equality'(15). Here is an interesting example of very basic

perceptions and of high philosophy both plucking at the same chord - even of the greater clarity of a negative proposition, for Runciman reaches the position that 'unjustifiable inequality' is more meaningful than positive 'equality'. 'Order' may not be used as a word, but it is perceived. A nine year old said to me ingratiatingly, 'It's so much nicer football on a Saturday since we had a referee, Bernard.' I first interpreted what lay behind this in Hobbesean terms, that is that they wanted me as order, referee, Leviathan, because without order there can be no football - 'proper football', anyway. But I soon discovered that once able to take *order* for granted, *fairness* usually proved the more dominant value. From seeing the need for and value of a referee, they would not pass at all easily to accepting my full, and somewhat desperate, Hobbist position, 'what the referee says, goes.' 'You don't know the bloody rules,' they bawl (nor do they neither); and they think it unjust if even a whole five minutes after a disputed throw in, decided quickly and decisively but wrongly by me, and play waved on, a goal is scored against the side that should have had it. 'It ain't fair.'

Anecdotage has to serve, for there is little work done on this, despite the fashion of political socialization research. Social anthropologists would do better. But I suspect one might find something if one could wade through a large number of papers and teachers' training projects in moral education.

Perhaps any clear set of basic-looking concepts is better than none. Something is needed for the new teacher to pull through and out of whatever material he is using, something far less elaborate, I believe, than Derek Heater suggests; something not in the form of a syllabus, but rather a sketch, a model, the smallest possible set of basic concepts that would constitute political literacy - for each teacher to marry to concrete examples (drawn from political conflict rather than constitutional rules) in each different teaching situation and at several different levels.

Some sort of concepts

All one can do is to specify something and see what people think of it, to explore whether it can be used in teaching, and ultimately to test and monitor what happens when it is used. Only at a far later stage of research will one be able to reconstitute it more definitely in light of knowing what children at different ages and levels make of it, and what other concepts they actually use.

What I suggest is something obviously drawn from reflecting on the tradition of political philosophy. This is a far older tradition than political science as a discipline, and so not surprisingly it is more part of the ordinary language, even of the language of politicians, than that most often used in the books of Almond, Apter, Eulau, Lasswell or Verba.

So, to put the matter ever so schematically, I would distinguish three levels of primary conceptions in politics: (i) perceptions of what is done to us - by government and external forces; (ii) perceptions of our human identity - what we think we are, what is due to us and what should not be done to us; and (iii) perceptions of different kinds of relationship between 'them' and 'us' or between 'order' and 'individuality' or 'government' and 'the governed'. Certainly the Tory horse must go before the Whig cart. There is always some pattern of order.

(i) *Government* is associated with three primary concepts: *force* (or power as coercive power), *authority* and *order*. Force and authority are obviously different perceptions. Power is the ability to achieve a premeditated intention, by any means, but force is when physical pressure or weapons are used or threatened, whereas authority is the respect and obedience given to someone in respect of his fulfilling a function which is felt to be needed and in which he is agreed to have excellence. That sounds complicated, but it is little more than 'he's throwing his weight about' contrasted to 'he knows what he's talking about'. Often authority proves stronger than armed force, in the sense of being obeyed; sometimes not. The question here is not one of generalizing - these concepts would then have become theories (a later stage), but simply of differentiating them. Either can coexist with *order*. Order is a very generalized concept, but it is always meaningful by contrast with disorder, or with uncertainty: order is expectations fulfilled.

(ii) *Human identity* can be seen in terms of four primary concepts: *rights, individuality, freedom* and *welfare*. *Rights* are what we think are necessary for us to be human (in affluent societies the specification of precise rights can become almost comic in their detail). *Individuality* is the perception, not equally shared by all cultures (which to that extent are more or less *political* in the Western sense), that a man is the ultimate unit of action and of moral responsibility, not, for instance, a family, a clan, a tribe, a race, some even say a class or a nation. *Freedom* is the perception of the area or space in which one can move and choose before becoming impeded by government or external forces. *Welfare* is the perception of benefits or hardships that one has by being under or associated with a particular government or form of government.

(iii) But between *Government* and *Human Identity* a large number of relationships can be perceived, but they can be grouped under three primary conceptions: *justice, representation,* and *influence* (or power as political power). *Justice* is the perception of fairness or rightness in the application of rules, the settling of disputes or the distributions of goods and benefits between people (hence both 'Law' and 'Constitution' are theories built upon this primary concept). *Representation* can be perceived in many different ways - a Government may seem as representative of

God's will, a race or caste, a tribe or family, a class, a nation, reason and/or skill, traditional areas, property, interests, the general will, or 'the people' or individual people (I think that exhausts the claims to be representative). *Influence* (or political power) can be perceived as persuasion, example and pressure (i.e. sanctions, threats and promises) which, in turn, can be economic, social or psychological.

Such a simple scheme could be elaborated as in the next essay. There are types of authority. Have I forgotten Weber?   Not at all, perhaps ordinary people do perceive traditional, rational-legal and charismatic authority as separate concepts rather than the learned alone seeing them as theories advanced to explain how authority relates to a particular kind of circumstance. Concepts of disorder can be elaborated as negatives of order, or it may be more sensible to treat them as a family of relational terms, perhaps on some such continuum as opinion, pressure, threat, strike, boycott, demonstration, parade, riot, rebellion, *coup d'etat*, revolution.

There are any number of possible variations, all infinitely arguable on grounds of actual usage, simplicity and of conformity to the traditions of political thought or of popular usage. I will argue for this particular scheme, which I have been thinking about for several years, at greater length elsewhere, and in so doing almost certainly modify it. But the adoption by a teacher of con-sistent usage of almost any such simple set of concepts might give a far greater coherence and professionalism in politics teaching.

Curriculum development

The method used should not be to draw up a syllabus with the concepts as the headings and in that order: but to see whether any curriculum can be used to illustrate and explicate these terms. They are not all of the same ease of comprehension, nor all equally fertile to lead into other things, even if found and elaborated from the pupils' usage. At some stage they could all be rendered fully explicit as a set for pupil as for teacher, but that stage, I admit, is likely to be that same sixth form stage into which most people appear committed to place a beautifully miniaturized polit-ical science. But some concepts could probably be explicated far earlier (here Bruner is, by analogy, convincing) than is usually believed - although, of course, only rarely will it be done by the specialized teacher of politics (just as basic concepts of Geography and of History are seldom introduced by advanced spec-ialists, but by the non-graduate teacher from colleges of education).

If built into the curriculum, such basic concepts are likely to enhance skills - the lack of a clear conceptual language must make politics seem not merely hard to comprehend, but hard to talk about, which is the beginning of action. Political literacy is only one type of literacy, but its importance is great.

To ask 'for what' in respect of political literacy is to invite replies with which we are all familiar - even if sometimes official words about good citizenship seem to confuse the Roman-French-Republican concept of 'citizen' with the more autocratic concept of 'loyal subject'. As I have said before, one of the difficulties with citizenship education is that it sometimes does produce citizens - active people trying to influence. But I think we could be more precise. It seems to me that there are basically three rival accounts of what political education is for, what I will call the 'Conservative', the 'Liberal' and the 'Socialist'. The Conservative theory is that the rise and fall of societies is to be explained by the character of the ruling class, the doctrine is that the experienced should rule, and therefore political education is seen as inculcating a respect for tradition and as learning the rights and duties appropriate to a law-abiding subject. The Liberal theory is that the rise and fall of societies is to be explained by individual invention and enterprise, the doctrine is that each individual should be left free (or helped, in the radical version) to participate as much as possible in public life, and therefore political education should foster skills of participation and influence. The Socialist theory is that the rise and fall of societies is to be explained by the economic relationships between workers and rulers, the doctrine is that there should be either a classless society or working-class rule, and political education should therefore expose present class interest and prepare for the future.

This is, of course, a very simple model; but both a kind that teachers can use and that corresponds to some basic popular perceptions. Not to repeat the argument in my essay 'On Bias', but to build from it, I would argue that not merely should the teacher establish empathetically the plausibility of these models, but he should see that the theories of education they imply can all form part of three logical and temporal stages of a comprehensive and objective political education.

(i) The purely and properly conserving stage of knowing how our present system of government works, what beliefs are thought to be a necessary part of it, what are the legal and customary rights of the subject, both in voting and in general dealings with the state and also those involved in membership of voluntary bodies.

(ii) The liberal or participatory level of development of the knowledge, attitudes and skills necessary for an active citizenship, that is when a man ceases to think of himself simply as a subject but as one who can influence public affairs; and this involves the recognition of different viewpoints, values and interests within society.

(iii) Beyond both of these there lies the more radical and

contentious stage of consideration of possible changes of direction or of alternative values and systems.

The last is a proper area of civic and educational concern that must not be dodged or evaded - so long as it is reached through the other two. But I am wholly sceptical about the effectiveness and the legitimacy of beginning the teaching of politics by introducing extreme or minority views. The precise educational value of reaching the third stage is that whereas the second level simply habituates the pupil to conflicts of values, the third level must habituate the student to the critical use of partisan sources - whether revolutionary, racialist, nationalist or whatever. He will meet them in the real world. Any good programme will include elements of all three objectives or stages. Political literacy, approached through knowledge, skills and attitudes and informed by some clearly defined set of basic concepts, is a compound of all three.

Of course, I have been talking entirely about knowledge of concepts and skill in their use. Not for one moment would I suggest that participatory skills do not need developing by whatever specific means are best: projects, gaming, simulation exercises, [16] debates, exhortation, example, discussions and even participation in democratic structures within the school. That is another question: all I am now arguing is that participation is not an end in itself unless informed by a greater sophistication about concepts. 'Attitudes' are also another and a difficult question. What right have we to impose attitudes? 'None, of a substantive kind, like the doctrines of the parties, but every right to try to impose procedural values like freedom of speech, toleration, fairness, respect for truth and respect for the giving of reasons and for reasoning; for without these there is neither civil polity, nor science', is the argument I would develop on another occasion. And this, anyway, is only clearing the ground towards, or trying to establish the outer limits of, precise curriculum development - which can only be precise in relation to identifying each different circumstance and ability level.

NOTES

1. See his Political concepts and the construction of a syllabus, *Teaching Politics*, 1 September 1973. The basic ideas and arguments are repeated in his essay in section three of this book, 'History teaching and political education'.

2. See R.E. Dawson and K. Prewitt, *Political Socialisation* (Boston, 1969) although L.O. Ward seems to see this point as less clear in his interesting survey 'Political Socialisation and the School', *Teaching Politics*, September 1973. But we soldier on, surely, for the school situation is the only one subject to the rational

influence of the teacher. So not to hope for too little, but certainly not to hope for too much and to take on a greater burden than we can possible bear. We cannot do as much harm as the 'leave it alone' brigade suggest, not as much good as we sometimes hope. Anyway, it could be argued that political education as distinct from political indoctrination *should not* have any effect on what attitudes are held, only on how they are held.

3. Peter Winch (1958), p.44.

4. Sheldon Wolin (1961), p.44.

5. Sir Karl Popper in his most illuminating essay, 'Sources of knowledge and ignorance' in *Conjectures and Refutations*, 3rd ed. (1969), pp.3-30.

6. Something odd I heard on the car radio, an M.P. speaking: and there was applause. I've no idea of the context.

7. Ernest Gellner (1973), see Chapter 2, 'Concepts and Society', p.18.

8. Ian Lister, 'A Negative Document: the political vocabulary test', *New University*, May 1969, and generally see his 'Political Socialization and the Schools', *Teaching Politics*, Vol. 2, No.2.

9. Stephen Toulmin (1972) pp.11 and 35.

10. But R.W. Connell's *The Child's Construction of Politics* (1971) is a very interesting exception. He does start from the bottom up.

11. Personally I would argue for some basic political education for *all* teachers, so that a greater political literacy permeates all subjects and levels, rather than beat a drum for more Politics' slots on the timetable. Before reading the political socialization literature, however, I was sceptical if political education, however incidental and informal, could begin before mid-adolescence, say 14-15; but the evidence is overwhelming that it could be begun far earlier, so by 'all teachers' I do include primary school teachers, even though it would always be done in passing, not as a formal lesson ' but 'in passing' does not mean casually or ignorantly.

12. Which we have now jointly elaborated as Working Paper No. 2 of the Programme for Political Education (funded by the Nuffield Foundation with supplementation from the Schools Council), obtainable free except for a s.a.e. from Hansard Society, 12 Gower Street, London W.C.1., or as part of their final report shortly to be published.

13. The Schools Council (1965), para. 68.

14. Ian Lister, Political Socialization and the Schools.

15. See John Rawls (1972) and W.G. Runciman (1966).

16. Again, I would retract three years later a tone of scepticism about simulation and gaming and testify now to a positive, if

discriminatory hope - at almost any level of education; I do not add the customary rider that such things are good for the younger and less able. Diane Bruce has influenced me in this. See her 'The use of educational gaming and simulation in political education' in T. Brennan and J. Brown (Eds) (1975).

17. The forthcoming Report of the Programme for Political Education (see note 12 above) should be helpful here.

REFERENCES

BRENNAN, T. and BROWN, J. (Eds) (1975) *Teaching Politics: Problems and Perspectives*, London: BBC Publications.

BRUCE, D. (1975) 'The use of educational gaming and simulation in political education' in T. Brennan and J. Brown (Eds) *Teaching Politics: Problems and Perspectives*, London: BBC Publications.

CONNELL, R.W. (1971) *The Child's Construction of Politics*, Melbourne: Melbourne University Press.

DAWSON, R.E. and PREWITT (1969) *Political Socialisation*, Boston: Little, Brown.

GELLNER, E. (1973) *Cause and Meaning in the Social Sciences*, London: Routledge and Kegan Paul.

HEATER, D. (1973) Political concepts and the construction of a syllabus, *Teaching Politics*, September

LISTER, I. (1969), A negative document: the political vocabulary test, *New University*, May

LISTER, I. (1973), 'Political socialization and the schools', *Teaching Politics*, May

POPPER, Sir Karl (1969), 'Sources of knowledge and ignorance' in *Conjectures and Refutations* (3rd Edition), London: Routledge and Kegan Paul.

RAWLS, J. (1972). *A Theory of Justice*, Oxford: Oxford University Press.

RUNCIMAN, W.G. (1966) *Relative Deprivation and Social Justice*, London: Routledge and Kegan Paul.

SCHOOLS COUNCIL, (1965) *Working Paper No. 2: Raising the School Leaving Age*, London: HMSO.

TOULMIN, S. (1972) *Human Understanding, Volume 1*, Oxford: Oxford University Press.

WARD, L.O. (1973) Political socialization and the school, *Teaching Politics*, September

WINCH, Peter (1958) *The Idea of a Social Science*, London: Routledge

and Kegan Paul.
WOLIN, Sheldon (1951) *Politics and Vision*, Boston: Little, Brown.

2.2
Basic concepts for political education

Bernard Crick

In Working Paper No. 2 on 'Political Literacy' of the Programme
for Political Education(1) it was suggested that 'A politically
literate person would possess, among other things, a knowledge of
those concepts minimally necessary to construct simple conceptual
and analytical frameworks. These need not necessarily be - indeed
are unlikely to be - concepts drawn from "the high language of
politics" (i.e. the arcane language of professional political
scientists), but rather from everyday life - yet employed more
systematically and precisely than is usual.'

This paper simply attempts to suggest one possible set of basic
concepts and to offer working definitions of them for the teacher
to apply to whatever materials he or she is using. Since there
is no possibility of final agreement either about which concepts
are minimal and which are basic (that is, not a compound of others),
this paper is inevitably more personal than some others in the
Programme. The Working Party endorse it simply as a useful contribution to discussion rather than as a policy document or as
carrying their agreement in every respect.

We perceive and we think in concepts. Concepts are, as it were,
the building blocks with which we construct a picture of the
external world, including imaginary or hoped-for worlds. So concepts are not true or false, they simply help us to perceive and
to communicate. To quote an earlier article of mine which offers
a fuller justification of this approach: 'I will argue for a
conceptual approach, that is I believe that all education, whether
in school or out of school, consists in increasing understanding
of language and increasing ability to use it to adjust to external
relationships and events, to extend one's range of choice within
them and finally to influence them. At all times we have some
general image of the world in which we live, some understanding,
however tentative, primitive or even false and the slightest degree

---

*   This essay was first published in *Teaching Politics*, September
1975.

of education consists in forming explanations of these images or
offering generalizations, however simple, about alternative images
or modifications of early ones, with some argument, some appeal to
evidence. The images are composed of concepts. Willy-nilly, we
begin with concepts and we try to sharpen them, to extend their
meanings, to see links between them and then to go on to invent
or accept special sets of concepts for new problems'[2].

By a 'conceptual approach' I do not, let me repeat, mean that
concepts themselves should be taught directly. The approach is
for the teacher, not necessarily the class; it is an underpinning
of curricula, not an outline curriculum. A 'conceptual approach'
only accentuates the positive, that we think and perceive in
concepts, and eliminates the negative, that we do not directly
perceive 'institutions' or 'rules' - these are imposed upon us,
taught to us or gradually become clear to us as patterns of behaviour, specific structurings of related concepts. The cluster
of concepts I will suggest does not constitute the skeleton of a
curriculum, unless for some advanced level indeed, but rather something for the teacher to have in mind and to elaborate and explicate
when occasion arises. The teacher will be better able to help
the pupil order and relate the disparate problems and issues of
the real political world if he or she has some sketch-map, at least,
of basic concepts. Most of the concepts I will specify do in fact
occur frequently in ordinary people's talk about politics, whether
or not the same words are used. Concepts can be translated into
many different language codes and conventions; but I do not believe
that any would be genuinely political (meaningful in any way, for
that matter), if they were not translatable. We do not need to go
beyond the language of everyday life to understand and to participate in the politics of everyday life and all those things that
affect it.

So to increase political literacy we need to work through everyday speech, sometimes tightening and sharpening it, sometimes
unpacking its ambiguities. Political Science as a discipline that
aims at generalization and explanation may, indeed, need a different and a more technical vocabulary. But for this reason it has
no direct relevance to increasing the political literacy of the
ordinary school child, and indeed I would doubt personally if it
has much to offer as a discipline in either teacher education or
sixth form work. I am surprised to find sociologists trying to
teach systematic Sociology in schools, rather than - perhaps - using
their skills for more relevant purposes. Political scientists
should not follow suit, but consider the different game of political
literacy.

My suggested concepts, or rather my explications of them, are
drawn from the tradition of political philosophy far more than from
political science or political sociology. Philosophers in talking
about politics have usually used the ordinary language of actors
in political events. (I am impressed that, for instance, John Rawls'

recent account in his seminal book *Justice* of justice as 'fairness', very much confirms or parallels how children of about 8 or 11 talk - about football, of course: not 'what's the rule?', i.e. law, but 'is it fair?', i.e. justice. Indeed they can have a valid concept of 'fairness' without ever having read the rules.) Political philosophy, however, *is technical*, of course, in so far as it goes beyond definition of *usage* and *meaning* and attempts to establish *criteria* for the *truth* of judgments. This is not for schools, at least in any systematic way, although perhaps it should be for teacher training. 'Political literacy' merely implies using concepts clearly and sensibly and recognizing how others use them. It does *not* imply solving the problems, getting them right; it only implies understanding them and trying to have some effect. So a conceptual approach to political education does not imply knowing or doing any political philosophy. It is simply a specialized vocabulary within 'the use of English' or 'communication skills' - which is, however, the beginning of reflection, only the very beginning but the necessary beginning. So not to set the sights too high: to improve the *usage* and *meaning* of concepts, not to judge the *truth* of propositions or assertions using them, should be our goal; and perhaps with the most able we can consider the validity of forms of political and moral argument but hardly their truth.

There is no reason why at an advanced level these concepts cannot be treated explicitly, perhaps as the basis for a syllabus[3]. But I cannot stress too strongly that I am not suggesting to teachers of the majority and of school-leavers of earlier age groups that they should teach these concepts explicitly or in any particular order. That is beyond my competence, and I doubt if it is desirable or possible in any systematic way. It lies in the nature of politics that there can be more plausible and sensible variations in approach than to almost any other topic (and possibly more unsensible ones too). Belief that a single method is best or that a single usage of a concept is correct, would come close to an imposed tyranny. All we can hope for is that a relatively greater conceptual awareness, clarity and consistency will improve teaching at every level; that the ability to conceptualize and distinguish concepts is a real persuasive, moral and political skill; and that concepts can be drawn from everyday speech.

A final and important reservation: this paper only suggests concepts which are genuinely *basic* or *primary*, that is only those from which others can be derived and on which theories, generalizations, explanations and moral judgments can be based; but they are not necessarily the most important or the most widely used politically. This reservation is important and must be understood. For example, 'democracy' is plainly one of the most important concepts used in political vocabulary. But it is plainly a compound of more basic concepts - such as liberty, welfare and representation, sometimes 'rights'; even 'justice' is built into the definition. 'Equality', on the one hand, and 'tradition' or

'custom', on the other, are similar compounds. Plainly it is not
much use asking 'what is *the* definition of democracy or of equality, etc.?', for straight away one is faced with several different
and plausible theories and doctrines about what should be done
or how things should be done. It is very important to ask such
questions but they can only be discussed rationally, that is, with
some agreement about meaning of terms and procedures of argument,
if there is some prior general agreement about what the component
basic concepts mean. Hence first things first. A politically
literate person must be clear what he or she means by 'democracy'
or 'equality', but in order to do so political education must
provide a basic vocabulary. Perhaps with advanced level pupils
it is possible to begin with complex, compound concepts like
'democracy' and to 'unpack them', to work backwards to their component basic elements; but with earlier ages and abilities it is
surely better to begin at the beginning.

The concepts in general

Surely the simplest perception of politics is that it is about
the relationship of rulers to ruled, the few to the many, 'them and
us', government and its subjects or the state and its citizens.
We may wish it not to be so, but it is so. It is about differen-
tial use of and access to power over others. We start from the
Fact of government. But government is not a madman sitting on
a sandcastle giving commands to the waves; it is men and women
commanding, controlling or persuading other men and women. Whether
government is prior to consent (either in time or logic), or consent prior to government is perhaps a chicken and the egg problem.
We want to know why such a question is asked before we try to
answer it. What is clear is that all leaders need to be followed
but equally clear that all large associations of people need and
produce leaders. Societies without government may be a speculative
possibility, but not the subject matter of ordinary politics.
(One may say that the object of all politics *should* be the happiness of individuals. But accounts of 'politics' which begin with
attempts to establish what are individual rights and how to get
them tend to be notoriously unrealistic - the old civil liberties
approach, which nowadays can be the potentially highly parochial
'community politics' approach.)

So we must start simultaneously with perceptions of what is
done to us by government and external forces; and with perceptions
of our human identity as people, what we think we are, what is
due to us and what should not be done to us. And then we consider
perceptions of all the different kinds of relationships there
can be between rulers and ruled. Thus the very simplest and most
fruitful model is:

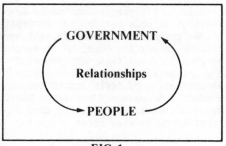

FIG.1

And right from the beginning the relationship must be seen as one of mutual dependence. Leaders must be followed (and pure coercion can rarely work for long, so immediately doctrines, ideologies and legitimation enter in) and people must have some reasonably settled organization for their welfare and protection. The more a government seeks to do, the more agents and support it needs (particularly to wage war or to industrialize); the more people seek to do collectively even for their own good and protection, the more instruments of government they create.

I suggest that a more elaborate model, setting out basic concepts associated with these very generalized perceptions, could be of this kind (which differs slightly from my earlier suggestion in *Teaching Politics*, January 1974, and in the previous essay).

GOVERNMENT

Power	Force	Authority	Order

RELATIONSHIPS

Law	Justice	Representation	Pressure

PEOPLE

Natural Rights	Individuality	Freedom	Welfare

FIG.2

If this appears ridiculously simple, (a) there are some advantages in simplicity, (b) not so when one begins to explicate *different* usages of these same terms and to show, for instance (as the political literacy diagram in Working Paper No. 2 suggests),* how different social groups or political doctrines interpret them differently. But I do claim that an understanding of the usage and *working* of these concepts in politics could take one far and that other, more elaborate, concepts can easily be derived from them. And, once again, let us walk before we try to fly. We should try to fly, but we must learn to walk first.

Two examples: what earthly relevance has this model to those who would say either that 'politics is all a matter of class structure' or that 'politics is all a matter of tradition'? Simply this, that 'class' is, anyway, a very complex and elaborate sociological concept. Its political relevance is as a perception of a form of ORDER (there are other perceived forms), and it can also be seen as a form of REPRESENTATION, the main kind of INFLUENCE and even in extreme cases as the definition or negation of INDIVIDUALITY. It is a very complex concept indeed, not as simple as it seems. We could not understand it without using more primary concepts, let alone evaluate its truth as a theory seeking to explain political behaviour. If taught first (i.e. 'before you can understand anything at all, comrade kids, you must understand the concept of "class"'), it is simply imposed knowledge, the very kind of structured socialization that radical teachers object to most. Similarly 'tradition' can be seen as a particular type of claim to AUTHORITY (the experienced should/do rule), and as a form of REPRESENTATION (history and our wise ancestors), even as a form of WELFARE (the well-being of a community is to be judged in terms of its historical continuity rather than the precise wealth or poverty of its members at any given time - otherwise, why shouldn't we sell out to the highest bidder?). It is a theory to be considered at a later stage, not a basic concept.

Let us now look at each of the terms in turn and some of their conceptual neighbours. What I cannot do is to suggest in detail what kinds of materials and what ability levels or what situations are best for illustrating which of these concepts. This can only be done by curricula development groups of actual teachers at the various levels and by monitoring actual teaching.

These 'definitions' are meant only to be useful, to furnish a starting point. 'Beware of definitions' sayeth truly Sir Karl Popper. Definitions are only proposals for usage or abbreviated accounts of usage. They cannot establish 'truth'. But I have tried to sum up a great deal of debate and to provide 'working definitions' for teacher and learner (and particularly learner-

---

*   See diagram at the end of the next essay 'Procedural values in political education.'

teacher) which are close to the centre of the clusters of meaning often revolving around these words. I'm not deterred by the fact that any of my colleagues would come up with something different. It is about time that someone had a go, came off the high horse and said, 'From the tradition of political philosophy and public debate about politics, in my opinion these concepts are indispens- able and have these basic cores of meaning.'

The concepts specified: (i) the governing concepts

POWER is, in the strongest sense, the ability to achieve a pre- meditated intention. Thus, to have power over people is to be able to affect them in definite and defined ways. Some have gone so far as to say that power 'is acting in concert' (Hannah Arendt) (4), that all political power is, in however narrow a sense, collective, needs to carry other people with it, whether by FORCE or by false or true AUTHORITY (of which persuasion is only one form). Even a Nero or Caligula needs to keep the Palace Guard sweet and even a nordic hero had to trust somebody while he slept. Bertrand Russell suggests that this strong sense of power as 'achieving an expressed intention' is often confused with a weak sense, that of (mere) 'unchallengeability'. It may be, for in- stance, that no one else can do it if the Prime Minister doesn't, but he may not be able to, e.g. prevent inflation. POWER as unchallengeability is often mistaken for POWER in the broader sense. If more power is accumulated in fewer hands, it does not necessarily follow that intentions can be fulfilled. Armies may fight better and workers work harder, for instance, if power is *devolved*. Sometimes so, sometimes not. Power can be used for good or for ill, there can be too much or too little at any given time for our own good; but a society with no concept of or use of power is inconceivable. And sometimes POWER requires FORCE, but some- times the force is unusable or irrelevant.

FORCE or *coercion* is when either physical pressure or weapons are actually used or when threat creates fear of use. Probably all government requires some capacity for or potentiality of FORCE or *violence* (a near synonym); but probably no government can maintain itself through time, as distinct from defence and attack at specific moments, without legitimating itself in some way, getting itself loved, respected; even just accepted as inevitable, otherwise it would need constant recourse to open violence - which is rarely the case. Again Arendt interestingly suggests that violence is at its maximum not in the concentration of political power but in its breakdown. When government breaks down, violence can thrive. Now FORCE, as such, is a neutral thing; it is an instrument which is used for clear or unclear purposes, for good or evil purposes. A few evil men (Fascists or types of anarchists) have made a cult of *violence*, but it is foolish or hypocritical to think that all *violence* is bad. The minority pacifist argument is to be

considered and respected but a majority of people would agree that
self-defence is justifiable, as is the use of violence in apprehen-
ding and containing criminals or in preventing greater violence.
All power is not violence; all violence is not unjustifiable; and
it is probably dangerous to believe that 'all power corrupts'. Such
a nervous view goes oddly with those who want, for instance, more
participation, i.e. more *popular power*. Max Weber did *not* define
'the State' (i.e. the modern State) as the monopolist of violence
but as the monopolist of the 'legitimate means of violence'. He
argued that the modern state at least ensures LAW and ORDER by
trying to abolish private means of violence. Besides, as Milton
remarked:

> Who overcomes by force
> Has overcome but half his foe.

AUTHORITY is the respect and obedience given to someone in
respect of fulfilling a function which is felt to be needed and in
which he or she is agreed to have excellence. If this sounds complicated it is no more than to contrast 'he knows what he's
talking about' - the exercise of a function - with 'he's throwing
his weight about' - the assumption of status. Thus every government seeks not merely enough FORCE to defend itself but sufficient
authority to legitimate itself. As Rousseau said, 'the strongest
is never strong enough unless he can turn power into consent,
might into obligation'. Oppressive despotisms, even, do not rule
primarily by naked force but by imposing on people beliefs, typically and historically through religion and education, that they
alone can fulfil functions which are thought to be *necessary* (e.g.
they embody the commands of the gods - who may not exist; they
defend the country against barbarian hordes - who may be quite un-
warlike; they ensure that harvests will be gathered and corn stored
and that irrigation takes place - when the peasants might anyway
do these things for them; or that they alone can preserve order -
when other forms of order, both better and worse, are readily
possible). Authority can be legitimate or illegitimate, false or
true, depending on how free people are to question the alleged
needs and functions of government, to recognize alternatives and
to judge how well the functions are being fulfilled. Authority -
is it needful to say? - is not necessarily *authoritarian*. All
authority is not bad, neither is it good *per se*. Authority is
thought of as legitimate authority when (a) its powers are derived
from commonly accepted procedures; (b) it does not suppress discussion of alternative ways both of defining and fulfilling needs;
and (c) does *not* seek to extend its functionally defined powers
generally into any or every concern. For example, the authority
I have as a university teacher is because students want to study
and, in varying degrees, respect my competence; but that competence
does not extend to laying down the law about their morals. The
functions of a primary school teacher, on the other hand, are far

more general and less specific: his or her authority is much more
general, and more like that of a parent. Hence the greater difficulties. The limits of proper authority are then far harder to
define. Or consider Dylan Thomas's old and blind Captain Catt in
Under Milk Wood: 'Damn you, the mulatto woman, she's mine. Who's
captain here?' And the implied answer is either that no one is
captain among whores in a tropical seaport, or else that a different kind of functionally defined competence would be called for
than that which gave him the unquestioned captaincy in keeping
his dirty British coaster afloat in mad March gales, etc.

ORDER is the most general perception that rational expectations
about political, social and economic relationships, whatever
they are, will be fulfilled. *Disorder* is when one doesn't know
what is going to happen next, or more strictly when uncertainties
are so numerous as to make rational premeditation or calculation
appear impossible. Faced with *disorder*, the radical philosopher
Bentham said, 'mankind will choose any kind of order, however
unjust'. ORDER is, in this sense, a prerequisite of any kind of
government at all, good or bad. JUSTICE, RIGHTS, WELFARE, all
need ORDER; and even FREEDOM (as we will suggest) becomes trivial
or simply ineffective if there is no reasonably settled context.
But the concept is completely morally neutral. It is simply knowing where one stands, however bad and oppressive the system ('at
least one knows where one stands' - which is no excuse, for the
same could be true in a better system). Only a lunatic would
attack order as such, or could possible adjust to a complete breakdown of expectations; but those who *justify* ORDER as such, rather
than simply point to its minimal necessity, are usually smuggling
into the concept their own particular ideas of the best form that
ORDER should take. And prophecies that 'all order will break down
if something isn't done about X' - whatever it is, are notoriously
rhetorical and alarmist. Concepts of *disorder* can best be elaborated as specific negations of ORDER. I mean that different types
of disorder are best understood in terms of what they are challenging rather than as things in themselves; and nor should we
necessarily assume that they are instruments to some other purpose,
their main purpose may be to protest against the existing form of
ORDER. I would suggest that these negations of ORDER could be
seen as some kind of continuum from *public opinion, pressure,
threat, strike, boycott, parade, riot, rebellion, coup d'etat, war
of independence, civil war,* through to *revolution*. And that each
of these concepts has specific and limiting characteristics. In
other words, *violence* is rarely uncontrolled and explosive, it is
usually intended and specific. 'Ungovernable fury' is usually
fairly deliberate. Ideas of how much types of violence threaten
ORDER are highly conventional and historically specific. Some
people today fear 'a breakdown of law and order' from a degree of
violence on the streets which was easily tolerable (if disliked)
in the eighteenth century. And in some of the Arab kingdoms of
the early Muslim era, civil war was the recognized institution for

settling the succession to the throne.

The concepts specified: (ii) the popular concepts

(So far looking, as it were, down; but now looking up; and we all want government both to do things for us *and* to keep its distance.)

NATURAL RIGHTS (or basic rights) are what we claim as the minimum conditions for a proper human existence. 'Life, liberty and property', said John Locke, or 'life, liberty and the pursuit of happiness', said Thomas Jefferson. Thomas Hobbes was even more minimal: man only had two rights, which were absolute - 'by all means to defend himself' and 'to seek peace and preserve it', in other words life itself, our basic human *individuality*, is all we have by natural right. As with ORDER, there is a great temptation to stuff into the concept everything one desires - the 'right to an eight-hour day and a five-day week', for instance; but clarity of discourse is likely to be greater the fewer basic assumptions we make. By all means demand an eight-hour day or eight-hour week, but such demands should be conceived as WELFARE, one possible thing that we wish for among others beyond our basic or natural rights.

Many of the things we call 'our rights' are, more correctly, seen as things the law allows us to enjoy (like free speech) or commands others to provide for us (like education); such legal rights are beyond number. And *political rights* are simply the minimum conditions needed for citizens (as defined by legal rights) to be politically effective - so these will vary vastly, depending on who are citizens and what the role of citizenship is thought to be. The Greeks of the fifth century BC valued political rights so much that they actually said that a man not fit to exercise them was not really or properly a man but was a natural slave. Yet 'a man's a man for a' that', as Robert Burns (following Rousseau) sees better than Aristotle. The basic concept must refer to what we think all legal and political systems should allow, indeed enhance; to what are our rights simply as human beings. But, of course, man is a sociable animal, so some would argue that groups can have NATURAL RIGHTS. Religions and nations are the most usual claimants. Opinions differ greatly but I am sceptical of this; they can be or should be justified on other grounds, they appear to me to be historically specific rather than universal (if they are RIGHTS then is there a right not to have a religion or not to be a member of a nation, or to change either?). The *family* is sometimes considered by some to have rights that are prior to those of its individual members (but this may be confusing biological and cultural need with moral judgment - I cannot avoid having been in a family and obviously should have some special obligation to it; but haven't I also on certain conditions, a RIGHT to break from it?).*

INDIVIDUALITY as a concept is closely related to the concept of NATURAL RIGHTS, but it is what we perceive as unique to each man and possibly to mankind. The content of the concept varies greatly from society to society. Ours is 'individualistic' in a sense almost unknown to the medieval or ancient world to whom in many ways group loyalties were more significant than individuality. We commonly believe that the object of our political activity is the happiness of 'individuals' and sometimes we even believe that actions and opinions can be justified for no other reason than that they are *authentic* manifestations of individuality, *sincere* expressions of personality. Marxists teach that 'the individual' is in an immanent category and will only be truly free and individual in the classless society when all oppression ends; and liberals preach that actual individual self-interest is the only possible measure, in the here and now, of the goodness of public policies.

Conservatives tend to be more sceptical about 'man as the measure of all things' and to share with some socialists a sense that *community* is more important than *individualism*. But *individualism* ('thou shalt be as individual as thou can be') or the cult of 'personality' may simply be a caricature or unnecessary extention of *individuality*. It is hard to conceive of a community that was not composed of, in some sense, biological units exhibiting INDIVIDUALITY, but they will not necessarily believe in individualism, certainly not in an economic liberal sense.

INDIVIDUALITY is one of the most difficult concepts to get across in our present society, for an almost militant individualism is so much assumed as natural. We should somehow respect individual differences while being fully aware how much we tend to exaggerate them. (I find that to discuss 'the attempt to dress differently' is a good way to sharpen this perception: the paradox that it all ends up so much alike and that the new clothes don't ensure new or radically different personalities.) No species in nature differs less in physical attributes from member to member than man, yet can differ more in character or psychology.

FREEDOM in its weaker or negative sense is being free form arbitrary or unwanted control or intervention but in its stronger or more positive sense it is actually making choices and doing things in a self-willed and uncoerced way. Modern liberalism has tended to stress 'freedom from', as if being left alone as an individual is the best thing to hope for. But the classical idea of FREEDOM was tied to the concept of citizenship, indeed to political activity itself; a free man was someone who took part in

---

*   It would not be moral of me to do so, irresponsibly, that is without considering the effect on others, but that does not negate the idea of a *right* to choose.

public life in an uncoerced way. Far from FREEDOM being 'the
recognition of necessity', things that we must do can hardly be
called free actions. 'Necessity, the tyrant's plea', said Milton.
Some FREEDOM in a negative sense may exist in autocracies, between
the gaps of the laws, the indifferences of the ruler or the in-
efficiency or corruption of the bureaucracy. In totalitarian
societies FREEDOM is actually denounced as an illusion (or else
praised to the skies as a great far future event), everything is
held in theory to be determined by economic or racial factors.
But genuine FREEDOM depends on some distinction and interplay
between private and public life. We have to believe that some
things (though they will vary from society to society) are private,
not of public concern, and that people are free to immerse themselves in private life; but FREEDOM is obviously endangered if
most or many do not choose to participate in public life. In
free societies participation is voluntary for each individual, but
it is - in greatly varying degrees - encouraged and it is functionally necessary for such societies that FREEDOM is exercised in
public affairs. FREEDOM, then, is neither isolation nor loneli-
ness, it is the activity of private men who help to maintain public
politics. Politics are the public actions of free men, free men
are those who do, not merely can, live both publicly and privately.
(My implication is that FREEDOM has to be practised, not just
enjoyed, that we have a duty as human beings to make use of our
rights; but, of course, when this actually occurs, it can be
disturbing for all who govern, manage or teach.)

WELFARE is the belief that the prosperity and happiness of
communities and individuals beyond mere physical survival should
be the concern of governments. The concept of *needs* is much the
same perception and like RIGHTS both seem to express something
which if minimal is almost self-evident, but when elaborated and
detailed become infinitely arguable - all the desirable things that
the state *could* do for us, at a cost (both of resources and liberty).
The 'common good' (which St. Thomas stipulated as an object of human
government) is close to WELFARE and as seemingly necessary but as
specifically ambiguous. The provision of 'bread' (or whatever
is the staple food) is almost universally agreed to be a legitimate
demand by individuals upon governments. 'Health' is a very recent
candidate - disease and pestilence were once seen as uncontrollable,
certainly by governments, perhaps not by prayer or sacrifice.
'Employment' is very modern - only in the 1930s did people begin
to believe that periodic cycles or spasms of unemployment were
avoidable at all, and some are still not convinced. Education and
minimal care of children are now hard to avoid; they are firmly
seen, both by governments and governed, as parts of WELFARE.

Everyone wants more WELFARE. It seems a self-evident good.
But there are two entailments of the concept which cause difficulties: (i) Whereas some RIGHTS may be basic to all humanity,
WELFARE is always a package with differing contents. What goes
into the package must be considered both economically and morally

in terms of a price to be paid in terms of other concepts, value
and goods: we live in a world of finite resources and potentially
infinite demand. (ii) It is possible for governments to smother
people in WELFARE in order to keep them quiet and politically
passive. A century and a half ago Alexis de Tocqueville imagined
that despotisms in the future would not exploit their subjects
so much as seek to satiate them or keep them full of wellbeing
and entertainment, to do almost anything for them, except to
let them govern themselves or enjoy FREEDOM. ('Bread *and* circuses',
as it were. Some see 'the consumer society' in this way.)
Ernest Gellner has recently called our society a 'Danegeld State',
and has earlier argued that the legitimacy of all governments in
the modern world almost entirely depends upon their ability to
increase the standard of living[5]. Of course WELFARE and RIGHTS
must progress and go hand in hand; but as concepts they are
distinct, and both distinct from INDIVIDUALITY and FREEDOM with
which they must always be balanced, compromised, related, synthes-
ized - use whatever word you think is best.

The concepts specified: (iii) the relating concepts

(Each of these concepts covers a wide range of institutions and
beliefs that relate governed to government, and each of which
looks different when viewed from on top or from below.)

LAW is the body of general rules, commands, prohibitions and
entitlements made by or recognized by government, published and
enforced by it and recognized as binding (even if not as JUST) by
those whom they can apply to. This definition is complex,
largely because I do not believe that people ordinarily regard LAW
simply as the particular command or will of a sovereign - this
is a pseudo-realism (LAW must be general, published and recognized
as binding, i.e. not 'Off with his head' but 'Be it enacted that
all those playing croquet who hit the ball of the Queen of Hearts,
whether by chance, accident, design or deliberate intent, either
of themselves or of others, whether people or beasts, shall forth-
with be beheaded, if it so pleaseth Her Majesty'). Yet the famous
'positive theory of law', that law is the command of the sovereign,
is at least half-right; if people do not ordinarily confuse LAW
with mere command, yet they do not confuse it with JUSTICE either.
Laws can be seen as valid and yet unjust. 'Off with his head' is
not law at all; but the 'Be it enacted ...' as above is clearly
a LAW, even if an unjust one.

Constitutional Law is a very complex concept, neither a basic
concept nor an especially suitable beginning for an understanding
of politics. And 'the Rule of Law' is either a truism, that
there should be laws (but about what?) or else is a politically
very tendentious assertion that we should ordinarily obey a law
simply because it is the LAW. Others would argue that we should
always consider whether or not laws are just before we obey them.

Somehow both positions seem extreme in practice.

Many people say that any civilized behaviour necessarily pre-supposes a belief in 'a rule of law', that is obedience to rules - so that even if the rules are unjust, we should only try to change them according to accepted rules. (Sometimes this is the *only* concept introduced into political education when taught - so incompletely - as 'British Constitution' or 'The Institutions of British Government'.) But two problems arise: (i) What if the rules are so constituted as to avoid change? (ii) Is it true that all complex activities presuppose legal rules? Consider again 'fairness' and the young footballer: he learns to play foot-ball by playing football, not by reading the rules (try learning to play croquet by learning the rules!) and his concept of what is fair (or just) does not in fact depend on knowing all the rules (only on observing behaviour and convention), nor logically need it - for the rules could be unjust, ambiguous or self-contradic-tory. Anyway, 'rules of law', like 'democracy' (the one usually conservative, the other usually radical) is arguably anything but a primary or basic concept.

JUSTICE or what is right is the most important and complex of concepts, into which everyone intrudes their own values; but gen-erally speaking what is just is what people accept as done fairly even if they are either ignorant of the outcome of the process or are even personally disadvantaged. 'Is this a *fair* way to decide?' usually means the same as 'is this a just way to decide?'. Anal-ogies and comparisons are more often invoked than *absolute stan-dards* or *first principles*. To deal with people justly or fairly is always to deal with them consistently relative to other cases and to changed circumstances. When absolute standards or first principles are invoked, they have to be applied to concrete problems; so inevitably the application will involve comparisons, relativities, calculations of the probably consequences, and - most important morally - consideration of other people's standards and principles. How easy it would be if 'idealism' were always confronted with 'naked self-interest'; but idealism is often con-fronted with idealism, morality with morality and 'naked self-interest' anyway usually wears fig leaves of many colours. 'To temper justice with mercy' is usually to confuse LAW with JUSTICE. For LAW, as general rules, needs mercy, forgiveness or justifiable exceptions to be morally acceptable; but the concept of JUSTICE ordinarily includes all these already. All political doctrines are concerned with *social justice*, or the proper distribution of goods, rewards and punishments of all kinds. Political doctrines are necessarily accounts of both what can or could be the case and of what should be the case. Hence nearly every relationship possible between ruler and ruled is perceived in some way as concerned with JUSTICE.

REPRESENTATION is the most general justification for why a few may rule many or for how the many try to control the few in

terms of embodying some external attribute. But there are many
more external attributes validating claims to represent than to
represent 'the people'. Historically most governments claimed to
represent the will of the gods or of God. Others have claimed
AUTHORITY because they are representative of a race or a caste,
a tribe or a family, a class or a nation; or of reason or of either
inherited or acquired skills; or of traditional areas, of property,
interests, the 'general will','the Party', 'the People' or of individuals. And all of the claims can be put either in the form that
representation is a mandated delegation, or else a responsible
discretion. The matter is complicated but not infinitely so. If
people have claimed that their POWER is representative for other
reasons, then I've missed them. My point is simply that the concept is of far wider applicability than 'representative institutions' in parliamentary or electoral senses. A 'representative
of the people' should also beware that he may be representing
government to the people quite as much as he represents the people
to the Government. 'Representative institutions', indeed, can
both control and actually strengthen governments. It is a two-
way business. REPRESENTATION is not just to be seen then as a
RIGHT of the people, it can also be a necessity of POWER.
'Because we wish to build the Federal pyramid to a great height',
said one of the participants in the Philadelphia Convention, 'its
roots must go deep.'

PRESSURE constitutes all those means by which government and
people can influence each other politically for specified purposes,
other than FORCE or LAW directly. Force or Law may both be used
as threats: if *expressed public opinion, persuasion, example,
economic, social* or *psychological influence* fail or falter, then
FORCE may 'have to' follow or the LAW will 'have to' be changed.
But public opinion, persuasion, example, economic, social and
psychological influence are the normal forms of PRESSURE. To
exert PRESSURE, organization is ordinarily called for, thus *parties*
and *pressure groups* are the most important institutionalized forms
of PRESSURE. But to stress institutions exclusively, as often
happens in introductory teaching, is to make the same kind of
mistake as when REPRESENTATION is remorselessly narrowed to
electoral systems from the word go: both comprehension and imagination are limited. Certainly there is an element of unreality in
assuming any longer that most political pressures in our society
come from the parties, even perhaps from the obvious pressure
groups. And pressure is not merely exercised through representative institutions, it is exercised through *the press* and the
other *media*, indeed, books still count surprisingly: and it is
exercised privately just by words and gestures. Types of *disorder*
(see ORDER above) are also, when used as threats for limited and
defined ends, types of PRESSURE. And there is not merely the
stick but also the carrot; praise is a form of pressure as great
as balme, criticism or threat. Almost any kind of PRESSURE, like
FORCE, can be justified *in some circumstances*, provided that the

object of the pressure is definable, specific and potentially realizable.

What is all that about?

Two words of warning. To understand concepts is not to understand a society, but only a preliminary step. To understand a society and its political system is to understand the *working* of its dominant concepts and their relationships.

I say again that I do not advocate the direct teaching or learning of concepts except perhaps at an advanced level (anyway definitions of concepts can be learned by rote quite as easily as constitutional rules and conventions). All I advocate is a far greater conceptual awareness in interpreting material in any study of politics from the simplest component of early secondary school Social Studies to Public Administration for D.P.A. And that curriculum development should build-in issues, cases and problems that establish and sharpen some such concepts and distinctions as I have tried to make. A large part of political literacy will consist in exposing the conceptual presuppositions of assertions about institutions and needs which claim to be purely factual and descriptive (but having exposed them, of course, it does not follow that all repressions are bad, as Marcuse once sweepingly assumed: some would do better for themselves if exposed to critical light, some not).[6]

The next essay will argue that there are five concepts which must be treated as 'procedural values', that is preconceptions of political literacy or necessary assumptions of any political education which is not simply indoctrination or imposed socialization.

NOTES

1. Obtainable free from the Hansard Society, 12 Gower Street, London W.C.1.

2. See the first essay of this second section of this book.

3. These concepts are specified in a new London GCE A-level syllabus in Political Studies which will replace the present British Government and Political System paper from June 1978 onwards. Presumably tests of their usage will be set, very much as in Use of English or English Language papers, not attempts to establish their truth.

4. See Hannah Arendt (1970) for a very clear set of distinctions in the power, force, coercion, violence cluster.

5. See Ernest Gellner (1975); and also his *Thought and Change*

TABULAR SUMMARY

GOVERNMENT

POWER

(the ability to achieve an intended effect either by force or more usually by claims to authority)

FORCE

(physical pressure or use of weapons to achieve an intended effect – latent in all government, constant in none)

AUTHORITY

(respect and obedience given by virtue of an institution, group or person fulfilling a function agreed to be needed and in which he or it has superior knowledge or skill)

ORDER

(when expectations are fulfilled and calculations can be made without fear of all the circumstances and assumptions changing)

RELATIONSHIPS

LAW

(the body of general rules made, published and enforced by governments and recognised as binding by the government even if not as just)

JUSTICE

(what is due to people as the result of some process accepted as fair irrespective of the outcome)

REPRESENTATION

(the claim for the few to represent the many because they embody some external attribute, of which popular consent is only one of many)

PRESSURE

(all the means by which government and people influence each other, other than by Law or by Force)

PEOPLE

NATURAL RIGHTS

(the minimum conditions for proper human existence – prior even to legal and political rights)

INDIVIDUALITY

(what we perceive as unique to each man and to mankind – to be distinguished from individualism, a purely 19th century doctrine)

FREEDOM

(the making of choices and doing things of public significance in a self-willed and uncoerced way)

WELFARE

(the belief that the prosperity and happiness of individuals and communities is a concern of government, not merely mere survival)

(1965), chapter 3.

6. See the title essay in my *Political Theory and Practice* (Allen Lane, 1973).

REFERENCES

ARENDT, H. (1970) *On Violence*, London: Allen Lane.

CRICK, B. (1973) *Political Theory and Practice*, London: Allen Lane.

GELLNER, E. (1965) *Thought and Change*, London: Weidenfeld and Nicholson.

GELLNER, E. (1975) The social contract in search of an idiom: the demise of the Danegeld State, *Political Quarterly*, April-June.

2.3
Procedural values in political education

Bernard Crick

The basic concepts discussed in the last essay are, in one
sense, value-free, when considered simply as concepts or as definitions of usage. But when they are put to use in political life,
they will always be value-charged. Every political doctrine will
adopt a usage or offer a definition which is partial, one part of
the cluster of meanings of the concept developed, bent, slanted,
twisted or pointed in a particular direction. If the twisting goes
so far, however, as to contradict the common core of meaning or
associations of meaning in other partial definitions of the concept, we are entitled to say that a person is talking nonsense or
simply failing to communicate, or being as proud and silly as Humpty
Dumpty who, we all remember, told Alice that words meant what he
said they meant. For example, the ordinary conventions of language come near to breaking point when people say, however well-
meaning they are, such things as 'In thy service, Lord, is the only
perfect freedom' or 'Freedom is the recognition of necessity'.
What in fact has happened is that something other than freedom is
being talked about, perhaps something more important than freedom
(the love of God or the laws of history, respectively); but then
it is better said through the direct use of these concepts; to drag
in 'freedom' is both rhetorical and confusing. And in morals and
politics it is very tempting, as Orwell was forever showing, to
try to take over a prestigious but awkward word, rather than to
argue either explicitly and rationally for its modification or that
it is irrelevant.

So whatever our objective, whether to understand political life
or to participate in it effectively, or better still, both, some
conceptual sophistication is needed wherever there is politics and
political activity. Of course every society will have its special
values and every society needs concepts more complex than those in
my box. All I claimed in the previous paper was that all the

*   This essay was first published in *Teaching Politics* January 1976
    and constitutes Working Paper No. 4 of the Programme for
    Political Education.

complex concepts that I have ever encountered can be built up from
them, and that they are a more suitable beginning than complex concepts, however important.

But though concepts are value-free in themselves, high degrees
of political literacy are, in fact, rare. Even in Western demo-
cracies much encouragement to participate is hot-air, or wills the
end, perhaps, but rarely the means; there can be positive discour-
agement; and there is also a sheer lack of political education. In
most other types of regime, political education is not allowed at
all, only indoctrination; and so much of that that it gives political education a bad name. Even in regimes with political education, there is often more unconscious indoctrination than is
supposed. We are socialized into many expectations even before we
think about them; but, of course, to realize this is to be able to
guard against it, to remedy or remove by critical thought some of
the bad consequences (for surely not all socialization is wrong or
un-free; much is trivial and much is convenient). If there is a
genuine political education, certain values are presupposed. I
will call these procedural values, for they are not substantive
values like various justifications of authority, like *equality* or
types of *justice*, but rather presuppositions of any kind of genuine
political education or free political activity. For one thing, the
politically literate person cannot just accept one set of values
as correct: he will see that the very nature of politics lies in
there being a plurality of values and interests, of which he must
have at least some minimal understanding.

In paragraph six of Document No. 1 of the Programme for Political
Education these procedural values were boldly and simply identified
as 'freedom, toleration, fairness, respect for truth and respect
for reasoning'. I claim that these are *procedural* values in that
there cannot be any reasonable study or practice of politics, other
than simple indoctrination, which does not presuppose such values.
As we will see, they are not specifically 'liberal' - except in a
very broad humanistic sense: they are compatible with many different doctrines and social systems. My omission of 'market values',
indeed of economic concepts in general, is (*vide* Sir Keith Joseph's
criticism)*, deliberate. For they are too specific and their
entailments, however justifiable, are too partial to be *the basis*
of any possible genuine political education (although they are part
of the subject matter which should be studied as doctrines, in the
societies in which they arise or to which they might sensibly
apply). We deal with conflicts of values. So we protest against
any attempts, Marxist or liberal-capitalist, to build into the whole
activity of political education the very assumptions that they wish
through practice to universalize. It is strange that those who
talk well about a 'critical sociology', a 'critical political

---

* See Sir Keith Joseph, Education, politics and society, *Teaching
  Politics*, January 1976, pages 1-10.

economy', or a 'critical politics', in fact seem to presume a far
more complete social theory than I can easily imagine to be possible, let alone desirable to teach as if it were true; or they see
'a true perspective', a theory quite as comprehensive as the liberal theory of the capitalist market which they attack. This
reduces criticism to a laboured, mechanical and uneducative account
of the discrepancy between their model and what they claim all
other people's models to be. Theory itself must be included in
criticism. This is another reason why we are for beginning with
issues, specifying 'political literacy' and working through basic
concepts, rather than beginning with theories and doctrines. Only
if the pupil, the student, the citizen finds for himself through
dealing with issues that patterns of explanation and response
emerge, will theory prove meaningful and useful. If it comes first,
it is imposed - whether in the names of Burke, Adam Smith or Karl
Marx.

I assume that a teacher should not ordinarily seek to influence
the substantive values of pupils - and that frontal assaults are
not likely, in any case, to be successful[1]. But I assume that
it is proper and possible to nurture and strengthen these procedural values precisely because they are educational values, rational
and public. Anyone can see that in real life and politics there
are many occasions when these values may have to be modified, because they can conflict with each other, or with substantive
values such as religious, ethical and political doctrines embody.
Part of political education is to examine just such conflicts.
But this does not in any way affect the primacy of these procedural
values within a genuine political education. The objection to them
is, indeed, more likely to be that they are pie more than poison,
nebulous platitudes more than harsh indoctrinatory concepts.

But has one any right, it will first be asked, to indoctrinate
even the basic assumptions of a genuine political education in or
for a political-democratic order? If we follow I.A. Snook's argument in his *Indoctrination and Education*, indoctrination is teaching something to be believed as true regardless of evidence. This
points to how indoctrination can be avoided even in the introduction
of basic procedural concepts. But what is the 'evidence' for a
concept, it will be argued. The 'evidence' for a concept is to
discover a common core of meaning amid a variety of different political usages, to bring out the implications of using it in different
ways and never to be categorical that there is one correct usage.
But no more than with the basic concepts am I suggesting that these
should be directly taught, still less taught first. Rather that
they should gradually be made explicit, being already implied in
whatever is done - if it is education and not indoctrination. At
the end of this paper, I set out a diagram specifying 'political
literacy', and superimpose on it the points where these procedural
concepts are most likely to be made explicit. Now to consider the
values themselves.

FREEDOM.   Freedom is the making of choices and doing things of
public significance or potentially public significance in a self-
willed and uncoerced way. This is not merely a basic concept and a
value, it is in a formal sense, a procedural value, for without
freedom there can be neither knowledge of nor voluntary participation in politics. True, some regimes deny freedom and thus knowledge of politics is low, but even the secret writing or the
samizdat is some sign of freedom, however minimal, of potential
importance; but it is hard to imagine (even in *Nineteen Eighty-
Four)* that there is not a functional necessity for some freedom of
action for some agents of the oppressor. Even in science-fiction's
despotisms, the computer and the robots need programming (and when
they begin, as is customary, to get their own ideas, we're back
where we started again with something like the dilemmas and de-
lights, the uses and abuses of human freedom). But to conceive of
a political education which did not seek to maximize freedom would
be paradoxical.

I prefer to use the word 'freedom' to the word 'liberty' simply
because it has a somewhat more positive connotation. It suggests
not merely being at liberty from specified restraints and interventions, but being free actually to choose between alternatives.
'They are perfectly at liberty to complain', is usually a very
qualified truth, whereas 'they are acting much too freely', may
well be true, but it does imply action. Easier to restrain excess
than to try to arouse habitual passivity. Liberty can be potential
or on licence, but freedom is an activity. No value is an end in
itself, however, or automatically overrides all other values.
Freedom is to be encouraged, and tested by whether it is exercised;
but it will be limited by other values. So if freedom is a component of political literacy, it carries an image of use about it,
not simply learning how our glorious liberties are preserved for
us by well-meaning gentlemen.

TOLERATION.   Toleration is the degree to which we accept things of
which we disapprove. The need for toleration would not arise if
there were not disapproval. It is inherently a two-dimensional
concept, both disapproval and restraint or forbearance are involved.
Thus to be tolerant is usually to express a disapproval, but to
express it in a fair way and without forcing it on another. But
absence of force does not at all imply absence of any attempt to
persuade. What is fair by way of persuasion will be relative to
the circumstance. (We surely, to make a small point in passing,
expect to be exposed to different sorts of influence and information in the classroom than in the party or union branch meeting.)
It is very important for political education to grasp the difference between 'toleration', in our sense, and 'permissiveness' - an
often futile debate. 'Permissiveness' may, indeed, imply not caring
whether something is done or not. But from the fact of a person
caring, it does not logically follow that he must be in favour of
restraints: he may be in favour of toleration, for instance of

allowing the behaviour but making his disapproval clear. Certainly
toleration should not be encouraged as an end in itself; it is
simply a response to living together amid conflicts of values.
Neutrality is not to be encouraged: to be biased is human and to
try to unbias people is to emasculate them. Bias as such is not
to be condemned, only that gross bias which leads to inaccurate
perceptions of the nature of other interests, groups and ideals[2].
Teachers, educational institutions and political regimes are not to
be condemned for bias or for anything as natural and inevitable
as attempting to maintain themselves; they are only, in terms of
reason and education, to be condemned if they do so in an intolerant manner, in such a way as to repress deliberately or to distort
unpleasant facts, contrary opinions, rival doctrines, challenging
theories.

Two important inferences can be drawn from the concept:
(i) someone who is politically literate will hold views of his own,
but will hold them in such a way that he is tolerant of the views
of others; and (ii) that as tolerance in part depends on knowledge
of the behaviour and beliefs associated with other viewpoints, this
knowledge should be taught and the pupil should be tested in his
powers of empathy[3]. 'State the case for ...', 'what would a
conservative/liberal/socialist want to do about this problem ...'
and 'Play the role of a Scottish Nationalist in this game ...' -
are all familiar devices which help strengthen an important component of political literacy.

Empathy is a skill to be developed quite as much as direct
participation, indeed the one strengthens the other: toleration is
neither simply an attitude nor knowledge, but is both together.
Even in political life, empathy has great tactical value. The dogmatic activist all too often fails to understand his opponents,
commonly hanging them all together as 'fascists' or 'Marxists', and
therefore adopts wholly inappropriate tactics.

FAIRNESS. 'Fairness' may seem vague compared to 'justice', but
it is the word of common usage. Also the most ambitious modern
attempt to state a philosophical theory of justice, John Rawls'
A Theory of Justice, resolves the overly legalistic, traditional
discussion of 'justice' into the more general considerations of
what is thought to be fair and what is fair. Earlier, though certainly influenced by Rawls, W.G. Runciman's work on equality,
Relative Deprivation and Social Justice showed empirically that
working people judged other peoples' wages by whether the differences were 'fair' or not (some were thought to be fair, some not),
and concluded that whereas equality cannot be stated precisely as
a social goal or justified in general terms as an ideal, 'less
unjustifiable inequalities' (or less unfairness) can. So it is
reasonable to demand that all inequalities should justify themselves.
(It is fair, says Runciman, to respect all men equally, but unfair
to praise them equally.)

Certainly 'fairness', however vague, is to be preferred to the

misleading precision of 'rule of law' which many would make a prerequisite both for political-democratic order and for political
education. 'What *rules* of law?' can be asked. If only there were,
but that begs the question. Must we adhere to 'rules in general'
so long as they have been legitimately made or derived whatever
their context or outcome? Perhaps, but then *have they* been fairly
made or derived? That may be the very question to ask; otherwise
making 'rule of law' a basic value begs the question and usually
smuggles into an argument about rules of procedures some highly
substantive content. Anyway, 'are the rules fair?' is a prior
question to 'is it fair by the rules?' You may have accepted the
Social Contract, but (a) I don't know what it is; (b) I haven't.
You must convince me that it is fair. A propensity to obey rules
in general is surely good if the rules are good. Plato, after all,
long ago distinguished between law and justice (by which he meant
righteousness). Socrates was a good man - who broke the law; so
did Jesus. We cannot hide behind such a vague formula; we have
got to come out, in the classroom as well as (hopefully) our leaders
on the platforms, and justify every instance that is challenged,
defend it or abandon it, not claim that they all hang together and
that the unjustifiable must be carried by the justifiable (which
is often what people mean by the 'rule of law'). Besides, it simply
is not true that we need to know what the rules are before we can
effectively and responsibly participate in politics or, for instance, play football. Football, even played reasonably fairly,
long preceded the existence of known or enforceable rules; and a
precise knowledge of them would not be high in the list of relevant
skills. Certainly, as we keep on arguing, knowledge of constitutional rules is a very poor beginning for a genuine political
education.

The simplest version of Rawls would seem to be that we should
accept an outcome as fair if we can imagine that we were party,
along with all others likely to be affected, in a state of equality
(or equality of influence) to establishing rules to settle disputes
without prior knowledge of the outcome. In other words, 'fairness'
follows from what in principle I would accept as a proper way of
making decisions without knowing whether the outcome of the process
will benefit or harm me.

This sounds very abstract. But the politically literate person
will question whether the distribution of goods, rewards and praise
is fair or not. And he will be satisfied (or not) that it is by
being asked and asking the further question, 'can you think of a
better way of doing it that would be acceptable to others?'

Tripped in the penalty area, penalty given and the vital goal
scored, there can be four reactions from the defenders. (i) 'Not
fair to lose by a penalty', both invalid as an argument and immoral;
(ii) 'That's the rule, what the Ref says it is', which implies a
passive fear of the referee or a dangerous assumption that one may
properly do anything if not seen or stopped; or (iii) a calm or even

grudging 'Fair enough' - which is fair enough and the best we hope
for. But if (iv) the defender improbably said, with happy civic
virtue and self-righteousness, 'Well I declare, that's a good example of what happens if we break the rules' we might judge this man
to be politically illiterate even if, of course, well-*taught*.

RESPECT FOR TRUTH.   If relevant truths cannot be told about how
government is conducted or what politics is about, then political
education is impossible. Anything that is even potentially relevant to how government is conducted, how decisions are made, how
the individual may perceive what his interests are and how he may
defend them, anything such must be capable of being stated publicly,
if believed to be true on some evidence that is stateable; and
stated at any level of education in which the questions arise,
however simplified it has to be. If the full truth is too difficult to grasp, or is simply unknown, what are strictly speaking
'myths' should never be put forward, either for mistaken social
or moral reasons or simply to have simpler models - i.e. the stork,
the Queen as ruler, the British Constitution, the Prime Minister
as above the battle, the cabinet as collective and dispassionate
wisdom, the House of Commons as 635 members elected for and by
constituents in the general interest (with no thought of Party),
civil servants only carrying out orders not helping to make policy
or that each social class has a clear mind of its own, etc., etc.
Simplification must not involve falsification, however innocent
the motives. When the teller of white lies is found out, it is
he who has discredited legitimate authority.

A politically literate person will ask awkward questions early.
Political literacy must involve knowing that the truth has to be
faced, however embarrasing or difficult. The child is surely
shocked by parents quarrelling openly with hysterical selfishness.
If he has to be made aware why this can happen in the world, this
does not imply habituating him to it. Individuals can only grow
and societies improve amid the tension between knowing what the
facts are and wishing to change them.

Formidable arguments based upon 'reason of state' were once made
that there are some things only knowable by natural rulers and that
there is some knowledge that must always be kept from the people if
order is to be preserved. This might seem utterly discredited. But
some modern concepts of 'ideology' are sophisticated versions of
this old 'politic' argument, i.e. that those who really understand
the ideology, the inner party, or the free-lance dialectitians,
know that it is best for everyone if propaganda and indoctrination
could replace the elitist, humanist practice of genuine critical
education - for the moment, of course, until conditions are right
for freedom and truth-speaking and non-censorship. Truth is what
is useful to the cause. The 'ideologically correct' is what the
truth will be tomorrow (if we can get our hands on you today,
rather than what you miserable, supine load of brainwashed brothers
happen to think is right now). But as modern writers like

Orwell and Koestler have argued, there is a simple sense in which a
lie is still a lie, and a half-truth is a half-lie, whether told
for country or party; and that regimes that depend upon systematic
lies are neither worthy of support, nor likely to be stable without
systematic coercive oppression. But if their opponents cannot
make enough capital out of exposing the untruths of autocracy but
invent their own counter-myths and ideologies, then this is a sure
sign that they are trying to make too much capital too fast and
before the shareholders wake up to see what is happening.

   Put positively, one necessary condition of a free and just regime
is/would be that the truth can be discovered and publicly told and
taught about how all decisions of government are made. There are
obvious practical limitations: security, anticipation of economic
decisions, confidentiality and libel. There are occasions in
which limitations on truth-telling, indeed on forms of expression
in general, are justifiable. But the literate person must presume
on a right to know and that everything should be told unless there
are compelling and generally acceptable reasons to the contrary.
If there are occasions when for the safety of the state truth
should not be told, in political education these must always be
presented as extraordinarily exceptional, as calling for very
special justifications and reasons. In hard times lying or just
not telling the truth can be regarded as a test of party loyalty,
but never of a political education.

RESPECT FOR REASONING.   It may seem pompously needless to include
respect for reasoning as a precondition for political literacy.
But it does need stressing that to be politically literate means
a *willingness* to give reasons (however ill-informed or simple) why
one holds a view and to give justifications for one's actions, and
to demand them of others - simply because to do so goes against
some other powerful cultural and educational tendencies of our
times. Some hold, for instance, that if an opinion is *sincerely*
held, it should not be questioned (a belief that all prejudices are
equal), nor should justifications be pressed for in respect to
actions that are held to be authentic expressions of *personality*
(a belief that no feelings should be hurt by being questioned).
Others regard reasons as unnecessary if actions can be certified
as authentic or typical emanations of some group interest -
'working class solidarity' or 'middle class moderation', for instance. Some progressives, after having properly attacked Burkean
ideas that prejudices drawn from experience and tradition are a
sufficient guide to political conduct, have now made a cult of
sincerity, authenticity or typicality. Sincerity, authenticity,
spontaneity, typicality, etc. are values to be cultivated, but not
as a cult or a one-crop moral economy; such values must grow alongside others. Since politics is so much concerned with consequences
on others, that reasons shall always be given and justifications
offered for effects unwelcome to some others, is of fundamental
importance.

Another reason why this great part of our Western political tradition that came from the Greeks, that politics involved reasoning
among ourselves, is not to be taken for granted is because invol-
untary political education as there now is usually comes not from
schools or media, but from waging of General Election campaigns
by leading politicians. The child might easily form the opinion
that politics is (a) a residual claim to govern on the simple
ground that the other side is inherently stupid and tells so many
lies; (b) simply the expression of social interests, and (c) simply
an auction of speculative benefits for probable support. So little
reasoning and canvassing of principles enters into current electoral campaigning that politics may seem just a question of 'who
gets what, when and how'.

Respect for reasoning comes from analogy and example: in the
polity, the home and the school. We are only discussing the
latter, but the context is always there. The teacher himself must
give reasons why things are done in certain ways, particularly
when he meets a new class or when changes are made. It is beside
the point to object that reasons given to young children may often
not be understood; for the real point is that the habit of giving
reasons and expecting them to be given is basic both to intellectual method (as distinct from memorizing) and to political democracy (as distinct from passive obedience). I don't understand
why I should do some of the things the doctor tells me to do,
but I do believe (usually rightly) that he could explain if I
asked (and I get worried if he refuses even to try). Of course
there is much more to it than this, for I know that there are
other doctors: part of political literacy is knowing that there
are both alternative means towards any end and alternative sources
of information.

The giving of reasons, even the obligation to give reasons and
to justify what one teaches and how, does not destroy legitimate
authority - on the contrary, the refusal to give reasons encourages
either passivity or rebellion. The indulgent, permissive view that
all reasons are equally subjective simply enshrines sincerity,
self-expression and authenticity as king, as against reason, truth
and love; so that then all authority is seen as bad authority. As
we have argued above, a basic part of political literacy is to be
able to distinguish between power and authority. Few types of
authority can subsist on coercion alone, but then some authority
is justifiable and some not. In general authority has been seen
by political philosophers as justifiable when it fulfils expertly
or skillfully some function widely agreed to be needed. To exercise authority is not, as such, to be authoritatian: to be authoritarian is when 'an authority' seeks to exercise power beyond the
admitted function. The most simple form of authoritarianism is
the extension of legitimate authority into topics and areas in
which it has no relevance and competence. Education, both in
home and school, can be seen as a process of increasing differen-
tiation of function; thus the authority of both the parent and the

school are originally very wide and generalized, but then they
become more and more specific. Within the accepted areas, the
authority can actually be stronger. But such authority depends on
the giving of relevant reasons.

Similarly it is not intolerant as such to disapprove of people's
viewpoints and to express the disapproval, only if the disapproval
(by 'authority', for instance) refuses to hear contradictions and
suppresses opportunities for dissent. 'Taking advantage of one's
position is not wrong, indeed usually proper, often a duty - if,
and only if, "the others are given a fair chance".'

Obviously a respect for reasoning and for legitimate (i.e.
specified) authority is part of all education, not specifically
political education. The question of how much political attitudes
are conditioned by the general organization of the school as distinct from particular teaching within the school is, we would argue,
an empirical question - on which little reliable research has been
done. But we are not impressed by the *a priori* argument that reforms of school organization are the *only* way to get a better
political education. The argument that the school is a good model
of the general political system, to be studied as such, must seem
of limited truth even in the United States where it is often heard;
here it seems faintly ridiculous. But *a priori* we might suspect
that important *negative* relations exist: the kind of presuppositions
to Political Literacy that we are discussing could hardly be expected to flourish in those few schools, for instance, where
children can still see a head teacher interrupt his colleagues
without apology or warning, and know that nothing is ever discussed between those 'authorities' whom they know and respect,
their teachers, and 'the authority', the one man of power, the
head.

Lastly there follows the diagrammatic specification for political
literacy from Document 2 of the Programme for Political Education
(and see page 105 below), with the 'procedural values' imposed on
it to show the kind of factors in an 'issues approach' which
might best combine to illustrate the actual working of the concepts
which I have been discussing. This is for the teacher's own benefit
but perhaps could usefully be made explicit with students who have
already done a good deal of work on social and political problems
by use of the 'literacy tree'. Again I stress that I am not advocating the direct teaching of concepts, 'basic' or 'procedural'.

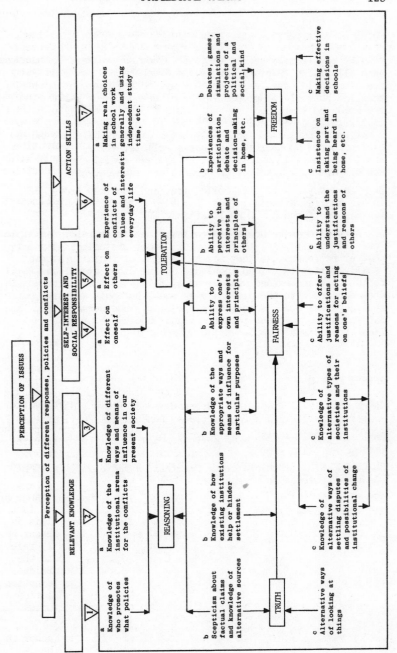

NOTES

1. The more exclusive and vicious values may appear, for example that all Blacks, Papists, Prods and Green-haired men (and women) are despicable, the less open they are to influence or reason of the kind possible or proper in the classroom. But *how* these views are held and expressed can and should be influenced. To go further is literally a personal matter - not in the sense that it is not a matter of public concern, but that ordinarily only one person can influence another in such basic beliefs, through great patience and time, short of processes of deliberate social change of which schools are more likely to be conditions than causes.

2. See essay 1.4 of this collection, and Jonathan Brown, 'Bias' in his and Tom Brennan's (eds) *Teaching Politics: Problems and Perspective* (London BBC Publications, 1975) pp.33-40.

3. A third consequence would follow, that it is rarely sensible (even if justifiable) to try to influence 'prejudices' directly, however reprehensible they may be/seem, i.e. racial prejudices. Usually better to extend knowledge of the other group, and to try to identify and extend what areas of tolerance there are; not to show concern with the prejudice as such, but only with its perceptual accuracy and its mode of expression. See Bernard Crick and Sally Jenkinson, 'Good intentions and muddled thinking', *The Times Educational Supplement*, 6 November 1970, 20 and 55.

REFERENCES

BROWN, J. (1975) Bias, in T. Brennan and J. Brown (Eds) *Teaching Politics: Problems and Perspectives*, London: BBC Publications.

RAWL, J. (1972) *A Theory of Justice*, Oxford: Oxford University Press.

RUNCIMAN, W.G. (1966) *Relative Deprivation and Social Justice*, London: Routledge and Kegan Paul.

SNOOK, I.A. (1972) *Indoctrination and Education*, London: Routledge and Kegan Paul.

3.0
Some Contexts

3.1
International studies at school level: the findings of recent British research

Derek Heater

Introduction and philosophy

The process of education, for all its centrality to the civilized mode of living, is but imperfectly understood. Yet if teaching is to be efficient, the preconditions for and means of
learning must assuredly be appreciated; and to this end educationists have started to unravel the awesome complexities of how
learning takes place - philosophers identifying the different
forms of knowledge, the psychologists the different mental activities involved and the sociologists the different contexts in
which learning can take place. As a consequence revolutionary
changes have been effected in the syllabus-content and teaching
methods of, for example, mathematics and the sciences. However,
the amount of research effort that has been deployed on the various
traditional school subjects varies considerably. But even the
task of surveying an established school subject most patchily
investigated would be more straightforward than an examination
of the work carried out in the field of international studies.

The problems presented by international studies are threefold.
First, it is virtually non-existent as a clearly identifiable subject on the timetable. Secondly, in so far as international perspectives may be studied in a wide variety of subjects, the
potential range of learning skills and contexts to be investigated
is for that very reason dauntingly vast. And thirdly, learning
about the world is by no means confined to the vehicle of school
lessons: knowledge and attitudes are bound to be assimilated from,
for example, the family and the media. The purpose of these preliminary remarks is not to make a value-judgment about the way
schools are tackling this particular teaching task; but merely to
explain the difficulty of research in this area. The elusiveness

* This essay was first published in *British Journal of
International Studies* 2, 1976. 'British research' is used here
to mean work undertaken in Britain about British children: the
nationality of the research worker is discounted.

of the subject-matter explains perhaps why the kind of survey attempted here has not been undertaken before. The only two summaries known to the author, admirable as they are in fulfilling their own particular objectives, are more narrowly (and, therefore, probably more clearly) conceived[1].

Because world studies, international relations, or whatever term might be applied, do not exist as neatly labelled learning packages, the bulk of the research that has been conducted has been motivated by a desire to understand only particular facets of the whole potential range. Broadly speaking, the work that is relevant to the present survey has been prompted by four main interests - although, of course, these categories are not mutually exclusive: many pieces of work covered in this survey have clearly been fired by two or three enthusiasms simultaneously.

First, there is the issue of race relations and racial toleration, forced upon the attention of educationists by the immigration and consequent communal and educational problems of the 1960s. This area of study has been excluded from consideration in this article both because it is a massive field in its own right and because of the intermingling and blurring of the personal, moral, local, national and the international manifestations of the topic. The second spring-board of interest has been the study of political socialization, which began in the United States in the 1950s. From asking questions about how people acquire party political orientations, it is but a short step to inquire how people develop perceptions about their own and other countries. Since one of the prime considerations in this work is to discover how far the child is father of the man, researchers setting out from this starting-point must take full account of Piagetian developmental psychology. However, many workers - and these form my third category - have started from a basic interest in the way children acquire, develop and refine concepts. A limited amount of work in Britain has been undertaken specifically on such central international concepts as peace and war; nevertheless, some portions of research in geography and history are, not surprisingly, very germane to our present enquiry. Finally, there is the most venerable interest of all, namely education for international understanding. Originally this role for education was promulgated by men and women who believed (or at least hoped) that education could be used to relax international tensions and even banish the scourge of war. This motive force still persists, but added to it is the charitable concern for the underdeveloped, third world.

The term 'education for international understanding' has in fact suffered from very imprecise usage. The task of unravelling the various nuances of meaning has been undertaken by David Bridges (1970). He discerns four distinct meanings: (i) knowledge and understanding of other societies than one's own; (ii) knowledge and understanding about international organizations and international relations; (iii) viewing events and situations from a global

perspective; (iv) education to support the achievement of international settlements between states. Bridges then examines the
justification given by the exponents of education for international
understanding (of whatever variety) for their work. He discerns
two quite separate approaches: we must teach international studies
because this is how the world is; or because this is how the world
ought to be. Moreover, he concludes that the normative view of
this educational process is the nub of the matter - that some
cosmopolitan better society is what it is all about. And he finds
the extensive literature on the subject disappointingly weak
precisely because of 'its failure to make explicit this kind of
moral purpose and judgments which underlie its recommendations and
to defend them for what they are'(2).

He concludes that:

> what is central to 'education for international understanding',
> central to the achievement of the cosmopolitan's conception of
> the good life and the good society, is a matter neither of
> psychotherapy nor of emotional re-adjustment: rather it is a
> legitimate, right, and proper extension of what might more
> ordinarily be recognized as moral education.(3)

The major topics investigated

The bulk of the research that has been undertaken has been concerned with the acquisition and development of attitudes and knowledge and the relative importance of the several learning
influences, such as formal school teaching. It will be convenient
to analyse the material here under three main headings: the major
topics of enquiry; the psychological developmental processes; and
the roles of the educating agencies.

Most research effort has been focused on four broad questions
regarding children's perceptions of the world: the child's conception of his own country; his attitude towards his own country;
his attitude towards foreign peoples and countries; and his concepts of war and peace. It is interesting to note in passing that
a significant proportion of the total work in the field has been
undertaken by researchers in Scottish universities. One of the
most distinguished of these is Professor Gustav Jahoda. Taking
some seminal work of Piaget as his starting-point Jahoda (1963)
tried to discover how far children were conscious of belonging to
a community and the relationship between the different levels of
community - i.e. Glasgow-Scotland-Britain. This work is clearly of
prime importance to international studies since a firm grasp of
the basic political unit, the state, is a precondition for any
more sophisticated learning. His work shows that, although many
eleven-year-olds have a remarkably mature grasp of these basic
spatial relationships, 'during the first two or three years of
their school career, most children have hardly begun to make sense

of the wider geographical, social and political setting around
them.'(4). He is, nevertheless, critical of the over-simple
rigidity of the Piagetian schema: for example, the child may
understand the geographical relationship between Scotland and
Britain (i.e. the former is a portion of the latter), yet be confused because of his inability to handle the more difficult concept of nationality which implies that one can be simultaneously
Scots and British (Jahoda, 1964).

Once we know that the child has securely identified his own
nationality we are then interested to know what his attitudes are
towards it. This is one of the questions posed in an ambitious
multi-national project which has generated a number of articles
to be cited in the present study. The British subjects in this
project were 6-12 year-old children in Oxford and Glasgow and the
main British contributors were Jahoda, Tajfel and Johnson. In the
nationality-preference test the researchers concluded that there
was a marked tendency for children to display a liking for their
own country, though with two major caveats: the tendency declines
with age and the Glaswegians did not conform to the general pattern, presumably because of the difficulty of achieving a clear-cut
national identification - i.e. Scots or British? (results from
Louvain were similarly atypical)(5). The team even discovered
that the Glaswegian children preferred English to Scots - i.e.
identification with the dominant rather than their own national
group - and concluded that there was 'evidence of the very high
sensitivity of young children to the more primitive aspects of the
value systems of their societies'(6).

Meanwhile a group of Americal scholars has been undertaking a
similar multi-national study with an older age group in Britain
surveying 8-17 year-olds in London, Colchester and Leeds(7). One
of their self-imposed tasks was to test the amount of pride these
young people had in their country and the sense of loyalty they
felt. Their findings reveal the 'unanticipated result' of a low
level of positive feeling compared with British adults and
American children. They conclude that, 'The old high patriotism
and respect for one's governing institutions appears at present to
be fragile. Not even children, who in such systems as the American
are typically well-disposed towards these objects, show much warmth
in England'(8). These results do not necessarily contradict those
of Tajfel and his colleagues: in the first place the strong
attachment sentiments were more in evidence with the infant age-
range not covered by the American team; secondly, their tests
related more to people than the more abstract political questions
of Dennis and his co-workers.

These studies raise the question of the relationship of children's attitudes towards peoples and countries, their own as well
as foreign. The attitudes of children to foreign peoples and
countries has been a popular topic for research. In particular,
there is the fascinating but difficult problem of the relationship

between knowledge and attitudes. The view, for example, that prejudice and emotion in children about other nations are based upon
knowledge that they have acquired (however inaccurately) has been
dismissed as a '"folk-psychological" assumption'[9]. Johnson's
group, Tajfel (1966) and Miller (1960) (in his survey of teachers-
in-training) conclude that emotions, socially moulded, are formed
before any really sound knowledge is acquired and without subject-
ing the resulting attitudes to any proper thought.

Thus, quite firm likes and dislikes are held in conditions of
quite primitive ignorance. In young children factual ignorance
is scarcely surprising, but it is unfortunate that strong attitudes are established at this time: according to Tajfel, 'thinking
about large human groups in a rational and adequate manner is a
complex conceptual achievement made even more difficult by the
early intervention of emotional biases of various kinds'[10].
In the process of developing attitudes the age of about eleven
years seems to be crucial. By this time young people combine quite
sophisticated conceptual understanding with a toleration towards
other people not yet undermined by adolescent hostility[11]. It
is at about this age, for example, that the interesting phenomenon
of reciprocity has been seen to emerge: this is the ability of the
child to understand that a foreign child experiences the same
emotions of preference for or loyalty to *their* country as the
British child experiences for Britain[12].

What clues, then, do we have about the kinds of attitudes children acquire about foreign nations? Germans, for the very young
and unsophisticated, living unwittingly in the penumbra of the
Second World War, are disliked. Similarly, because of Cold War
orientations, Russia and China are generally rated low in popularity and America high[13]. Even the child is not an island unto
himself. Not only are his stereotypes replicated from adult views,
but he is also capable of catching changes of nuance. Jahoda
(1962) writes:

> Perhaps the most striking finding concerns the impact of con-
> temporary events on the children's ideas and attitudes. Many
> even the youngest ones had heard about the Russian sputnik, and
> this in turn had some effect on their conceptions and attitudes.
> At the time of the fieldwork their image of Russia as austere,
> but technologically advanced contrasted favourably with the
> chromium plate and candyfloss picture of America.[14]

And that young people have been very conscious of the Cold War east-
west divide has been well established at the levels of lower
secondary, upper secondary and higher education[15].

We come finally to the two pieces of work that have been undertaken in Britain on children's comprehension of the two basic
conditions of international politics - war and peace. Cooper's
(1965) important paper was based on a study of some 200 English

school pupils ranging in ages from seven to sixteen, while Mercer's sample was of over 2,000 pupils (14-17 years) pursuing the Scottish Modern Studies syllabus[16]. Both researchers were interested in the evidence for concrete and abstract levels of thinking and about perceptions of responsibility. Over the longer age span, Cooper discovered a shift from the immediate, concrete conception of war as a 'big fight' with emphasis on the 'hardware' of conflict to an appreciation of a more truly political and international conception. In contrast, less progress seems to be made in the understanding of peace, because perhaps it is intrinsically a more negative, abstract concept. On the question of responsibility there is a massive shift through the age-span from a rejection to an acceptance of war as an inevitable part of the international scene - a finding Cooper feels to be sobering for those who would wish to use education as a means of achieving a more pacific world. Nevertheless, the increasing capacity of the older children to achieve a developed understanding of war and peace is very relative, and Mercer, taking a more concentrated age-range, emphasizes rather the failure of young people to achieve any significant cognitive advance:

Not only have we found that the concrete aspects of war show no inclination to decline with age, but further when looking at 'peace' we find that the more abstract perceptions only advance in a most inconsistent manner, while the concrete categories generally hold in an unsteady equilibrium ....We are left wondering how far this tendency to underemploy one's cognitive capacity is a feature in the perception of international conflict alone or rather more generally applicable to politics[17].

The psychological developmental process

Despite some reservations it is evident from commonsense, let alone research findings, that infant children have a more primitive understanding of international affairs than secondary adolescents. What we must ask now is what levels of knowledge, attitudes and understanding have been uncovered by the research and how far cognitive and affective development are related to such variables as religion, sex, socio-economic status, intelligence and the sheer process of maturation with advancing years. The point must be made initially that testing separately for knowledge, attitudes and understanding is very difficult. Supposing, for example, a child provides an inadequate definition of communism. Is this because he lacks certain crucial factual information; or because he has a prejudice, for or against, the system; or because his total grasp of the concept is shaky; or even because he lacks the capacity to verbalize understanding which is basically sound? With this proviso in mind, what do the research findings tell us about the development of knowledge, attitudes and understanding?

Some of the research has uncovered the most abysmal ignorance and misunderstandings at every level. In a test of factual knowledge administered to 7-11 year-olds, Johnson and his colleagues (1970) discovered some quite 'gross errors'; for example, one third of the children thought that Germans were non-white. At the other end of the age-scale, three batteries of tests supervised by Lister (1973) with sixth-formers revealed a depressingly low level of understanding of basic concepts. 'The saddest descriptions of all,' he reports, 'were of the Third World: these included - "The world to come" (the most common misconception) ... In fact even with generous assessment, the correct response rate on this question was as low as 13 per cent.'[18] In a more sophisticated test with university students to assess the mental picture they had acquired of a communist society, Jahoda found that 'The Ss cognitive maps not only tended to be inaccurate, but ... on being told (the right answer), some found it difficult to conceal their incredulity.'[19]

In contrast, however, Morrison and French (1972) in their very important survey of over 1,000 14-16 year-old Scots pupils, were able to paint a more encouraging picture: they obtained mean scores of '34 for boys and 21 for girls out of a possible 50; for a group of honours graduates doing a Dip. Ed. course the mean score was 42 out of the possible 50. These comparisons suggest that many of our pupils performed rather well on a modestly difficult test.'[20] Mercer (1971) too, discovered impressive gains in knowledge from the age of twelve to seventeen. Indeed, for all the disappointments, even howlers, one comes across, there is a fairly general agreement that information is very steadily accumulated with age. In assessing the relative influence of the different variables, few would quarrel with Johnson et al (1970) and theirsuccinct summary that, 'Not only does knowledge increase significantly with age, but also boys score significantly better than girls and middle class children much higher than working class. The social class difference is greater than the sex difference.'[21]

But one must distinguish between the accumulation of concrete facts and the development of abstract concepts. Piaget has laid down the classical formulation of the conceptual stages whereby children progress from concrete to abstract thinking. The validity of his scheme has been questioned for social education generally (indeed, much of his work has been in the field of mathematical education); and those researchers who have amended his conclusions have in turn been criticized. Besides the work of Jahoda, Mercer and Cooper already mentioned, the research theses of de Silva (1969) and Hallam (1966) in history and Wood (1964) in social studies are particularly relevant to the problem of concept development. All show that movement to thinking is a difficult business, that the natural process of maturation with age is essential, although it can be accelerated by high intelligence and social class. It has been argued, notably by Hallam, that the very subject-matter of social subjects (in his case history) is so abstract as to retard

the achievement of the level of formal operational thinking
(Piaget's highest level) until the age of sixteen. And Mercer
(1971) suggests a regression to the concrete mode of thinking
when pupils are faced with the too difficult concepts of political
studies. But the most sophisticated work in this field is perhaps
de Silva's. Although he approached the problem from the point of
view of a history teacher, a number of concepts he was testing
were of an international kind - e.g. tariff, nationalism, cold
war, gun-boat diplomacy. He concludes that there are a variety of
levels of mental operation in deducing meanings from contexts,
that the most sophisticated process is not achieved until about
fifteen (for many probably not at all) and that teachers should
help more consciously in the process of gradual concept building.
The 15-16 age-range thus appears to be the most fruitful time for
teaching international studies if one is to achieve most effective
understanding, though always recognizing that understanding, as
with knowledge-acquisition, is affected by intelligence and social
background.

The fact that sound knowledge and more particularly effective
understanding of basic concepts develop comparatively late in a
person's school life may not be especially surprising given the
sophisticated nature of the material we are considering. Nevertheless, it becomes a worrying consideration when we realize that
attitudes become quite firmly entrenched before they can possibly
be supported by proper understanding. For example, Morrison
(1967) discovered quite firmly held Cold War attitudes among children of junior secondary age: 'Thus, long before any formal instruction had been given on this topic, all the children to some
degree have been modelling their attitudes upon those of adults.'(22)
Moreover, there is some doubt whether people, even quite academically oriented people, readily amend their attitudes in the light of
developing knowledge and understanding. Thus, in his study of
trainee-teachers' attitudes towards other national and racial
groups, Miller (1960) concluded:

> This investigation has shown that the attitudes of many students
> are influenced by their religious affiliations and their social
> class; these influences are probably linked with the reduction
> of social needs. The influence of education, the reading of
> newspapers, the study of geography, seem to be less important
> with many students in the formation of attitudes.(23)

This problem has disturbed Mercer (1971) particularly: he was
drawn to the conclusion that the Scottish Modern Studies syllabus
for 14-16 year-olds is too little and too late to have any noticeable effect on the pupils' attitudes. Tajfel (1966) too, has
written about the early assimilation of evaluations about peoples
'in a conceptual vacuum'.

None of these comments are meant to imply, of course, that the foundations of attitudes remain static from, say, the age of six. We have already seen from the studies of children's attitudes to other nationalities and races that the mental processes become more complex, sophisticated and realistic. Very young people have a mental picture of foreign countries as exotic and strange, which they shrug off as they grow up. On the other hand, even when a more realistic basic picture has been built up, Americans continue to be liked and the Russians and Chinese disliked. It is widely agreed that the process of changing attitudes is very difficult. Has the teacher any real opportunity to be effective?

The roles of the socializing and educating agencies

A wealth of evidence in the general field of socialization research emphasizes the fundamental importance of family and class background in establishing predispositions and attitudes. In addition, the influence of the media - television and comics particularly - must be taken into consideration. The task of separating out the relative impact of the several influences that impinge upon the child's mind is, of course, enormous. The pioneering work of Professor Himmelweit and her associates (1958) on the impact of television on children remains an invaluable source precisely because it was conducted at a time when there were a sufficiently large number of families without TV sets to act as controls. Generally, however, they concluded that the effects were limited: a slightly more objective attitude towards some peoples especially at the 10-11 age-levels; but disappointingly low levels of knowledge-acquisition about current affairs.[24]. Children's comics have, of course, a wide circulation. Johnson's (1966) investigation has shown that boys' and specifically war comics emphasize international hatred and that the readers (mean age 9.2) have sharply polarized views about the axis and allied powers of the Second World War. He concludes that 'It seems likely that the effect of readership of war material by young children is far from trivial. It may, of course, also be long lasting.'[25]

Against this background of natural maturation and social influences, the opportunity for the teacher and the school generally to make much of an impression may seem to shrink to comparative insignificance. If attitudes develop in isolation from sound knowledge how can school lessons influence attitudes? If age, intelligence and social class affect the speed of conceptual development so crucially, can the teacher do anything more than follow rather passively in the wake of this development? The bulk of the research that has been undertaken presents us with a gloomily negative picture - both from the point of view of what the schools are doing and what they can do. For example, in drawing conclusions from his survey of trainee-teachers, Miller asserts that the whole matter of the involvement of teachers in the process of racial and national attitude-formation has been neglected for too long: many

of his subjects had never been forced to think about the attitudes
they held. Moreover the major survey of school work for international understanding undertaken by the Canadian researcher,
D.C. Smith (1966) revealed a similar failure to seize opportunities,
even lack of interest in the matter. Thus,

> In very few schools, perhaps less than one tenth, was there any
> evidence that the curriculum was organized intentionally to
> foster world understanding.... From these discussions with head-
> masters and headmistresses it was apparent that for most of
> them the interview represented the first time they had given
> serious thought to the problems of educating for world under-
> standing.(26)

Even more of the researchers harbour grave doubts about whether
schools can achieve anything in terms of thoughtful attitude formation or adjustment even if the will is there. Lister (1973)
claims that schools are institutionally ill-fitted for the task;
Brennan (1961) and Hamer (1955) argue that the academic nature of
school teaching is irrelevant to the emotional bases of attitude
formation; Mercer (1971) and Morrison (1967) believe that the
concentration of most teaching about world affairs in the secondary school involves a postponement until attitudes have already
hardened beyond the teacher's power to reshape. The reasons for
these conclusions of professional impotence have already been
expounded.

But are teachers really so ineffectual in this vital sphere of
education? Some teachers, particularly of geography, have faith
in the potential of their classroom work. Some early research by
two members of the London Institute of Education showed the value
of personal contacts: good negro teachers inspired more favourable
attitudes towards negroes generally(27). Carnie's (1963) work
drew him to similar conclusions, but also that - in default of
natives of the country under study - visual aids are an effective
second-best. Ingram (1972) in turn, has emphasized the need for
teachers to encourage international understanding by their own
evident commitment and to help young people very gradually to
'build bridges from personal situations' in which they feel naturally involved to the wider world which at first seems remote from
their personal lives. The emphasis must lie, it would therefore
seem, on the how rather than the what of teaching (although admittedly Williams (1961) has suggested that attitudes can be affected
more by teaching social rather than physical geography.) In the
words of Miller, 'teachers need to set up an environment, and
develop a school community, which help the younger and less able
children to acquire good attitudes.'(28)

In terms of everyday classroom practice much of this research
is tantalizingly scrappy and tangential. This renders the work
of Morrison and French (1972) all the more valuable as the only

thorough investigation of the effects of teaching a coherently
planned school course on international affairs. It is, therefore,
worth summarizing the work as a whole. The syllabus is the
Scottish Leaving Certificate in modern studies, ordinary grade,
covering contemporary national and international affairs. Conventional geography and history syllabuses coexist with this and
pupils following these traditional courses were used as controls
in this research. All told some 1,200 pupils from twenty-five
schools were involved.

Tests of knowledge and ability to verbalize concepts at the
start of the course revealed wide disparities. Boys from non-
manual backgrounds scored highest, girls from manual backgrounds
lowest, though with significant variations between schools independent of the tested variables. It is heartening to record
that there was an overall gain in information and comprehension
during the eighteen months of the investigation - but with some
important negative pointers: the girls seemed unable to make up
the leeway detected at the start; variations between schools
remained noticeable; and although modern studies pupils achieved
greater gains in information compared with the controls, they
did not improve in comprehension. Attitudes to countries, on the
other hand, appeared unaffected either by any of the variables or
any of the teaching. However, many pupils following the modern
studies course felt that their opinions on a number of topics had
changed during the span of the course and there was some correla-
tion between this perceived change and the level of enjoyment
experienced in the study of the various topics. Indeed, a high
proportion of the modern studies pupils recorded enjoyment of the
course, even though few were stimulated thereby to any attentive
reading of the press.

In addition to data on the impact of the course on pupils, the
research uncovered useful material on teaching methods and teachers' views. Morrison and French started their research in 1969
and at the time of writing they are still engaged in work in this
field. One can only express the hope that they will publish their
findings and recommendations in a widely accessible form. In the
meantime, Arnold Morrison's tentative conclusions are worth
recording:

> The teaching of International Affairs within Modern Studies is
> firmly established, the majority of pupils appear to get con-
> siderable satisfaction from their courses, and for many pupils,
> Modern Studies is making a contribution to their knowledge,
> opinions and interests which they would not get otherwise.(29)

Conclusions

What conclusions, then, can we draw from this work? First, the
point that has been emphasized throughout this survey - the lack of

synchronization between the psychological processes of attitude-formation on the one hand and knowledge-acquisition and concept-development on the other. Secondly, apart from the work undertaken in Scotland in the context of modern studies, very little system-atic teaching or development is taking place. The list of what needs to be done in the field of education in development studies, compiled by the Wrights (1974) is an impressive monument to the thoroughness of their work and a weighty condemnation of the weak-ness of the British educational system in this area of teaching. And thirdly, teachers must recognize more clearly the normative dimension of such studies and come to grips more resolutely with the problems of opinion-formation without the taint of indoctrina-tion.

The research here surveyed suffers from a number of weaknesses and gaps. We must, of course, be grateful for what has been achieved in the face of the major difficulties of separating out the relative significance of the various influences and the lack of clearly identifiable school programmes. A great deal of diff-icult work still needs to be undertaken. To secure greater confidence in the research findings we need investigations with larger samples than have often been used hitherto and particularly more longitudinal studies - studies of the changes in knowledge, attitudes and understanding in the same children over a long period of time.

Secondly, we need to know more about the particular pedagogical and conceptual problems that stem from the interdisciplinary nature of international studies and the interrelatedness of international situations and events. Perhaps the time has come to investigate 'network' rather than 'linear' modes of thinking. While emphasiz-ing the greater realism of such an approach to the subject-matter, John Burton (1972) has expressed himself confident of the ability of young people to cope with these complexities: 'Recent experience in teaching International Relations to first year undergraduates gives reason to believe that an analytical, interdisciplinary approach to behaviour in world society is well within the compre-hension of school-leavers.'(30)

Having established the required content and conceptual range of international studies teaching in theory, the next research task is to investigate the most effective means of teaching. This is a massive but vitally important practical undertaking. Researchers in the field need to take account not just of the obviously relev-ant research such as that surveyed here, but to investigate the potential spill-over from other fields. For example, if Bridges is right, or even if he is only partially right, that international education is an aspect of moral education, then the translation of the work in that field into specifically international studies might well yield profitable results.(31)

Only after this work has been accomplished will the teacher in the classroom have secure guidelines for his lessons and be equipped with a set of clear objectives and well tested methods for achieving them. And perhaps it is the very lack of such guide-lines - and the consequent hit-and-miss nature of so much teaching in this difficult field - that explains the apparent lack of effect of school learning in so much of the research reported here. Teachers and pupils need and deserve such help.

NOTES

1. See A. Morrison and D. McIntyre (1971) and also J. and D. Wright (1974).

2. D. Bridges (1970) page 70.

3. D. Bridges (1970) page 79.

4. G. Jahoda (1963) page 152.

5. H. Tajfel *et al* (1970).

6. H. Tajfel *et al* (1972) page 243.

7. J. Dennis *et al* (1971).

8. J. Dennis *et al* (1971) page 47.

9. N. Johnson *et al* (1970) page 232.

10. H. Tajfel (1966) page 11.

11. J.M. Carnie (1963) pages 130-1; and see also J.M. Carnie (1972).

12. M.R. Middleton *et al* (1970).

13. H. Tajfel (1966).

14. G. Jahoda (1962) page 107.

15. See A. Morrison (1967); A. Morrison and D. McIntyre (1966). See also A. Morrison and K. French (1972a and 1972b).

16. G. Mercer (1971) and see also G. Mercer (1974).

17. G. Mercer (1971) page 101.

18. I. Lister (1973) page 16.

19. G. Jahoda (1966) page 14.

20. A. Morrison and K. French (1972b) page 4.

21. N. Johnson *et al* (1970) page 35.

22. A. Morrison (1967) page 201.

23. H.W.L. Miller (1960) page 156.

24. H. Himmelweit *et al* (1958) pages 255, 272-3.

25. N. Johnson (1966) page 12.

26. D.C. Smith (1966) pages 610, 621.

27. H.E.O. James and C. Tenen (1951).

28. H.W.L. Miller (1960) pages 157-8.

29. A. Morrison (1973) page 10.

30. J.W. Burton (1970) page X.

31. This approach is being used in the area of political education. See, for example, P. Tomlinson (1975).

REFERENCES

BRENNAN, T. (1961), Teaching for international understanding in a secondary modern school, *Researches and Studies*, No. 21.

BRIDGES, D. (1970), *Education and International Understanding - A Philosophical Examination*, M.A. thesis, University of London.

BURTON, J.W. (1972), *World Society*, Cambridge: Cambridge University Press.

CARNIE, J.M. (1963), *The Contribution of School Geography to the Improvement of International Understanding*, M.A. thesis, University of London.

CARNIE, J.M. (1972), 'Children's attitudes to other nationalities', in N. Graves (Ed), *New Movements in the Study and Teaching of Geography*, London: Temple Smith.

COOPER, P. (1965), The development of the concept of war, *Journal of Peace Research*, Vol. 2.

DENNIS J. *et al* (1971), Support for nation and government among English children, *British Journal of Political Science*, Vol. 1.

DE SILVA, W.A. (1969), *Concept Formation in Adolescence Through Contextual Clues, with Special Reference to History Material*, Ph.D. thesis, University of Birmingham.

HALLAM, R.N. (1966), *An Investigation into Some Aspects of the Historical Thinking of Children and Adolescents*, M.Ed. thesis, University of Leeds.

HAMER, S.M. (1955), *An Experimental Comparison of the Effect of Two Methods of Teaching upon Attitudes Related to International Understanding*, M.A. thesis, University of London.

HIMMELWEIT, H. *et al* (1958), *Television and the Child*, Oxford: Oxford University Press.

INGRAM, D. (1972), *A Study of the School's Role in Attitude Formation and Change with Particular Reference to International Understanding*, M.A. thesis, University of London.

JAHODA, G. (1962), Development of Scottish children's ideas and attitudes about other countries, *Journal of Social Psychology*, Vol. 58.

JAHODA, G. (1963), Development of children's ideas about country and nationality, *British Journal of Educational Psychology*, Vol. 33.

JAHODA, G. (1964), Children's concepts of nationality: a critical study of Piaget's stages, *Child Development*, Vol. 35.

JAHODA, G. (1966), Impressions of nationalities - an alternative to the 'stereotype' approach, *British Journal of Social and Clinical Psychology*, Vol. 5.

JAHODA, G. and TAJFEL, H. (1967), Development in children of ideas about their own and other countries, *New Era* Vol. 48.

JAMES, H.E.O. and TENEN, C. (1951), Attitudes towards other people, *International Social Science Bulletin*, Vol. 3.

JOHNSON, N. (1966), Children's comics, *New Society* Vol. 8.

JOHNSON, N. *et al* (1970), The relationship between children's preferences for and knowledge about other nations, *British Journal of Social and Clinical Psychology*, Vol. 9.

LISTER, I. (1973), Political socialization and schools, with special reference to the knowledge of political concepts of English sixth-formers, *Teaching Politics*, Vol. 2.

MERCER, G. (1971), *Political Learning and Political Education*, Ph.D. thesis, University of Strathclyde.

MERCER, G. (1974), Formal political education and the perception of international conflict, *Journal of Moral Education*, Vol. 4.

MIDDLETON, M.R. *et al* (1970), Cognitive and affective aspects of children's national attitudes, *British Journal of Social and Clinical Psychology*, Vol. 9.

MILLER, H.W.L. (1960), *A Study of the Use of Attitude Tests and of Attitudes of Students to Peoples of Other Countries and Other Racial Groups*, M.A. thesis, University of Birmingham.

MORRISON, A. (1967), Attitudes of children to international affairs, *Educational Research*, Vol. 9.

MORRISON, A. (1973), The teaching of international affairs in secondary schools in Scotland, *MOST* No. 2.

MORRISON, A. and FRENCH, K. (1972a), *The Teaching of International Affairs in Secondary Schools in Scotland - First Report*, Mimeograph, University of Dundee, (unpublished).

MORRISON, A. and FRENCH, K. (1972b), *The Teaching of International Affairs in Secondary Schools in Scotland - Final Report to S.S.R.C. and to Schools*, Mimeograph, University of Dundee, (unpublished).

MORRISON, A. and McINTYRE, D. (1966), The attitudes of students towards international affairs, *British Journal of Social and Clinical Psychology*, Vol. 5.

MORRISON, A. and McINTYRE, D. (1971), *Schools and Socialization*, Harmondsworth: Penguin Books.

SMITH, D.C. (1966), *Education for World Understanding: An Estimate of the Impact on the Secondary Schools of England and Wales in 1964 of its Influences Since 1945*, Ph.D. thesis, University of London.

TAJFEL, H. (1966), Children and foreigners, *New Society* Vol. 7.

TAJFEL, H. *et al* (1970), The development of children's preferences for their own country: a cross-national study, *International Journal of Psychology*, Vol. 5.

TAJFEL, H. *et al* (1972), The devaluation by children of their own national and ethnic group: two case studies, *British Journal of Social and Clinical Psychology*, Vol. 11.

TOMLINSON, P. (1975), *Political Education: Cognitive Developmental Perspectives from Moral Education*, Mimeograph, University of York (unpublished).

VENESS, T. (1972), 'The contribution of psychology', in N. Graves (Ed) *New Movements in the Study and Teaching of Geography*, London: Temple Smith.

WILLIAMS, H.M. (1961), Changes in pupils' attitudes towards West African negroes following the use of two different teaching methods, *British Journal of Educational Psychology*, Vol. 31.

WOOD, D.M. (1964), *The Development of Some Concepts of Social Relations in Childhood and Adolescence Investigated by Means of the Analysis of Ten Definitions*, M.Ed. thesis, University of Nottingham.

WRIGHT, J. and D. (1974), *The Changing World in the Classroom*, London: U.K. Commission for UNESCO.

3.2
History teaching and political education

Derek Heater

The civic education tradition of History

So many of the great historians said it, and those who did not often took it for granted - that History and Politics were virtually identical subjects, distinguishable only by the particular time perspective through which the subject-matter was viewed. Until quite recently it was taken as axiomatic that the historian's prime concern was with the political events of the past and that present political activity was History-in-the-making. Sir John Seeley's snappy aphorism is well known. However, the following comment by him is even more illuminating: 'Politics', he said, 'are vulgar when they are not liberalised by history, and history fades into mere literature when it loses sight of its relation to practical politics.'[1]

This sentence expounds a relationship that can be traced back as a continuous thread to Thucydides.[2] And the key word is 'practical'. For just as 'History' has the dual meaning of 'the past' and 'the record of the past', so the word 'Politics' has come to mean both 'political activity' and 'the study of political activity' (since terms like Political Science and Political Studies are not universally acceptable). Seeley's emphasis was thus on the relationship between History as the record of the past and Politics as an activity: History records that activity, and politicians, in their turn if they be wise, will learn from that record. By accepting the validity of this relationship one con-

*   I am very grateful to the kindness of my friend, Dr. W.N. Coxall of East Sussex College of Higher Education, in reading the original typescript and making many valuable suggestions for its improvement. The essay was first published by the Politics Association in 1974 as *Occasional Publication 1*. Work on the utilisation of History as a vehicle for political education has continued in the context of the Nuffield-funded Programme for Political Education. Its forthcoming report will include some practical syllabus suggestions.

fers upon History a utilitarian function - it is not 'mere literature'. This is an unpopular interpretation today, when it is widely considered that History should be studied 'for its own sake'. This latter point of view can lead, for example, to a Regius Professor making decidedly offensive remarks about a Minister of Education for expressing a belief that the study of Vietnam should be given priority over 'all the details of the Wars of the Roses'[3]. Let Professors of Politics advise foreign governments on the writing of constitutions or even recommend the reform of our own parliament; such practical activities, however, are not quite proper for historians.

But if political wisdom *is* to be gleaned from a study of the past, many would argue that the most fruitful field of study is the recent past. A politician is a fool if he does not master the background of any issue he may be tackling; and it is only the immediate background that is normally necessary. So it has come about that much of the history consciously written for political edification has been Contemporary History. Hence Clarendon's great *History*, for example. Nevertheless, the historian is right to utter a warning against neglecting more remote times if a full appreciation is to be made of some problems: Northern Ireland is a present reminder of the cogency of this argument. And Machiavelli, of course, considered that the most pertinent political lessons for Renaissance Italy could be learned from a study of Republican Rome.

History is not, however, just a professional study - for the delight and enjoyment of historians and the education of politicians. It is also, and has been for something like a century, an important school subject. At this level, too, there has been a parallel acceptance of the close interrelationship between History and Politics. At first, in the Victorian public schools, the relationship was exactly a junior, preparatory version of the adult relationship between historian and politician already outlined. It was expected that a significant proportion of the boys would enter public service in some form, and History was introduced into the curriculum to provide the necessary education in political matters. Of course, as this study of History spread throughout the state secondary schools, this particular justification could not be sustained. Nevertheless, although the products of Fenn Street Secondary Modern School were clearly not destined for senior Foreign Office appointments, they were all going to be equipped in due course with the rights of citizenship. And what is sauce for the government is sauce for the governed. Citizens as well as civil servants require political education. History would provide.

For many History teachers any proposal for divorcing historical from political education has been quite unthinkable. The subjects are, in this view, as inseparable as bubble-and-squeak, the flavour of the one ingredient being irreparably harmed in the

event of the other being excluded[4]. One of the very earliest
textbooks ever written in this country, in the sixteenth century,
Anglorum Poelia, was a history of English involvement in military combat from the Hundred Years War onwards. The Privy Council
ordered that it should be read in all schools in order to promote
a patriotic spirit[5]. Today the government is not quite so
interventionist. Yet official statements in recent times reiterate the belief that History is the proper vehicle for political
education. It is through History, asserted the Norwood Report of
1941, 'that we believe the best contribution can be made in schools
to the growth of an informed democracy'[6]. The D.E.S. expressed
a remarkable faith in the efficiency of History teaching for this
purpose as recently as 1967: 'Even pessimists argue that ... it
will be as well to give (the next generation) as good a political
education as may be, which means giving it an education in
history.'[7] Moreover, History teachers themselves tend to have
a certain professional, proprietory feeling towards political
education. "Civics and current affairs are regarded as mere
splinters unnecessarily struck from main timbers of the history
syllabus', declared the Grammar School teachers a decade ago[8].
'Most (History) teachers tend to stress the preliminary training
which the subject provides in responsible citizenship', reported
the D.E.S. a few years later[9].

The traditional relationship between historical and political
education would seem to have been fairly firmly established; and
an essay to argue in its favour might at first sight appear
to be a supererogatory task. In practice, however, the tradition,
deeply rooted as it has been, has been seriously undermined. And,
what is more, there have been very good reasons for this. Firstly,
there has been the evolution of Politics as an academic discipline
separate from History. Secondly, there is the aridity of much
that has passed for Political History. Thirdly, the belief that
History should provide a rounded picture of the past, not merely
one segment. Fourthly, the view that the great value of History
is its provision of perspective: and that this is eroded by
studying the past for the sake of the present. Fifthly, the fact
that Political History entangles the teacher in the webs of bias
and indoctrination. And finally, the conviction that Politics is
unrelated and irrelevant to the child's experience. Each of
these cases must be examined later. However, it is sufficient
here to notice the strength of the reaction against the traditional
employment of History for political education.

Even so, despite the cogency of these arguments, I believe it
to be important to revivify the former role of History as a trans-
mitter of political education. After all, a tradition that is
planted as firmly as I have tried to indicate cannot surely be
entirely devoid of value. So let the valuable features of the
union be identified and preserved. This is not to be blind to
the drawbacks of the old kind of Political History in its school

form any more than it is a partisan defence of the scholarly nit-picking that has marred Political History at a more elevated level. Just as Professor Plumb (1973) perceives 'a new renaissance (for Political History), an end to the desiccation and sterility of the last two decades' - basing his optimism on the emergence of work combining a breadth of perspective with scrupulous scholarship - so we may hope for a new Political History in the schools, which, while not renouncing any useful and necessary attention to detail, will illuminate by its evidently broad relevance to political understanding.

It is one of the purposes of this essay to try to define the main features that might characterize this new Political History in the schools. Before reaching this level in the discussion however, there are still a number of preliminary matters to be raised. For example, it has rather been taken for granted up to this point that political education, in some form or other, is an important, even necessary, function of the school system. It cannot be taken for granted; the case has to be argued.

The importance of political education

'The expression "political education" has fallen on evil days; in the wilful and disingenuous corruption of language which is characteristic of our time it has acquired a sinister meaning.'(10) A much-quoted sentence from Michael Oakeshott's inaugural lecture. Twenty years later, one of his former colleagues, Bernard Crick, saw the problem as dullness rather than danger. He is equally quotable: 'To teach the constitution,' he has written, 'is like teaching elementary anatomy or biology instead of the nature of sexuality. They may be necessary first steps, or collateral studies, but by themselves they would either be an evasion, or quite simply something else.'(11) Nevertheless, just to quote two professors on the subject, however learned, is to do less than justice to the variety of the arguments marshalled by the opponents of political education (or as in these cases, its perversion).

Firstly, one may trace the arguments based upon the supposed ineffectiveness of programmes of political education: either that there is no evidence that instruction in political matters leads to greater interest or sense of civic responsibility(12); or that the schools cannot hope to compete with the media, which will be utilized by those who have the interest in any case. Secondly, there is the belief that, paradoxically, faith in and support for the democratic system is undermined by teaching about it. This belief is based on the assumption that the model that is taught gives a false impression of the ordinary citizen's power to exert influence and that the discovery of the practical truth is attended by disillusionment. The third set of reasons for rejecting political education in the schools is the fear that the teachers will not, indeed cannot, be impartial. And this attack is mounted on all sides: 'Ideological indoctrination,' cry the Right; 'Defence of the Establishment,' complain the Left; 'An unwarranted invasion of a family responsibility,' claim the Liberals. And finally there is the most dangerous, albeit rarely heard, argument of all - the argument that political apathy is politically healthy. The reasoning goes as follows: political education leads to political interest; political interest leads to political activity; most people are not politically wise (even if 'educated'); therefore a politically active mass will support dangerous demagogues who offer superficially attractive promises - just look at the political mobilization achieved in Nazi Germany. Ergo, let us not have political education.

It is possible, of course, to neutralize each of these arguments by quite simply asserting that, although any of these situations *may* result from political education, they are the conditions or effects of *bad* political education. Even so, this argument is not good enough on its own; we must counter-attack by arguing the positive value of good political education.

We must start by rejecting out-of-hand the fourth objection in the above list - namely, that political consciousness is conducive to totalitarianism. In their influential book, Gabriel Almond and Sidney Verba have argued cogently that the existence of a civic culture, in which 'the norms of interpersonal relationships, of general confidence in one's social environment, penetrate political attitudes and temper them'[13] is a necessary feature of a stable democratic society. What is needed, in short, is a sense of responsible competence - the golden mean that neither surrenders freedom for fear of exercising it nor gives rein to political passion, intolerant of others' views and needs. This means using the system, not being used by it; using the system, not undermining it. But it is a complex system (one of its virtues). To withstand or promote change we may engage in a variety of activities - voting, lobbying M.P.s and councillors, writing to the press or local officials, supporting pressure groups and trade unions. And precisely because the system is complex, the citizen has to learn how to work it. Ignorance of the system and a sense of powerlessness before the system are at the moment widespread because the schools are shirking this social and educational responsibility.[14]

True, most secondary schools teach some Political History or Current Affairs or Social Studies or British Constitution or Civics. But it is rare to find a coherently thought-out programme for all pupils (and, after all, *all* pupils are going to be citizens at the most two years after leaving shcool). Not that this neglect is the sole responsibility of the teaching profession, for teachers have neither been professionally trained for the task[15] nor professionally encouraged to undertake the task by such authoritative bodies as the D.E.S. or the Schools Council.[16]

It is time, therefore, not merely to assert the importance of

political education as an article of faith, but to clarify what
specific advantages are likely to accrue from such teaching. In
order to operate effectively as a citizen of a democratic society
one needs to have a certain basic knowledge of how the system
works. In addition, one needs ideas - in order to examine one's
own attitudes; to be honest enough to change them if, under scrutiny they turn out to be untenable prejudices; and in order to
assess the validity of information and opinion presented by the
'persuaders'. The teaching of such material would equip young
people to cope with three important problems: firstly, participation in the democratic process; secondly, defence against manipulation by the media and politicians; and thirdly, an interested
commitment to ward off apathy and alienation.

'Participation' was the key political word of the late 1960s,
whether on the campus or in the community. There has been widespread agreement that an increasing proportion of the population
expect avenues of consultation to be opened up and that our society
will be made more healthily democratic by expansion in this two-way
traffic - within reason, of course, since direct democracy is
scarcely a practical possibility on the national level, let alone
a European. However, people do not participate without encouragement: they need the confidence that derives from knowledge of the
machinery and faith in its relevance to them. In many ways people
can only learn to participate by participating. Nevertheless,
invaluable preparatory work can be undertaken at school both by
the provision of basic information about the institutions and
processes accessible to the adult and - though this is a sensitive
matter - by involvement in consultative processes within the
school itself[17]. We live in a sophisticated society. Participation does not mean just voting in national elections every four
or five years. A variety of actions are open to the citizen and
he needs knowledge of this variety and the ability to judge their
appropriateness in given circumstances. What do you do? Why do
you do it? When do you do it? If such questions are valid in
the context of Sex Education, are they not just as valid in
Political Education?

There is considerable evidence that people selectively glean
from television and newspapers material that confirms their already
established point of view rather than are swayed by what they read
and see[18]. Yet there is no room for complacency. The use of
commerical advertising techniques to 'sell' personalities in US
elections and the deliberate projection of his magisterial personality into the living-rooms of France by President De Gaulle should
be sufficient warnings of the potential for political manipulation
through the media. Participation requires that people should be
endowed with discrimination as well as knowledge. The challenge
presented by the media should lead us to foster the development
of open, alert and critical minds.

So, we have our pupils knowledgeable and insulated from the

persuasiveness of the media. But our task is uncompleted if,
Dalek-like, they utter the 'Destroy' of the alienated or groan the
'What-the-hell' of the apathetic. In other words, we should encourage them to understand the system is a worthwhile one - but
encourage gently by teaching, not irreversibly by an unprofessional indoctrination. Alienation and apathy are not so very
different qualities in origin. Rather they are the two faces of
a Janus-like disillusionment. 'The faceless bureaucrats run our
lives'; 'The politicians are only in the game for their own
benefit'; 'The individual is powerless.' How many times are such
comments made - by cynical adults, let alone disillusioned youth?
Both forms - active alienation or passive apathy - are equally
corrosive of the democratic system, which needs the underpinning
of public support. The teacher's task, therefore, is to convey by
the infection of his own enthusiastic, even if critical, commitment the belief that the democratic system we have is worth using
and preserving. Not perfect to be sure; and in need of organic
adaptation; but the best we have. It is a delicate task not to
be undertaken lightly.

The importance of history as the vehicle

    All - or at least some - of this may seem rather remote from the
kind of job many History teachers thought they were undertaking
when they started in the classroom; or, indeed, far removed from
what they actually do engage in in the classroom. Many a History
teacher may well feel that such tasks as outlined above are
either uncongenial to him or that he is in all honesty professionally just not equipped for the task. If political education is
to be undertaken in schools, he may argue, it ought to be the
responsibility of a teacher academically trained in Political
Science and teaching a version of his own subject - labelled
British Constitution or Civics. And such an argument would gain
considerable support from graduates in Politics - and not just
because there are too many of them searching for too few teaching
posts! After all, if the job is worth doing properly, it ought to
be handled by the expert. However, the formal qualifications of
the teachers are not the central issue here. The real question is
whether political material should be taught from an historical an-
gle, no matter by whom.

    If one looks at the CSE and GCE syllabuses in political studies
- generally called British Constitution, British Government and
Politics, Public Affairs or Civics - it is clear that the overwhelming emphasis is on the contemporary, though admittedly an
expectation is often expressed that candidates will have some
historical background knowledge, especially for A-level. An
overtly historical approach, like the Oxford and Cambridge A-level
options in 'British Constitutional History since 1830' and 'Political Thought' (texts ranging from Rousseau to Leo XIII), is rare

indeed. It is difficult to generalize because the scene is constantly shifting as examination boards adjust their syllabuses
(for example, as from 1974 four A-Level boards change the titles
of their papers from 'British Constitution' and allow the dreaded
word 'Political' to creep in.) The trend, however, is to introduce questions of a sociological and comparative rather than an
historical nature. These emendations are admirable in their own
way. But it does mean that we are left with the question, 'What
important insights are lost by the pupils being deprived of the
historical dimension?' In a sense, of course, no teaching of
political material can entirely ignore the past. For example, it
would be a narrow-minded and uninspired teacher, indeed, who
taught about the House of Lords without mentioning the schemes for
reform in both composition and powers that have been debated and
sometimes implemented since 1911. Clearly individual teachers
differ, according to interest and knowledge, in the weight they
give to historical matter. In the question posed above, then, we
must understand by 'historical dimension' not passing references
and allusions but solid historical depth built as an integral
perspective into the whole teaching scheme. What benefits can
we expect to be derived from the teaching of political studies
in this way?

Firstly, there is the invaluable benefit of History in any
form - the benefit of perspective. From historical study comes
the understanding that the present is the result of a complicated
network of past decisions and happenings; the understanding that
our own society is different from other, past societies - and not
necessarily better; the understanding that change is the essence
of human society and that just as the present is different from
the past so the future will be different from the present. To
place oneself thus in the flow of time is to prevent oneself
from exaggerating either the importance or the permanence of the
present. In the study of matters political this sense of perspective is surely vital. Assuredly it can be dangerous too. The
perception that different societies have different political
arrangements may lead to an attitude of relativism in which the
student suffers an ethical paralysis, unable to make judgments
about different regimes and policies, including those that pres-
ently affect him as a citizen - the curse of the liberal and the
historian of being able to appreciate every side of an argument.
Alternatively an understanding of the process of change may lead
to political passivity: let us bide our time and things are bound
to change for the better. But these are risks worth taking.
Better the bewildered understanding of the multi-dimensional man
than the blinkered impatience of the man who sees only a static
present, and is impatient to build defences against change or to
effect changes precipitately. Viewing contemporary politics
through an historical perspective must become a natural habit, not
a conscious effort. The habit must be nurtured at school.

The second benefit to be derived from the historical approach is the immense interest-potential of the biographical and narrative material that may be quarried by the teacher. How much more interesting to tell the story of the Cuba Missile crisis than to teach abstractly about the powers of the US President as the Chief Executive; how much more interesting to tell the story of Little Rock than to teach the theory of State v. Federal powers; and how much more realistic. The exercise of imaginative re-creation is both fascinating and educationally valuable in its own right.* Teaching about political, especially constitutional, matters can be very drab and abstract - and sometimes even misleading, because the way things are supposed to happen is not always the way things actually happen. Actual historical case studies can help breathe life into the textbook statements.

The range of illustrative historical material available to the teacher of Political Studies is, of course, huge. And in the last resort it is the individual teacher's selective skill that will determine what is chosen and its effectiveness. General principles for relating political concepts and historical events will be discussed later in this pamphlet. What must be noted here is that the two principles of perspective and realism may pull in opposite directions. For example, the role of the Privy Councillor in Elizabethan times and the relationship between Privy Councillors on the one hand and the Queen and the Commons on the other may make a fascinating contrast to the present-day system of Cabinet government. But it is the loyal sheep-dog activities of Edward Heath as Chief Whip or the ruthless purging of ministers by Harold Macmillan that provides the effective understanding of present-day Prime-ministerial power. History must therefore not be used haphazardly: the teacher must be clear what his objective is in selecting his illustrative material. Otherwise he invites confusion and anachronistic thinking.[19]

Problems

The problem of selection is not such a special difficulty for the teacher of History: it is a professional hazard whatever syllabus he chooses or constructs. There are other problems, though, that are specific to the teacher who decides to use History as the medium for political education. It has been argued here that political education is an activity that the teaching profession should undertake and that an historical perspective to this work is desirable. But it would be dishonest not to recognize that the prosecution of this duty by this means raises considerable

---

* This is closely related to the important mental quality of empathy, insufficiently emphasized here. It is central to the History section of the report of the Programme for Political Education.

difficulties.

The six major cases were listed in the first section. Let us
now examine each in turn. Firstly, the emergence of Politics as
a separate discipline, in the general process of the differen-
tiation of knowledge, has probably helped to nurture the belief
that civic education now has its own specific discipline with its
own specialist practitioners and that the continued use of History
is an indirect, even amateurish, approach to the matter. The
first half of the 1960s witnessed a remarkable expansion of university facilities in the subject: there were only 10 chairs in
1960; 38 by 1966. This development has been paralleled by a
considerable growth in the number of candidates for A-Level
British Constitution. Yet to use this as a strong argument is to
miss two points. Firstly, that the development of Politics as
an academic discipline at the scholarly level has not been
matched by its development in any full sense at school (the
A-Level British Constitution example is very partial evidence
indeed). It *may* be desirable that Politics should be taught as
a separate subject in schools (the point is debatable); the fact
is that it is not. The second point is that Politics as an
academic subject makes frequent use of historical material and
perspectives. And while Politics and History can certainly no
longer be viewed as virtually synonymous subjects, they enjoy an
overlap of matter than can be usefully exploited for civic education in schools.

Secondly, a great deal of the Political History taught in the
past has been incredibly arid - dusty and barren facts bearing not
a germ of fertility to stir imagination or understanding to budding
life. We shake our heads in superior incredulity at the sheer
professional incompetence of History textbook writers of the late
nineteenth century who could produce the following catechism
about Henry VIII: 'Q' Was he a good king? 'A' No; he was one of
the worst kings that ever reigned in England.'[20] We titter over
howlers like 'Wolsey shot the Pope'; then tut over the teacher's
failure to present his historical material in a comprehensible
way. After all, it is so many years since Whitehead warned us
against inert ideas. And yet, how many O-Level pupils each year
learn off the terms of the 1832 Reform Bill or the causes of the
Second World War in as uncomprehending a way as their forebears
learned of the relative worth of by-gone kings or the motives
of ambitious cardinals? Because so many teachers believe that
there is too little difference, they have concluded not that the
teaching approach is wrong, but rather that the very subject-matter
of Political History is inappropriate fare for many pupils.
Social History has thus come to replace Political History in many
schools on the ground that this version of the past is about ordinary people's lives and thus more easily understood by ordinary
pupils. Furthermore, since Social History is about the activities
of the bulk of the population, whereas Political History is, by

and large, about the actions of a tiny elite, it is felt that
Social History is a much more 'real' kind of History. The response
to this argument is merely to reiterate the faith already expressed
in the last section that there is nothing more fascinating in
History than the imaginative re-enactment of dramatic political
events of the past or the study of the lives of great men.
Handled with the proper attention to detail, it is for most children the most interesting kind of History.

The third problem is a closely associated issue, namely the
belief that History is, properly construed, a synoptic subject.
History is a complex canvas of the past painted in many hues.
By filtering out all but the political colour, one impoverishes
the picture. And impoverishes the student too - because the unique
value to be derived from History is precisely the appreciation it
affords of the complex web of interactions of which life is composed. Artistic expression, scientific discovery, literary exposition, commercial endeavour, military exploits, technical
invention, everyday life - as well as the maneuvrings and achievements of statesmen and politicians - contribute to the fabric of
History. And all these must take their place in the student's
reconstruction and therefore understanding of his chosen period
of study. The political picture is rejected as too partial a view
of historical reality. Any proposal to turn the clock back and
reinstate Political History at the expense of the other varieties
is clearly not only impracticable but undesirable. But let us
keep a sense of balance about this. It may have been misguided in
the past to teach Political History with the ordinary people left
out; but one does not correct that error by teaching, with
Trevelyan, 'the history of a people with the politics left out.'[21]
Bindoff and Elton may overstate their case when they argue the
primacy of Political History, but it must surely be admitted that,
without a reasonable wodge of Politics, one gets a rather thin
slice of the past.[22] At least, the teacher who wishes to engage
in political education through History must fight for the recognition of this point of view. He must also struggle with the
intractable problems of fitting in enough Political History without
displacing too much valuable material from the other varieties,
while at the same time striving to rehabilitate the name of Political History from the smears suffered from years of bad teaching
and choice of material.

But even if Political History is restored to pride of place (and,
of course, in some schools it has never been displaced), this development would not necessarily in itself promote civic education.
There is no necessary transfer of understanding from the political
past to the political present. The civic education function of
History can only be performed by studying the past in such a way
as deliberately to illuminate the present. And this presents us
with our fourth problem. The opposition is based upon the belief
that the essence of History lies in the detached re-creation and

observation of the past - an activity which leads the historian
in his study of a past period 'to understand its people better than
they understand themselves.'[23] The function of History is to
understand the past, not the present. The most consistent and
insistent defender of the purity of school History in recent years
has been W.H. Burston[24]. He argues indeed very forcibly for
an historical perspective as a means to an effective understanding
of the present - either by the study of the remote origins of
contemporary situations or by a study of the recent historical
context. Nevertheless, alongside this there must be, he insists,
a separate study of the past for its own sake - in order to preserve History from the distorting lens of the present. But more
than this, he sees the preservation of the autonomy of the past as
a civic duty of the History teacher, sustaining a critical mentality against a Whiggish self-satisfaction with the present that is
the danger of a myopic study of the present. This is a subtle
argument and needs to be treated with respect. It is not the naive
proposition that the study of History has nothing to do with an
understanding of the present: this kind of 'History-for-its-own-
sake' argument we can probably afford to dismiss without discussion. Burston's argument is, rather, that History is a necessary tool for shaping our understanding of the present, but that
if we use the tool with blundering brute force the tool itself
will malfunction and our understanding will be consequently mis-
shapen. The curricular implications are that the study of History
and the study of Contemporary Affairs must be kept distinct - a
sort of pure and applied History. I wonder, though, whether it is
not beyond the wit and honesty of History teachers to present a
patch of the past in a detached manner and subsequently draw from
this study matter relevant to an understanding of the present.
And even if the whole range of subject-matter in a History syllabus
is selected for its overall ability to cast light on the present,
provided the initial approach is clearly aimed at an understanding
of an independent past, could not Professor Burston's fears be
allayed?

These fears are in some measure the fears of distortion, of the
biased presentation of material which may, in certain circumstances
lead to indoctrination. And so we come to our fifth problem.[25]
Just as a saint fears the temptation of the thought of sin and the
damnation of its commission, so the History teacher is alert to
bias as a professional hazard and indoctrination as unprofessional
conduct. The issue of bias and indoctrination, while germane to
the whole subject of History, tends to increase in sensitivity as
one nears the present. The History teacher may hesitate about
how to present the character of Richard III but at least he has
little fear concerning the social or political effects on his pupils
whichever interpretation he presents. Such bland indifference
might not perhaps be so appropriate for the teacher dealing with
the Cold War or the recent history of race relations in Britain.
The teacher of Contemporary Affairs frequently feels himself,

indeed, in an exposed position. He may be attacked from the
Right for encouraging a critical approach to established institutions and ideologies. Yet, what is an education worth if it is
not critical? At the same time, he is abused by the Left for being
a lackey of the Establishment:

> What did you learn in school today, sweet little boy of mine?
> What did you learn in school today, dear little boy of mine?
> I learned our government's very strong,
> Always right and never wrong.
> Our leaders are the best of men
> And we elect 'em again and again.   (Tom Paxton)

Yet, what is an education worth if it does not induct the pupils
into the ways of their society? The History Teacher may be forgiven for concluding that he just cannot win on a twentieth-century
wicket and retiring to the placid croquet-lawns of feudal England -
a cowardly ducking of the issue. Indeed, more than that - it is a
jettisoning of an opportunity to teach controversial matters in a
manner least likely to result in indoctrination, since an historical approach rather than a strictly contemporary one is more
likely to reveal every side of the question. In any case, the real
fear of indoctrination generates much more heat than the actual
minimal danger warrants. We do well to remember, humbly, that the
teacher is but one influence among many that shape the child's
political views. And yet, among all the moulding influences and
pressures, should not the teacher's be the most responsible hand?
Should it not be a matter of professional pride for the History
teacher to provide a political education that fosters critical
understanding, responsible independence of thought and tolerant
social behaviour? If the teacher pursues these qualities as his
goals; if he is honest enough with himself and his classes not
to infiltrate his own prejudices and beliefs; if he is learned enough to understand the complexities of his subject-matter, there
will emerge from his care independently thinking people, not indoctrinated automata. And let the teacher remember that he alone has
the opportunity of providing a fully rounded political education.
What most pupils pick up from the media will be fragmentary; what
they pick up from their parents will be loaded. These sketchy
patterns are already etched into the pupil's mind even by the time
he leaves the primary school.[26] The teacher who would stay his
hand, fearing to despoil a tabula rasa, may act with greater bold-
ness in this knowledge.

   This brings us to the final problem. Evidence that even quite
young children have some political understanding, however hazy, has
emerged in recent years, especially from the research into political socialization undertaken since the late 1950s in the USA.
This has done much to undermine the previously widely-spread
belief, which still however lingers, that children are not capable
of having some understanding of political matters - a point of view
that has handicapped development in this field. The basic

objection - that 'political science is not a proper study for the
young. The young man is not versed in the practical business of
life from which politics draws its premises and data' - is as old
as Aristotle, from whom this quotation is, in fact, drawn[27].
The 1944 Education Act firmly placed the task of civic education
not with the schools but with the County Colleges, which did not
materialize[28]. And powerful voices at the time, like those of
Livingstone and Barker, reiterated the message. Moreover, evidence of lack of interest, easily culled, would appear to reinforce
this view. 'History was all right at the beginning, but when I
got to the beginning of the fourth year we had nothing but politics,
politics, politics' was the reaction of one of the Newsom
Committee's respondents[29] - a view that accords with the low
rating given for 'Current affairs, social studies' in the follow-
up investigation by the Schools Council: out of fourteen subjects,
tenth in the order of preference for boys, seventh for girls[30].
Yet, as the Newsom Report asserts, 'we are not confronted with a
psychological barrier which prevents people of below average
intelligence, that is to say half the nation, forming a responsible
and reasoned opinion about public affairs. Optimism is possible.'
(31). As is so often the case in teaching, it ain't what you do,
it's the way that you do it, if I may crib from a swing tune of
my childhood days. One obviously sound piece of advice is to
present material in as concrete a way as possible. Local studies,
depth studies, biographies, simulation exercises - all are splen-
did. But ... when you have captured their interest, what do you
do with it? It is not an end in itself, despite the views of some
educational pundits. Interest is really not of much value unless
it is used as a springboard to deeper understanding. And understanding will remain at a primitive level if generalizations and
abstractions are not grasped. The authors of the Schools Council
Working Paper No. 2 on *Raising the School Leaving Age* are anything
but faint hearts in this regard. 'It is the large ideas that are
seminal', they declare, 'not the details.'(32) Ideas which they
list as essential for 'members of a civilized society' to grasp
include the rule of law, government by consent, freedoms of speech
and action. This may well appear a pretty tall order to teachers
with Rosla recalcitrants. How realistic is it to set about teaching such 'seminal ideas'? The clue to the problem lies in the
development and formulation of concepts.

Concepts

Two educational psychologists went out prospecting quite separately and struck veins of ore that subsequent miners have found
rich in utilizable content. The psychologists were Piaget and
Bruner; their discovery, concepts. It is nevertheless important to
realize that their uses of the notion of concepts are not identical.
Piaget (and those like Coltham, de Silva, Hallam, Peel and Wood,
who have built on his work in the field of History)(33) is

interested in the way children acquire and manipulate basic ideas
and how age and ability levels affect this understanding. Piaget's
model is that of a developing mind. His message for teachers is
that they will be battling unsuccessfully against a natural process if they attempt to teach too sophisticated concepts too early,
before the child's mind is ready to handle them. At its simplest
the word 'concept' in this sense is used to denote the mental
picture that someone *in fact* has; it is a personal understanding,
however inaccurate or sophisticated, of a word or a phrase. The
vast complex of concepts that we have at any one time is the prism
through which we view reality. Bruner, on the other hand, uses
the notion of concepts differently. His starting point is the
discipline or school subject, each of which, he believes, is
structurally composed of concepts. Used in this sense, concepts
have to be purposely taught. Taught skilfully they can enable us
to pigeon-hole and cross-refer information, since any given subject will be perceived as a pattern of conceptual units rather than
as an amorphous whole.

In effect, what we have is both a range of children's concepts
and the battery of the scholar's. The distinction here is similar
to Bernstein's distinction between restricted and elaborated codes
and Vygotsky's spontaneous and scientific concepts. The child's
concepts are picked up and often developed in a haphazard way,
especially in social subjects like History and Politics where the
school is by no means the only source of such ideas. Thus, even
quite young children will have notions of what a war or a king is
without ever having received any formal instruction about these
matters. These concepts will evolve in sophistication with the
growth of the child as a natural process of maturation. And it
should be noticed in passing that this process is not necessarily
a shift from a false to a true understanding, though admittedly
this is sometimes the case. Rather is it that early formulations
identify only the concrete outer shell of an idea: a child conceives of a king as someone who lives in a palace before he has
any notion of the political system of constitutional monarchy.
In Piaget's view the teacher's function is thus restricted to
developing those concepts the child already has at the pace suited
to the child's natural intellectual development and to introducing
new concepts at an equally appropriate level.

In contrast, Bruner sees the identification of structural concepts as a specialist task - 'The decision as to what should be
taught ... is a decision that can best be reached with the aid
of those with a high degree of vision and competence in each
(field).'(34). It is necessary to comment a little more on the
Bruner-type concepts than the Piagetian, because, firstly, neither
he nor anyone else has developed the notion in any detail; and
secondly, because the notion is central to the conclusions to be
drawn in this paper. Bruner's basic thesis - the idea of a spiral
curriculum in which concepts are illustrated at ever-increasing
levels of sophistication as one ascends the ability grades - is

now too well-known to be laboured. And some of the advantages of
using this framework are clear: reinforcement of learning by repe-
tition; intellectual 'stretching' by the use of increasingly
advanced illustrative material; and, perhaps most importantly, the
whole range of the discipline and subject-matter is seen in perspective - learning is eased by the immediate perception of relationships. What must be emphasized here, since Bruner himself
does not make it clear, is that if his system is to work, the word
'concept' must be understood in a special way. Concepts, in his
sense, are decidedly not what children happen to have in their
minds. They must have four essential characteristics. In the
first place, they must be categoreal concepts. They are a perhaps somewhat artificial device for classifying the data of a
subject - rather like placing a grid over the subject or constructing a set of pigeon-holes so that the material of the discipline
can be sifted into the constituent categories or concepts. Perhaps
the concepts do not exist in any objective sense: they are mental
approximations to reality to aid the learning process. Secondly,
the concepts must be transferable so as to enable the student to
glean examples from a wide range of situations as he progresses
along his corkscrew syllabus. And thirdly, the total range of
concepts, once identified, must be all-embracing so that the potential data of a subject may find a home somewhere; yet at the same
time they must be limited in number or they will themselves become
cumbersome mental burdens. The final characteristic is that each
concept must be capable of sub-division into lower-order concepts.
The first stage of analysis is the identification of what might
be termed the primary concepts (by analogy with the artist's primary colours). These are the truly basic concepts - just as red,
yellow and blue are not themselves composed of other colours.

What are the implications of these two views of concepts for
the present issue, namely the teaching of Politics through
History? Firstly, concepts in the sense of the child's perceptions.
Many of the concepts tested in the research projects referred to
above were, in fact, political - e.g. king, war, parliament, prime
minister, nationalism. It seems evident that it is inadvisable to
leap straight into an abstract or complex presentation of a concept: the student needs to be led carefully through the stages of
understanding. History teachers are, indeed, too prone to use
terms (both political and economic) without specifically laying the
ground-work of explanation. The results are anachronisms, failure
to appreciate the subtleties of meaning or plain, shrieking howlers.
Lister's investigations among Sixth-form History students, which
showed just how ignorant they were of the most common and *necessary*
words, is guaranteed to cure any complacency. The failure of much
History teaching to undertake really systematic concept-building
is particularly worrying in the light of the evidence presented by
Coltham (and reinforced by Hallam in a different context) that
understanding in History lags behind parallel developments in some
other subjects because of the impossibility of actually experiencing
the matters being studied.

Secondly, the implications of Bruner's model of a spiral curriculum. He believes that the most effective way of teaching any
subject is to analyse it into its component concepts and to construct one's teaching programme round these. Now, as I have argued
elsewhere[35], I believe that any attempt to identify historical
concepts *in this sense* is doomed to failure since History is more
a mode of thought than a structured subject: every subject may be
studied historically. Furthermore, time, causation, the Renaissance - often cited as historical concepts - are not concepts in
this structural, transferable sense. This is not to say, however,
that History teachers cannot benefit from Bruner's advice. On the
contrary, the Social Sciences, including Politics, can with profit
be analysed into their constituent concepts; and, in turn, these
concepts are probably most effectively taught through the medium of
Historical exemplifications. Indeed, many concepts frequently referred to as historical are in reality political, economic or
sociological concepts (e.g. revolution, trade, class).

For the teacher who wishes to use History as a vehicle for civic
education the conclusions to be derived from this discussion of
concepts are vitally important. In drawing up his syllabus the
teacher must have clearly established what political concepts he
wishes the pupils to learn - the number and level of abstraction
and complexity for each given age-level. The aim should be to
furnish all pupils with a complete map of political understanding
by the age of 16, though obviously the level of detail will vary
according to ability. The unveiling of this map must, however,
be a gradual process: the pupils must be taken step by step from
the easy to the difficult, from simple to complex, from concrete
to abstract. For the teacher should not be too ready to conclude
from the research findings that because political and historical
concepts *are* only primitively developed in many young people,
they must necessarily *stay* at this level. I would align myself
with Wood and urge that this kind of teaching can and should be
improved: '... many children,' he writes, 'do not have concepts of
"democracy" adequate for responsible democratic life. Concepts,
however, cannot be regarded as entities which are either possessed
or not possessed; they start as partial understandings and may be
progressively enriched and systematized.'[36] It is the teacher's
responsibility to ensure that these processes of enrichment and
systematization are properly undertaken. If they are, the result
should be the progressive refinement of the child's political
concepts in his History lessons so that his own, rough-hewn ideas
are eventually welded together, struck apart and finely shaped to
re-emerge as the basic concepts that the teachers of Politics
have identified as composing the overall structure of their
subject.[37]

*The range of political concepts**

One of the major criticisms levelled at the teaching of GCE
British Constitution - the most common political syllabus that has
a clear articulation - is that it is too closely focused on
institutional minutiae. Such teaching, some believe, is consequently academically stultifying ('a soft option') and intellectually
misleading ('it's not the reality of politics'). This is not the
place to enter into this debate. I raise the matter because it
seems to me that if Politics teaching is to be more than institutional analysis - if students are to appreciate that politics is
a complex business and that there are a wide variety of methods
used throughout History and the world today to influence and change
governments and to resolve genuine differences - a framework of
concepts would seem an admirable aid to this end.

The problem is that the identified concepts must at one and the
same time be limited in number for easy handling and all-embracing
for flexible usage. The rest of this article is an essay in
the identification of a handful of primary concepts and their sub-
divisions plus some illustrations of the ways in which they might
be exemplified by historical material.

For purposes of discussion (and this is certainly not meant as
an arrogant *ex cathedra* statement), I suggest that the subject-
matter of Politics can be analysed into six primary concepts. Let
us label them: Ideas, Administration, Leadership and Decision-
Making, Role of the Individual, Techniques of Change, and Conflict.
I claim (or rather hope) that all political material can be incorporated into one or more of these concepts and that the analysis
of the discipline in this way clarifies the subject-matter. Let us
investigate each of these concepts in turn.

Firstly, Ideas. The topic of Political Ideas is the *logical*
starting point in the study of the subject, even if *psychological*
considerations would normally make us postpone it until a grasp of
more concrete material has been achieved. For, although Politics
is concerned with action, action must be undertaken within a
framework of thought - however ill-digested that thought may be.
There are, it might be argued, three ways of studying Ideas; or
rather, to use the terminology of this paper, the primary concept
of Ideas may be further analysed into three subordinate concepts.
These may be labelled Philosophy, Historical Background and
Practical Effects. A system of Political Ideas may be based on a

---

* The ideas in this section were first published as Political concepts and the construction of a syllabus, *Teaching Politics*,
September 1973. This article is referred to by Bernard Crick
in two essays in this collection - 'Basic political concepts
and curriculum development', and 'Chalk-dust, Punch-card and the
Polity'. The original article is not reprinted here since it
would be too repetitive.

fundamental philosophy, be it dialectical materialism, belief in
equality or whatever. Moreover, in studying the philosophy it is
necessary to study not merely the original doctrine but also to
understand its evolution, and perhaps distortion, through time.
This time factor is, of course, crucial to the second subordinate
concept, Historical Background, by which is meant the original
circumstances in which the doctrine was first formulated as well
as the historical framework within which it evolved. Finally,
ideas do not exist in a vacuum: they have practical effects. One
can study the initial impact when an idea is first absorbed by
opinion or first becomes a rallying-cry. Then, more specifically,
one may study the adoption of ideas by groups or political parties
and the importance of the acceptance or at least the reiteration
of ideas in explaining politicians' retention of power. This is
shown in Figure 1.

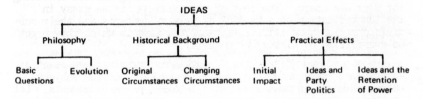

FIG. 1

Just as action presupposes ideas, so disembodied ideas are
powerless without an administrative network to bring them to
realization. And I use the term Administration because I wish to
embrace within this concept both the institutions and the personnel
who operate them. In analysing institutions it is clearly necessary to differentiate between those that operate on an international,
a national and a local level. At this high plane of generalization
it is necessary to identify further sub-divisions. International
institutions may be of either a global nature (e.g. UNO) or confined to a region (e.g. EEC). Also, at the national level it is
important to distinguish between federal and unitary systems of
government as different techniques of arranging the exercise of
authority. In turning our attention to the second subordinate concept, namely personnel, we must study the functions of both
politicians and civil servants; and, moreover, the relationship
between them in the formulation and execution of policy (See
Figure 2.)

Both Ideas and Administration, although perhaps the most crucial

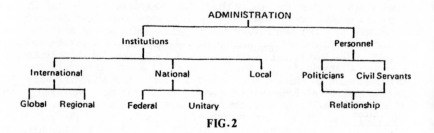

FIG.2

concepts in Politics, are comparatively simple in structure:
there are a limited number of subordinate concepts needed in order
to understand the range of material contained by them. An analysis of the concept of Leadership and Decision-Making, however,
requires a slightly more complex process. The two high-order
subordinate concepts are already contained in the dual label
devised for the primary concept. In studying the concept of
leadership, however, it is necessary to look at the rise of the
leader, which in turn involves a study of his social origins and
the process of his rise to power. Secondly, it is necessary to
understand the activity of the leader in power, the nature of his
personal authority over his colleagues and subordinates; the nature of his control over or support by the mass of the population;
and the ways in which he utilizes the machinery of power.
Leaders may concentrate in their persons all important decision-
making or, in an effectively democratic polity, decisions may be
affected by the corporate opinion of the members of constitutional
bodies like Parliament. In analysing the concept of decision-
making it is therefore important to make this distinction.
Further, one needs to clarify the extent of this power, however
exercised; and, in both cases, to examine the processes available
for giving and taking advice. (See Figure 3.)

The fourth concept is the Role of the Individual. Clearly the
importance of this concept in the study of a society is in large
measure dependent upon the degree of participation allowed for
in the political system. Nevertheless, even in a society where
the citizen is comparatively passive, this condition must be understood. The concept of the Role of the Individual is particularly
important for this essay because it subsumes not only the subordinate concepts of voting and activism but of socialization also.
I believe that in any programme of political education a consciousness of the nature and process of socialization is of central
importance.   The student must understand not only the process of

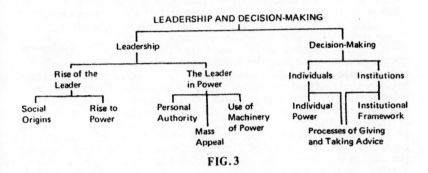

FIG. 3

socialization but the sources of information which are open to the individual and which can help to formulate attitudes. Under voting it is necessary to differentiate between elections and referenda. Under activism one must note the operation of the individual as an individual through the constitutional machinery (e.g. a letter to his M.P.), the organization and activity of pressure groups and finally the resort to violence. (See Figure 4.)

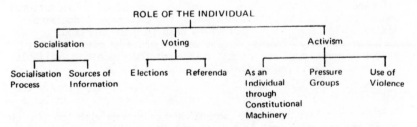

FIG. 4

Techniques of Change is the next concept to be analysed. Political change can, of course, be brought about either peacefully or
violently, and these alternatives provide the obvious subordinate
concepts. But the sub-concept of peaceful change itself needs
considerable refinement if it is to be satisfactorily understood.
We may note three ways of achieving change peacefully. Firstly,
there is the moulding of opinion. This can be effected either by
the government itself or by independent information media. Secondly, there are the pressure groups. And here we must distinguish
between their organization and their techniques. Thirdly, change
may be brought about by new laws. These have to be enacted by
the judiciary. Let us now turn our attention to the violent means
of change. This may be sub-divided into two categories: the change
of policy by a government in the face of violence and the change of
government as the result of violent action. In the first category
the violence may take the form of a demonstration or, more seriously,
a rebellion. In the second category, a government may be changed
by coup d'état or by revolution. (See Figure 5.)

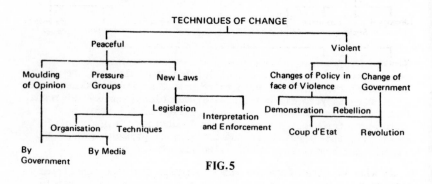

FIG.5

Closely allied to and in some ways overlapping with the concept
of Techniques of Change is the concept of Conflict. In discussing
this, our sixth and final concept, we may distinguish between
internal and international conflict. Internal conflict may conveniently be viewed either from the point of view of causes or of
its nature. Four kinds of causes may be identified, namely,
ideological, social, economic and political. In its nature a
conflict may be peaceful (i.e. verbal or written debate) or violent.

If violent, it may take the form of civil war, revolution, coup d'état, rebellion or demonstration. In the international field we may distinguish three kinds of conflict: ideological, imperial and a naked power-struggle. An imperial conflict may be the result of either process in the history of imperialism - colonization or decolonization; while a power struggle may be in the form of an arms race, economic competition or conflict to retain or upset the balance of power. (See Figure 6.)

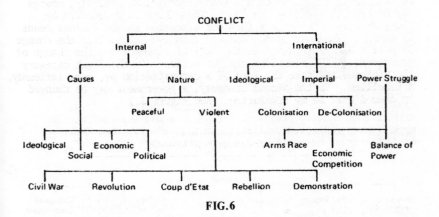

FIG.6

It will be clear from the above analysis that the identified primary concepts are not water-tight compartments. For example, Revolution and Coup d'Etat are included under both Techniques of Change and Conflict. And what about a topic such as the Separation of Powers? This might well be placed under Ideas or Administration or even Decision-Making. Such overlaps may make the learning process less easy because less tidy - but do they undermine the principle? I think not. No categorizing formula can be entirely watertight, since any formula is an artificial construct that can only be an approximation to reality: reality is more complex than any model can represent. In order to learn we must simplify, indeed oversimplify. Only when the simple framework is mastered is it possible for the student to proceed to an understanding of the complexities of interconnections and exceptions.

This is the conceptual network of Politics as I understand the subject. And I believe that an understanding of this network (or something similar) should be in the minds of teachers when constructing a syllabus in order to clarify their views of the understanding they wish their students to have at the end of a course.

This schema may be thought by some to be too ambitious - to credit young people with too great a sophistication for understanding the structure of the subject. For example, Bernard Crick argues cogently instead for working from the bottom up; that is, for starting with the simple, lay view of politics. He identifies three starting points: '(i) perception of what is done to us - by government and external forces; (ii) perceptions of our human identity - what we think we are, what is done to us and should not be done to us; and (iii) perceptions of different kinds of relationships between 'them' and 'us' or between 'order' and 'individuality' or 'government' and 'the governed'.(38) The first is concerned with force, authority and order; the second with rights, individuality, freedom and welfare; and the third with justice, representation and influence. It is an attractive alternative model. Mine seeks to mobilize interest through the dramatic narrative of History, Crick's through personal experience; mine seeks conceptual cohesion through an ultimate pattern, Crick's through initial perceptions.

Exemplification of political concepts

So much for the Politics. But where, it might well be asked, does the History come in? It would be tedious to plod through the whole range of concepts. Nevertheless, it is important to clothe the tabular skeletons with some historical flesh and sinew.

If, for example, one were teaching British History since 1945, Ideas would be handled in a discussion of the doctrinal differences between the major parties. Administration, in turn, would come to be understood by reference to the parliamentary and local systems of government, probably with an emphasis on reforms of the systems. A study of prime ministers would illuminate the concept of Leadership. The Role of the Individual would emerge in the discussion of elections and such movements as CND. A study of the media, trade unions and the IRA would provide a wide variety of exemplification for Techniques of Change. The Northern Ireland situation, of course, well illustrates the concept of Conflict; and on the international plane, Suez would be a fruitful study.

It has already been suggested that History could be most conveniently used for teaching Politics if examples were drawn from most recent times. Although there is probably considerable truth in this, it would be wrong to discount the possibility, and indeed at times desirability, of utilizing more remote periods of History for the purposes of political education. Medieval History can illuminate Ideas through the Becket controversy, for example; Administration through the evolution of the justices system; Leadership through a study of William the Conqueror; the Role of the Individual can be seen in village administration; the question of Techniques of Change is thrown up by the Peasants' Revolt; and Conflict by the troubles of John's reign.

Figure 7 shows how one of the primary concepts could be illustrated in some detail by revealing how Techniques of Change operated in France at the time of the Revolution. I would hope that both historical and political understanding would be enhanced if a teacher had this pattern in his mind while dealing with the French Revolution; though whether it is advisable for the pupils to have the material in this form is another matter.

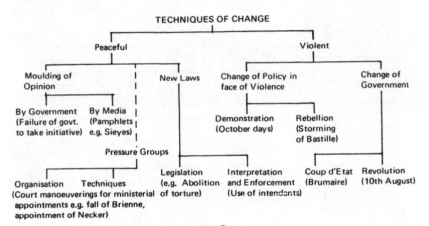

FIG.7

The problem is thus raised of how the teacher actually presents his political/historical material in the classroom. The first essential point to be made is that there cannot, in the nature of things, be a single, all-purpose syllabus. The individual teacher must adapt his syllabus according to two significant variables which will in large measure determine the practical implementation of the model here advocated. These variables are the relative importance given to historical and political education and the level of understanding of which the pupils are capable.

Hence, the teacher who sees his main function as teaching History will probably wish to construct a syllabus based upon some chronological principles and mention parenthetically what political concepts are being illustrated by any given events. On the other hand, the teacher may wish to engage in political teaching much

more overtly and thus deal with each of the concepts in turn,
drawing upon the historical examples that are most apt or interesting. In each of these approaches a certain degree of coherence in political and historical understanding respectively is
bound to be sacrificed. It is fairly clear, for instance, that
a teacher who selects modern English History as his basic course
will be hard put to it to find an example of a coup d'état
(perhaps 1688 is the most recent example). Coverage of the concepts is likely to be both incomplete and unsystematic. But then
the alternative approach could well lead to a haphazard scatter
of historical material.

However, this is to assume extreme cases. Sensible compromises,
I feel confident, are possible. For example, I do not think it
would be wise for the concept framework outlined in this paper to
be translated direct into a syllabus - except perhaps for the most
able students. It represents more an ideal pattern of understanding which a student must master if he is to perceive the subject
whole. A teacher may nevertheless gauge it inappropriate to present the whole subject to his class; or, again, he may choose to
approach the abstractions obliquely so that they emerge only after
considerable learning of concrete examples. The important consideration is for the teacher to understand the network of concepts
into which the subject may be analysed and consciously to construct
a syllabus so that at least a selected proportion are grasped by
his pupils. In practical terms it may well be that a fairly traditional organization of material is the best - either through
coverage of topics or exemplification by case studies, either by
reference to the British system or by a more deliberately comparative approach. But - and this would be the important modification -
time would be allocated at given intervals for 'stock taking'.
This operation would take the form of a recapitulation of learned
material with the express purpose of drawing out the generalizations from which the concepts would emerge. Once a class has been
introduced to the technique, the pupils themselves, by skilful
question-and-answer teaching, could be encouraged to analyse and
categorize: they would be actively thinking rather than passively
memorizing.

My own preference would be for a basically historical syllabus,
but with the material carefully selected so that the political
concepts form a natural part of the whole construction - not
artificially 'stuck on'. It would not, it must be noted, be necessary to teach all the concepts at once. I would envisage, to be
rather repetitious, that the teacher would set aside certain times
in the course to review each particular concept and discuss the
range of examples that had been covered in the History syllabus to
that point. Alexander the Great, the Roman consular system and the
Anglo-Saxon monarchy might be compared half way through the first
year as examples of Leadership; while a fifth-form syllabus on the
twentieth century would be a good opportunity to look at Communism,
Nationalism and Conservatism as Ideas, at the same time taking a

backward glance at Divine Right and the Separation of Powers. It
is quite possible, of course, that one would wish to refer to the
same historical topic at different points in the course to illustrate different concepts. For example, one term after teaching
about Louis XIV one might wish to refer back to the topic to
illustrate the concept of Leadership and three years later to
illustrate the concept of Ideas (Divine Right).

There is then the tricky problem of deciding if there is a
preferred order for dealing with the concepts. Two considerations
must determine this decision: one is the relationship between the
concepts; the other, the level of conceptual difficulty each represents. To take each of these in turn. It would be difficult to
grasp, for example, the concept of the Role of the Individual
without having been introduced to the institutional framework
which, in any given society, the individual can operate. This is
the relationship consideration. Secondly, however, it is clear
that the concept of Leadership can be made much more concrete and
comprehensible than the inevitably abstract Ideas: hence it would
seem sensible to leave Ideas to a late part of the syllabus. This
is the point at which teaching becomes an art - where the teacher
must present his subject-matter in the way he deems most effective
in the light of his knowledge of a given set of pupils and his
experience in handling the material in different ways. A great
deal of experimentation is needed.

I would not wish to argue that a pupil taught in this way
would be a wholly politically literate person - whatever that
might be. What I think one could reasonably claim is that, even
if the concepts had been taught at a fairly superficial level, the
pupil would emerge with a clearer understanding of what politics
is about than is generally the case at the moment, and also equipped
with an aid to further understanding of the political news that
will impinge upon his consciousness from the media in adult life.
However, understanding is only one contribution to political education. A critical appraisal of the system in which he lives and
views about the rights and responsibilities of participating in
it are attitudes that need also to be fostered. This raises the
whole question of the relationship between cognitive and affective
learning and how far the latter can be promoted by classroom teaching (as opposed to the organization and ethos of the school) -
matters beyond the scope of this essay. But even if History
teachers cannot achieve every objective of political education,
they can at least increase the efficiency of the learning that it
is within their competence to promote.

It is time that History teachers resumed their burdens of political education: too long have they been cast aside or carried in a
cumbersome, awkward fashion. Hefted into a comfortable position
the loads will become not onerous weights to be suffered out of a
sense of duty but badges of civic responsibility borne with proper
pride.

NOTES

1. Quoted in Inaugural Lecture on the study of History, Lord Acton (1956) page 25.

2. For a full discussion see G. Connell-Smith and H.A. Lloyd (1972).

3. H. Trevor-Roper (1969).

4. For a convinced exposition of this faith, see Sir Norman Angell (1966).

5. Ministry of Education (1952) page 6.

6. Quoted by W.H. Burston (1948).

7. DES (1967) page 2.

8. IAAM (1965).

9. DES (1967) page 2.

10. M. Oakeshott (1962) page 112.

11. B. Crick (1969) pages 5-6.

12. See K.P. Langton (1969) Chapter 4; also G. Mercer (1972).

13. G. Almond and S. Verba (1965) page 360.

14. For an illuminating discussion of the question of political ignorance see J. Blumler (1974).

15. D. Heater (1969) 'Teacher Training'.

16. See my essay in section one of this book, 'Political Education in Schools: the official attitude'.

17. For a discussion of the school as a political microcosm, see H. Entwistle (1971).

18. J. Blumler and D. McQuail (1968).

19. For a thorough exposition of the argument in favour of teaching Social Studies, including Politics, through History, see M.M. Krug (1967).

20. Ministry of Education (1952) page 7.

21. G.M. Trevelyan (1942) page vii.

22. S.T. Bindoff (1962) and G.R. Elton (1970).

23. H. Butterfield (1931).

24. W.H. Burston (1948). See also W.H. Burston (1962).

25. This issue is too complex to be dealt with in detail here. See B. Cohen (1969); I.A. Snook (1972). See also Bernard Crick's essay *On Bias* in the first section of this book.

26. See, for example, A. Morrison (1967).

27. Aristotle, *Nichomachean Ethics*.

28. The Education Act (1944) paragraph 41(1).

29. C.A.C.E. (1963) paragraph 213.

30. Schools Council (1968) figure 7.

31. C.A.C.E. (1963) paragraph 500.

32. Schools Council (1965) paragraph 68.

33. See D. Thompson (1972).

34. J.S. Bruner (1960) page 19.

35. D. Heater (1970).

36. D.M. Wood (1964) page 228.

37. This notion of the fusion of the two kinds of concepts through teaching has already been propounded by Vygotsky: see D.G. Watts (1972) pages 24-26.

38. See Bernard Crick's first essay in section two of this book.

REFERENCES

ACTON, (1956), 'Inaugural lecture on the study of History' in *Essays on Freedom and Power*, London: Thames and Hudson.

ALMOND, G. and VERBA, S. (1965), *The Civic Culture* New Jersey: Princeton.

ANGELL, N. (1966) 'History teaching and the voter', in M. Gilbert (Ed) *A Century of Conflict 1850-1950: Essays for A.J.P. Taylor*, London: Hamish Hamilton.

ARISTOTLE, (1955) *Nichomachean Ethics*, Harmondsworth, Penguin Books.

BINDOFF, S.T. (1962) 'Political history' in F.P.R. Findberg (Ed) *Approaches to History*, London: Routledge and Kegan Paul.

BLUMLER, J. (1974) Does mass political ignorance matter? *Teaching Politics*.

BLUMLER, J. and McQUAIL, D. (1968) *Television in Politics: Its Uses and Influences*, London: Faber.

BRUNER, J.S. (1960) *The Process of Education*, New York: Vintage Books.

BURSTON, W.H. (1948), History and education in citizenship, *History* October.

BURSTON, W.H. (1962) *Social Studies and the History Teacher*, London: Historical Association.

BUTTERFIELD, H. (1931) *The Whig Interpretation of History*, London: Bell.

C.A.C.E. (1963) *Half Our Future*, London: HMSO.

COHEN, B. (1969) 'The problem of bias' in D.B. Heater (Ed) *The Teaching of Politics*, London: Methuen Educational.

CONNELL-SMITH, G. and LLOYD, H.A. (1974) *The Relevance of History*, London: Heinemann.

CRICK, B. (1969) 'The introducing of politics' in D.B. Heater (Ed) *The Teaching of Politics*, London: Methuen Educational.

DES (1967) *Towards World History*, London HMSO.

ELTON, G.R. (1971) *Political History: Principles and Practice*, London: Allen Lane.

ENTWISTLE, H. (1971) *Political Education in a Democracy*, London: Routledge and Kegan Paul.

HEATER, D.B. (1969) 'Teacher training' in D.B. Heater (Ed) *The Teaching of Politics*, London: Methuen Educational.

HEATER, D.B. (1970) 'History and the social sciences' in M. Ballard (Ed) *New Movements in the Study and Teaching of History* London: Temple Smith.

IAAM (1965) *The Teaching of History* Cambridge: Cambridge University Press.

KRUG, M.M. (1967) *History and the Social Sciences*, Waltham,Mass: Blaisdell.

LANGTON, K.P. (1969) *Political Socialization*, Oxford: Oxford University Press.

LISTER, I. (1973) Political socialization and the schools, with special reference to the knowledge of political concepts of English sixth-formers, *Teaching Politics*.

MERCER, G. (1972) *Political Learning and Political Education*, Ph.D. thesis, University of Strathclyde.

MINISTRY OF EDUCATION (1952) *Teaching History*, London: HMSO.

MORRISON, A. (1967) Attitudes of children towards international affairs, *Educational Research*.

OAKESHOTT, M. (1962) 'Political education' in M. Oakeshott *Rationalism in Politics and Other Essays*, London: Methuen.

PLUMB, J.H. (1973) The world beyond Westminster, *New Statesman*, 16 February.

SCHOOLS COUNCIL (1965) *Working Paper No. 2: Raising the School Leaving Age*, London: HMSO.

SCHOOLS COUNCIL (1968), *Enquiry 1: Young School Leavers*, London: HMSO.

SNOOK, I.A. (1972) *Indoctrination and Education*, London: Routledge and Kegan Paul.

THOMPSON, D. (1972) 'Some psychological aspects of History teaching' in W.H. Burston and C.W. Green (Eds) *Handbook for History Teachers*, London: Methuen.

TREVELYAN, G.M. (1942) *English Social History*, London: Longman.

TREVOR-ROPER, H. (1969) The past and present: History and Sociology, *Past and Present*.

WATTS, D.G. (1972) *The Learning of History*, London: Routledge and Kegan Paul.

WOOD, D.M. (1964) *The Development of Some Concepts of Social Relations*, M.Ed. thesis, Nottingham.

3.3
Chalk-dust, punch-card and the polity

Bernard Crick

Anniversaries are times for embarrassing reflections. I want
to reflect on our lack of explicit concern for political education
in its quite ordinary senses. Our amateurism and irresponsibility
in these respects is, at times, extreme. There has scarcely been
any discussion in this country in recent years of the educational
responsibilities of university and polytechnic teachers of politics,
not even for their own institutions, still less for schools and
colleges of further education. Of course, if nothing that we
rationally and consciously do has any effect, if, as some say,
everything is only a matter of understanding, appreciating and continuing tradition, or if everything is all a matter of socialized
knowledge exclusively serving the interests of the particular
class structure, as some others say, then there would be no problem. But it is likely that there are important links between our
scholarly perceptions of what politics is all about and the
general education of the whole of society. And it is also likely
that what goes on in the *teaching* of politics in the universities
and polytechnics (as distinct from scholarship and research) has
relevance and responsibilities towards the tasks of the chalk-dust
teacher in our schools - though this relevance is seldom acknow-
ledged. So many of our students go on 'to teach', but seldom does
it cross our minds that we have responsibilities in their direction
or that basic concepts can be defined as to what can and should
be taught at the most elementary levels which are conceivable and
workable.

There have been considerable debates about science and politics,
theory and practice, the influence of students of politics on
government and, last but not least, the influence of politics on
political science. But there has been little or no debate among
university students of politics about political education in its
practical sense[1]. Schools have simply appeared in political

* This essay originally appeared in the Twenty-fifth anniversary
number of *Political Studies* June/September 1975. I have removed
and shortened some footnotes referring to books or articles
already cited in this book of essays.

science as data-hordes or stores to plunder for raw facts and
captive audiences in political socialization research[2]. Such
good folk have carried on with their researches stubbornly and
resourcefully, despite abundant evidence, from these very same
researches, that the shaping and conditioning of basic political
attitudes depends far more on all other social influences and
institutions outside education and school than on those of formal
education in school.

Perhaps the traditionalists are half right: when the continuity
of political institutions and customs seems assured, there is seldom any demand for political education. School syllabuses in
America in the early Republic were much the same as those in
Great Britain; they only changed with the era of mass immigration,
and possibly through the effect of the self-doubt engendered by the
carnage of the Civil War. Only in the 1870s did that great movement begin to Americanize the immigrants', the conscious teaching
of the American way of life and of good citizenship in the high
schools - indeed, a wave of founding and extension of high schools
intended precisely for that purpose[3]. In France, civic education
was regarded as inherently the offspring of the Revolution, either
stridently patriotic or it was suppressed entirely from the Restora-
tion until after 1870 when everywhere it became part of the curriculum, part of the attempt to revive national feeling, civic pride,
the path of national recovery from military defeat and dishonour.
In Western Germany the famous *Politische Bildung* was part and parcel
of denazification; it was as much a conscious break from the past
by the middle and younger generation as was the famous materialism
and business energy[4]. Only now in our national history do we
feel the need to raise this question of political education, indeed
can one see things beginning to happen in schools. And in many
ways thinking in the schools is, to say something that is not
likely to be popular, streets ahead of anything in the universities
about the aims and objects of education, how to organize it, how
to construct syllabuses and curricula. There is a university myth
of the terribleness of all studies of education and teaching of
teaching, which is all too often arrogance compounded by ignorance.
How many times has one listened to that formidably mechanical
debate among groups of university teachers about whether it is
better to 'take thought first' or 'take institutions first' in the
first year introductory course - which just about exhausts curriculum thinking. The syllabuses and teaching materials of the Open
University have set an entirely new and really very, very high
standard in this field[5] - a standard that no one is likely to
follow openly because of the rooted prejudice of the university
teacher that he should do his own thing, be completely his own
master, however same, ordinary, habitual and muddled the result
often is. I use the harsh word 'muddled' simply because alternatives, when seen as no wider than whether or in what proportion to
teach institutions ideas or behaviour, simply beg every question
the sensible schoolteacher is forced to face. What are the real
objects of a particular subject? What are the best methods to

obtain those objects? What are the main concepts needed to understand the theories of the discipline? And what are the main theories? How few of us would dare to specify for fear that some
armour-plated nit-picker showed that any generalization, simplification or abstraction has its grandiosities and sillinesses,
if put in some false or half-light.

University aims

    If we all really believed that in forty or fifty university
institutions there was room for original research in each subject,
there would be less reason to worry. Someone is doing original
research to the advancement of knowledge, which is surely what
the university is for, and we then just hope that his teaching
will be reasonably competent, perhaps quite interesting, simply
because he is doing research: but anyway his teaching is a secondary activity. Yet from scepticism that anyone can teach teaching,
it does not follow that we can all be good teachers just by in-
stinct or mimesis. We commonly, all of us, talk in a different
way when career prospects and promotional struggles are involved.
Then it turns out that everyone who is not plainly a scholar is,
by some law of nature of cybernetic device of the educational
system, plainly an excellent teacher. A man may go on reading long
dead notes straight from standard authorities to an audience which
is too courteous or hasn't got the guts to walk out, but this is
still regarded as teaching.

    The 'real researcher', the real punch-card and data man, actu-
ally claims that it is the business of university education to
provide the next generation of punch-card and data men. In other
words, his research depends upon having cheap postgraduate assis-
tants when the scientists would have technicians. He could
actually do more good than he intends, in that his retreat from
education about the nature of politics into training in research
techniques may actually force his more intelligent students into
reading, going to the library and learning for themselves - which
is, after all, the best part of education. Think how often,
particularly in the civic universities, though London is far from
immune from this fault, the syllabus is constructed by thinking of
conventional areas that are taught by particular people; and by
the time Tom and Jerry have been given equal parts on the stage,
there is little time left for the audience to read the programme
notes, let alone the basic texts. Teachers of Politics are far
from being the worst sinners in this respect, but it is particularly
odd that we so commonly overstructure in terms of time when, in the
nature of politics, it is recognized that we live in a world of
conflicting values, interests and choices. Why is it that we are
often so indecisive and indulgent concerning the sheer quantity of
matter than can be formally taught; and are so poor at making up
our minds about what really are the basic concepts of the subject
that have to be discussed, debated, shown how they vary from book

to book? Why do we so often wade through all that infinite
accretion of facts about political institutions which are far
better taken from books than from lecture notes?

If we had more concern about teaching methods in the universities, even in the very broad and simple sense of trying to define
general aims rather than just adding-on sub-subjects, we would
almost certainly have more concern for teaching methods in the
schools; and we might discover that we had something to learn.
There are times when the tail should wag the dog. Is it not wholly
bad that youngsters straight from school, straight from their First
or Upper 2, can do a Ph.D. or a taught M.A. without any pedagogic
element or even supervized teaching experience; indeed, teaching
experience quite apart, without any break? Can any social scientist really be trusted who has had no experience of working in
the real world - the world that he studies?

We should debate what are the responsibilities of political
scientists to society. Bleak if the answer is none. I admit to
seeking almost desperately for some middle ground between the
belief that we should have no effect (because we plainly do, even
by holding such a belief) and the belief that there are those
amongst us who, as political scientists, have something unique,
some technique or *arcana imperii* to give as political advisers to
ministers: the *reductio ad absurdum*.

My main worry is, however, that we are not willing to take
seriously enough the importance of our practising politics ourselves and of our thinking in a political way for the general civilized, cultural values of our society. We are too diffident. So
many of the non-political things that everyone values depend upon
getting political things reasonably right; so we should seek to
have more influence in general education. The need is obvious,
for there is a political philistinism among British intellectuals
which is every bit as chronic as cultural philistinism. For reasons that I do not fully understand, French, German and American
intellectuals will commonly own to some interest in politics, some
knowledge of political ideas and theories in a way which is far,
far more rare among English intellectuals (and I am not impressed,
either, by the myth that English intellectuals were once much more
politicized in the 1930s; indeed, to the extent that a few were
then heavily committed, indeed over-committed, it was almost a
reflection of their lack of political culture that they went so
far and then pulled right out). Our diffidence as political
scientists to pursue political education may have had a very simple
connection with the politics of establishing Politics as a university subject and an independent department in the immediate post-
war era. For particularly in civic universities, a subject was
held to consist either in x-1 of Honours examination papers (the
one being any old subsidiary subject going, which was then held
to be a sufficient sacrifice to 'general education'); or else a
definite and substantial proportion of a combined degree or a

joint Honours degree. Almost everywhere those teaching Politics
sought to establish themselves as fully - and hence as isolated -
as anyone. It was like the doctrine of autarchy in international
relations. But just suppose that the price for a more general
intrusion of political thinking into education could be, now that
the subject is respectable and established, a retreat from the
claim to be a full or part degree subject like any other. Certainly Politics when taught broadly can be as good a general education as any other. But that is not quite the point. And equally
certainly the practical case is stronger in some other subjects as
to why they should command the students' time all but exclusively.
That is not quite the point either. The point is whether we dare
say that no student should go out from the University into the
world of occupation, employment and political decisions without
some smattering of a political education. Is it fanciful to
think we might want to trade the prestige of an Honours for a
few small, but important, political elements in other subjects for
everyone or many to be, in a word, the universal super-subsidiary?
Certainly it is sad to see that so many Social Studies or General
Studies Departments set up in Polytechnics and Technical Colleges,
in the days of the 'bridge the two cultures' snowstorm, have now
achieved independence and their own degree; and hence isolation.

Such an argument raises two embarrassing questions that we
should be prepared to face (at least on these grim anniversary
occasions). Firstly, why is so little credit commonly given to
those few who actually specialize in teaching 'Subsidiary Politics'?
Have we not got peculiar reasons for refusing to accept the universal hypocrisy that every university teacher, amid so many universities (too many to fit this ideal definition), can also make
'original contributions to the advancement of knowledge' - or
whatever the Terms of Service say? Secondly, what would we all
want to put into such a course if we all knew that, say, ten lectures and five classes were all the formal teaching in Politics
that people were going to get, but that nearly everyone was going
to get it? This is perhaps the kind of thing that should occasionally be discussed, quite as much as written about, at conferences -
rather than so many of those ghastly and time-wasting rituals of
listening to learned papers that are better read, papers heavily
defended by barbed-wire and minefields, quite beyond the point of
discussion or criticism, fit only for print, built-in fillibusters
to prevent any attempt for us to pass below the salt, each one
of us among the others, to discuss the seemingly taboo subjects of
the aims and objects of our teaching - indeed of our whole subject.
We would then recognize that we all, amid the vaunted uniqueness
of every university department, have, of course, much the same
problems.

Political literacy

Let me at least describe something that is being worked out for

trial in schools by a working party of teachers and the educationalists as a 'Programme for Political Education'[6] The ideas
might be of some use to the university teacher, or might interest
him for the very basic conceptual problem involved. For it is,
after all, around the elementary assumptions of a subject that
great mistakes or advances are made; with the greatest respect
to whoever it hurts, any learned fool can after a sufficient number
of years'training work at an advanced level. Graeme Moodie once
suggested that 'politeracy' should be seen as the most general
object of political education. I prefer to talk about 'political
literacy' (slightly more literate), but the paternity of the term
is clear, although the elaboration might now amaze and dismay its
innocent inventor.[7]

     Political literacy is to be seen as a compound of knowledge,
skills and attitudes to be developed together, each conditioning
the other. Straight away one sees that the school cannot limit
itself simply to knowledge, although one doubts very much whether
the effect of studying politics at university is simply cognitive;
in any case, some subjects have to develop skills and do so very
well, and several are aware - particularly medicine at the moment
- that attitudes, indeed values, must be discussed, alternatives
demonstrated, criteria pondered. Knowledge alone, then, was rejected by the working party as an object of political education
in schools, but so was participation - though some teachers hold
a fashionable fierceness in this respect. But 'participation
how?' and 'participation for what?' always have to be asked. The
politically literate person must be one who can use his knowledge,
or at least see how it could be used and have a proclivity for
using it; a pupil should be given opportunities for applying it,
or the opportunities that they themselves sieze should be analysed
and aided. Equally his or her desire to participate must be informed by as much knowledge of what he or she is going into and
of what consequences are likely to follow from actions as is
needed to make participation effective. All actions affect others,
so he or she must be aware of what effect actions are likely to
have, and then also to be able to justify them. Better than teaching responsibility is to demonstrate effects; that there are no
purely'self-regarding' actions in politics. Some consistency, both
in explaining consequences and in justifications, must be assumed.
Hence to that extent, but to that extent alone, a politically literate person will show some consistency and subtlety in the use of
political concepts. But the concepts are likely to be drawn from
everyday life and language: a politically literate person may be
quite innocent of the more technical vocabulary of the social sciences. (Derived from the social sciences, one can certainly conceive,
as it were, an advanced literacy which would put far more stress
on genuine explanation rather than on practical understanding and
ability to participate; but this is simply not the primary concern
of the teachers.) One may think that a politically literate person
needs to know what the main issues are in contemporary politics
as he himself is affected, and will need to know how to set about

informing himself further about the main arguments employed and how to criticize the relevance or worth of the evidence on which they are based; and he will need as much, but no more, knowledge of institutional structure as he needs to understand, first, the issues and the plausibility of rival policies; and, second, how to defend and obtain his rights within the system - but the latter without the former is, indeed, mere ameliorative quietism. To summarize: 'A politically literate person will then know what the main political disputes are about; what beliefs the main contestants have of them; how they are likely to affect him, and he will have a predisposition to try to do something about it in a manner at once affective and respectful of the sincerity of others.'(8)

Now, for the university teacher, it would be nice if he could assume that such political literacy already existed in society and in the schools so that he could treat it as a prerequisite. He could then begin his explanatory and scientific study or his political philosophy and analyses of complex concepts upon the basis of such knowledge - and he might grudgingly recognize that skills and attitudes as well as knowledge can be quite helpful too. But we know that this is not the case. We are in a constant state in British education, because of the vast varieties of choices available both in what schools do at all and in the many syllabuses in the various subjects, of having to mount rescue operations for what we all believe should have been done earlier - even the primary school teacher curses the neglect in the home(9). We cannot even assume by 17+ (let alone for the mass of school leavers) even a simple familiarity with current affairs. This has an immediate consequence for a genuine university education in politics; It means that a large element of contemporary history is a necessary part of the course, but a contemporary history designed to bring out what the student of politics regards as the most important political problems and to deal with them, using the terms, concepts and theories with which he is familiar - in other words, it will have to be done by ourselves.

A school cannot ignore attitudes, some responsibility for shaping or sustaining those that are necessary for political participation and literacy. From the school level, any attempt to turn such a brief specification of political literacy into a curriculum immediately faces the problem of whether the teacher expects all the time in the world: in other words has a subject slot on the timetable over two years at least, which gives him time to *cover* the subject; or whether he realizes that even if he could do this he will inevitably reach but few people, and anyway might better give a good deal of his time to developing small modules of basic concepts and problem materials that could enhance political literacy, even in a very small compass of time, wherever political aspects of other subjects occur. Politics occurs in History all the time and in aspects of Geography and Social Studies. But above all it occurs in English. In English so many political, social and moral problems are raised. They are raised obviously in relation to certain texts, like *Animal Farm* and *The Lord of the Flies*, which may not be compulsory as yet, but which are, in fact, nearly universal for the 15+ school-leavers[10]. Less obviously, yet of more social importance, materials about political and social problems, commonly published in multi-media form or assembled by individual teachers or in the new teachers' resource centres, are used with lower ability or attainment levels and with industrial day-release students in Further Education as stimulants to interest and effort in the great, good and primary fight to enhance 'use of English'.

This is why the teacher will almost inevitably want to begin with a particular political problem or issue, but to treat it in such a way that it might be able to illustrate the general nature of politics or, more comprehensively, to enhance political literacy. Seldom will he have what is to him the relative luxury of setting out some conventional view of the whole 'subject' and then showing how it can be applied. The weakness of this kind of teaching has been, as in General, Liberal, or Social Studies, a tendency to jump frantically from one damn problem to another; from crime, abortion, political violence to the United Nations, with no particular system in mind or end view - almost as poor a political education as newspapers[11]. The strength is greater when handled more systematically in that it can appeal to the imagination of the pupil or student far more, and lead him into learning what are the main concepts and doctrines of politics and about institutional forms and restraints, rather than simply having them taught to him. And if the formal structure of the subject is ever applied to actual political problems in any systematic way in universities, it is more often by luck or by the initiative of the students than by design.

Where the teacher of politics in schools could be much helped by the university or polytechnic teacher, is in the provision of refresher courses and of materials, but to do both well means knowing something of the level, mixing much more with teachers and their teachers. For example, there is the very simple, but technical and quite tricky business, of specifying various reasonably objective procedures by which political problems are identified. We are all commonly rather offhand about this. It is not that our good judgment and our own consciences should not be respected; we should certainly be able to name a few of the cards in the hand ourselves as a kind of reward for slog and teaching; but we are commonly rather lazy in using the objective data that are available. And that data are often particularly difficult for the school teacher to get access or to handle. There is a wealth of reportage in the press of political opinion polls, both of voting intentions and attitudes to problems; but there are also in nearly all the major surveys over a series of years a store of open-ended responses when people are asked what *they* think the main problems are[12]. These are in published survey reports but are rarely found in school or in local public libraries. The limitations,

even perhaps dangers, of such procedures as a way of defining
what problems go into the curriculum are obvious. But so long as
they are obvious, so are some of the advantages. The school teacher is, not surprisingly, under far more constraint than the
university teacher about what branches of a subject he teaches,
sometimes about how he teaches it. Head teachers and officials of
local education authorities can be genuinely worried not so much
that teachers raise and discuss political issues in their
classes, but worried as to how they decide what are the issues -
gross bias is as often on the level of deciding what the problems
are as in a one-sided and totally unemphatic approach(13). The
manifestos of the political parties are now readily available
over a long period of time; but that alone would also be a curious
method of deciding what real political issues are. Public opinion
surveys. The same comment goes. There have been too few dull
but systematic content-analyses of newspapers to see what the
press think the main issues are; and these are genuinely useful
to the teacher. It is crude and as commonsensical as that if there
were three sources available, the teacher could then accept as
legitimate those 'problems' occurring on all three lists. There
is no particular reason, to my mind, why particular political
problems - housing, immigration, inflation or whatever - should
not be named even in formal GCE examination syllabuses, if the
procedures of choice can be specified and justified. The difficulties are purely technical ones of the time it takes to change
syllabuses and of the machinery for announcing that minor changes
are being made.

An attempt to specify how any political issue or problem could
be studied so as to enhance political literacy is expressed in the
following two diagrams(14). These diagrams may seem to some univ-
ersity-isolated minds both crude and over-schematic. The reply is
not merely that for secondary education one needs simplified
structures, but that for any level of political education it is
more likely that there will be effective discovery, innovation,
freedom of discussion within some definite intellectual structure
than within what is all too often the dab and flounder anarchy
of every conceivable sub-division of the subject being offered and
being taught in a different way, and not even with a single
genuinely introductory core course. Furthermore, I would argue
that the actual chain of reasoning in these two diagrams is a
sensible one. Somebody who becomes aware of all these factors
and could develop these skills would be a politically literate
person. Personally I am more keen on the eighteen or twenty-one
separate factors than on the general headings and the sealing wax
that is supposed to hold or pull all the strings together - but
that is probably a matter of taste more than intellectual method.
(Nothing should seem to suggest that 'effective participation' or
'political democracy' is guaranteed by any particular process of
reasoning or education. There's even a lot of luck in it. It is
simply the rational best we can do.)

A Specification of Political Literacy

Perception of issues

Perception of different responses, policies and conflicts

Relevant knowledge

Self-interest and social responsibility

Action Skills

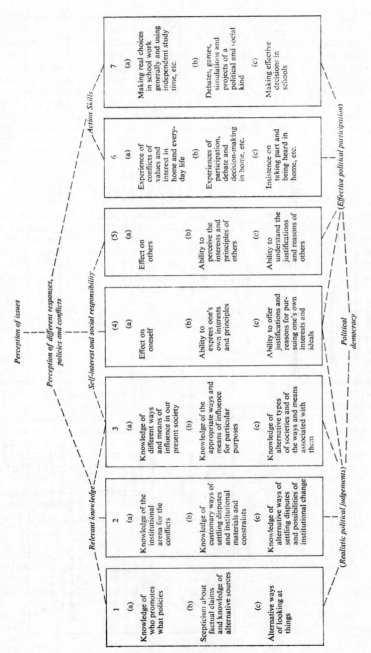

1

(a) Knowledge of who promotes what policies

(b) Scepticism about factual claims and knowledge of alternative sources

(c) Alternative ways of looking at things

2

(a) Knowledge of the institutional arena for the conflicts

(b) Knowledge of customary ways of settling disputes and institutional materials and constraints

(c) Knowledge of alternative ways of settling disputes and possibilities of institutional change

3

(a) Knowledge of different ways and means of influence in our present society

(b) Knowledge of the appropriate ways and means of influence for particular purposes

(c) Knowledge of alternative types of societies and of the ways and means associated with them

4

(a) Effect on oneself

(b) Ability to express one's own interests and principles

(c) Ability to offer justifications and reasons for pursuing one's own interests and ideals

5

(a) Effect on others

(b) Ability to perceive the interests and principles of others

(c) Ability to understand the justifications and reasons of others

6

(a) Experience of conflicts of values and interest in home and everyday life

(b) Experiences of participation, debate and decision-making in home, etc.

(c) Insistence on taking part and being heard in home, etc.

7

(a) Making real choices in school work generally and using independent study time, etc.

(b) Debates, games, simulations and projects of a political and social kind

(c) Making effective decisions in schools

(Realistic political judgements)

Political democracy

(Effective political participation)

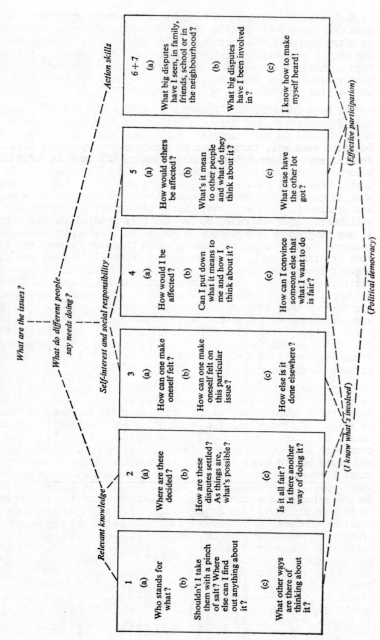

A Specification of Political Literacy
Simplified Diagram for Classroom

What are the issues?

What do different people say needs doing?

Action skills

Self-interest and social responsibility

Relevant knowledge

1

(a) Who stands for what?

(b) Shouldn't I take them with a pinch of salt? Where else can I find out anything about it?

(c) What other ways are there of thinking about it?

2

(a) Where are these decided?

(b) How are these disputes settled? As things are, what's possible?

(c) Is it all fair? Is there another way of doing it?

3

(a) How can one make oneself felt?

(b) How can one make oneself felt on this particular issue?

(c) How else is it done elsewhere?

4

(a) How would I be affected?

(b) Can I put down what it means to me and how I think about it?

(c) How can I convince someone else that what I want to do is fair?

5

(a) How would others be affected?

(b) What's it mean to other people and what do they think about it?

(c) What case have the other lot got?

6 + 7

(a) What big disputes have I seen, in family, friends, school or in the neighbourhood?

(b) What big disputes have I been involved in?

(c) I know how to make myself heard!

(I know what's involved)

(Political democracy)

(Effective participation)

Such a specification can be applied at almost any level. Children are capable of handling abstract concepts far earlier than is often supposed,[15] although there may be other educational and social priorities greater in the early age groups. It is more than a whimsy that political puberty is not reached much beyond that variable time when children begin to read the front half as well as the back sections of the newspapers.

The need for political literacy is a general need for a whole school population, but there is nothing to stop such a concept being applied to the A-levels. For in any case, few A-levels in Politics seem well thought out as university preparatory work. Few, if any, universities actually require GCE work in Politics before studying Politics for a degree. Most departments would surely welcome a greater political literacy rather than the somewhat long odds that the particular GCE syllabus which the pupil has studied is what will slot neatly into their own first year syllabuses. (In any case, no one has ever studied whether there is any congruence between GCE A-levels and first-year university courses, indeed no one has ever given a thorough 'across the board' look at either level, let alone compared them.) Perhaps our very neglect leaves the schools in a freer position in this respect. Politics departments do not make those precise demands that the sciences, and even Geography and History, make upon schools; and nor have we that dubious feeling almost of mission with which some economists and sociologists try to extend or try to get into the sixth forms. (It is only fair to add, however, that economists are having second thoughts, many of them openly preferring candidates who have done Maths in sixth form to those who have done Economics without Maths.)

If, indeed, one were to explore school studies intended to be preparatory to university, I would have to admit to some scepticism about their value in our case. There is still too much learning of rules and procedures of something called 'the British Constitution', mirroring a long-dead style of university teaching; and even with some of the better GCE syllabuses there are many of us who would not be too unhappy for universities to have to start from scratch in teaching all of the social sciences; or who might be more happy with something like the combination of social sciences to the value of one Advanced level which the Scottish system has in 'Modern Studies'. (As usual, England has a lot to learn from Scottish education.) In my own experience as a persistent teacher in the first year both at London School of Economics and at Sheffield, where the standard of entrants was high, it was rarely any advantage for a student to have taken 'British Constitution' at school, even from one of the improved syllabuses, often a handicap. I admit that this is a subjective assessment based on no research, even the simplest study of A-levels as a predictor of university performance in Politics has not been done. My hunch is that a student is best prepared, in our present ludicrously over-specialized sixth form, if he has done History, English and either

Maths or a modern language, depending on what kind of Politics
he wants to study. Essex, Strathclyde and Lancaster must demand
more numeracy; Manchester, Glasgow and London School of Economics
must demand more literacy. An interest in politics might more
naturally spring from an old friend, Current Affairs, which should,
in any case, be a prominent part of secondary education throughout,
especially if a minimum political literacy for all was adopted as
a goal. The tendency of the universities to try to get schools
to do their work for them is deplorable. The social sciences
should not enter into a competitive race, both with themselves
and with other subjects, for compulsory prerequisities; for one
thing, this perverts the purposes of secondary education, and for
another it is quite unnecessary; the social sciences are popular
enough already, despite the absence of prerequisite requirements
and offerings in the schools on like scale to the old, established
school subjects. If I were handling admissions I would say: 'one
social science A-level, good; two, dubious, three deplorable.' No
tabula is completely *rasa*, but I preferred to start from scratch
as regards any disciplinary assumptions or *Wissenschaftlich*
knowledge in the First Year.

So we political scientists should not 'get into A-level' on a
larger scale, rather that we should be interested in the general
political education of secondary schools at all levels and as a
component part of many subjects because it is important in its
own right and because it is important in the public interest, not
as a feeder to the university Moloch.

If it were done at all, it must be well done. The starting
point is all-important. The starting point surely has to be the
nature of political activity itself, that in all societies known
to history some differences of interest exist, even in the simplest
tribal societies with minimal government and even in the most complex and suppressive totalitarian regimes. Only if it is accepted
that it is natural for men to differ about interests and ideals
and that it is possible for them, in many circumstances, to so
differ and yet co-exist, is the basis both for the reasonably
objective study and for the reasonably tolerant practice of politics assured - otherwise the whole study can easily be bent, as
some students eagerly expect, to seeing how politics can be overcome; just as some students turn to economics in the hope of discovering how scarcity can be overcome. Such an abstract starting
point is necessary, because there is a very concrete entailment.
If politics is the recognition and tolerance of diversity, so must
be a political or civic education[16]. We wonder that the young,
in a growingly complicated and less and less confident society,
sometimes want to rebel against, but are more often merely cynical
about, teaching which simply asserts *the* values of their society,
the consensus, *the* parliamentary system and *the* Constitution - or
even *the* Revolution. To have stressed deliberately 'what we have
in common' and underplayed differences is both a false account of
politics and a cripplingly dull basis for a political education.

It is extraordinary to consider how often Government and Politics
has been considered a dull and safe subject in school; perhaps
those who drew up some syllabuses simply over-reacted against obvious doubts, but over-reacted they certainly did.

Therefore the two diagrammatic explanations of 'political
literacy' stress the need to identify, even to empathize with,
a variety of viewpoints at the very first stage, and to discover
alternative sources of information, however simple. For some, this
may mean no more than looking at another newspaper from time to
time, deliberately talking politics to someone whom one knows one
will disagree with, rather than avoiding discussion in such quar-
ters: for others it will mean using alternative reference books
or developing critical faculties about textbooks and standard
authorities. But at any level, there are always some alternative
sources of information; and at any level, there are always some
perceptions of alternative viewpoints. Why should it not be fair
game actually to test and examine students not on their ability to
memorize and recall the stages of a Bill, nor to provide standard
answers to impossible constitutional riddles, but on their ability
to imagine how somebody of a specified political position would
view a certain issue, try to resolve a particular problem, and how
he would seek to justify himself?

Basic concepts

The teacher of politics in school, unlike the teacher of
politics in university, will more often be on his own, will have
a sense that he has little time in which to do something very
difficult, and will have a greater - if sometimes needlessly exag-
gerated and worrying - sense of responsibility; for he believes,
wrongly or rightly, that he can have an effect on the attitudes
of a pupil. Perhaps only the hardiest or the most obtuse of us
in the universities now think we can have, let alone should have,
much effect on the attitudes of our students. This means that
it is much more important for the individual school teacher to be
clear what he is doing. At a university department or a polytechnic we can always hedge. We can either be terribly strong-
minded and committed, either politically or methodologically
(sometimes both), or we can toddle along for ever in a delicious
academic dither of indecision about nearly everything, but in both
cases feeling fairly confident that there is safety in numbers -
that if the ball slips through our fingers, someone else will pick
it up.

So it is not any desire for an over-schematic pedantry, but very
sensible considerations, that leads the school teacher to ask such
embarrassing things as '*What* basic concepts should we teach?' I
would like to put that cat among the pigeons. The request is
frightening, but it is sensible. It calls our bluff. It is a
challenge that the political philosopher should be willing to take

up. He is likely to be more helpful in what is wanted in secondary education, more close to ordinary language, than is the political sociologist with his special vocabularies and scientific
concepts. And the political sociologist, despite all he has had
to say about socialization (often hinting that it is a bad thing),
usually has simply studied the attitudes of children to concepts
imposed on them, for the sake of the questionnaire of the depth
interview, by the sociologist himself. Very rarely has anyone
adopted the techniques of the anthropologist to try to produce accounts of what are, in fact, the concepts used by children in
political discussion, in disputes generally, or in situations analogous to political ones[17].

In fact, I doubt if it is possible simply to build up from
observed primary concepts-as-perceptions and then try to sharpen
them, tighten them, reconcile them to the concepts-as-explanation
of a tradition or a discipline. Certainly we need to build up
from what it is *possible* for the child to perceive and from his
own experiences; but his indigenous concepts are likely to be
too limited to prepare him for the real political world. Some
kind of compromise has to be struck between the derived concepts
of the discipline, reaching down and being simplified, and the
primary concepts of the lore and language of school children
reaching up and being sharpened and extended.

The political philosopher should be able to say to the school
teachers, here is my (reasonably authoritative) suggestion as to
a minimal set of concepts which would provide a language for
understanding the political world; but he would be able to do
this better and would be listened to more respectfully if he were
willing to make some acquaintance with the little literature there
is, much of it in Educational and Social Psychology, about concept-
formation, even the few empirical studies of what concepts children
actually use in argument. In the end, quite crudely, almost
any starting point is better than none. We should be bold and prescribe, and leave to the educationalists the devising or procedures for monitoring the effectiveness, in terms of specified criteria, of teaching based on such concepts. (Again, we are amateurs
in methods of assessment, using few, and using them ritualistic-
ally.)

This is not to argue, quite the contrary, that political philosophy can be introduced into schools - that is quite a different
question. Political philosophy must surely be concerned with
criteria for making judgments and with truth conditions - very
difficult matters indeed. But before one can be sensibly concerned
with truth, one must have established meaning. The primary concern
of the political philosopher may not be relevant, but he has an
essential secondary skill: sensitivity and accuracy, one hopes, in
the use of concepts. He *should* be concerned, like an intellectual
historian, in discovering what concepts are actually used. My
main complaint about the linguistic school of political philosophy

is not the technique as such, but that all too often their idea
of what constitutes usage is extremely limited, random, even
eccentric; rarely do they make serious attempts to discover what
terms actors in political events and ordinary people actually
use, how consistently they use them, or what precisely they mean
by them. The kind of work that Pocock and Quentin Skinner have
done in the 17th century needs to be done in our own society,
particularly among the mass of people who would have to be talked
to, perhaps even - strange suggestion - lived amongst, before
their concepts would become clear; for the bias is obvious if all
such studies were based purely on the written word. This is both
intellectually interesting and politically important. There are
interesting books and articles on the logic of political argument;
but no one seems concerned to do the social anthropologists'
work for us of establishing just what are the terms of ordinary
political rhetoric and argument and how they are used. One can
stop a long way short of Basil Bernstein's somewhat paradoxical
view about mutually incomprehensible language codes, and yet
still realize that many of our political and educational problems
appear so insoluble because many leaders no longer know how to
talk to those who they would have follow them. Certainly not to
assume that the fault is always a fear of speaking above the heads
of the general population, for often when talking with ordinary
people, surprisingly illiterate ordinary people, one hears a rage
that '*they* are talking down to us'. The problem is the general
breakdown in the political ruling classes of any clear sense of
what concepts ordinary people use and what they mean by them, so
that sometimes politicians overshoot, sometimes they undershoot,
but more often they undershoot simply because of their uncertainty.

It should be possible to suggest concepts that are basic, that
is those perceptions from which others could be derived and on
which theories, generalizations, explanations and moral judgments
can be based, but to be clear that they are not necessarily the
most important. They are simply the primary ones. For example,
'Democracy' is plainly one of the most important concepts used
in contemporary political discourse. It also happens to be one
of the most inherently unclear, simply because it is a compound of
more basic concepts: liberty, equality, representation; sometimes
rights and even justice (almost anything) can be built into the
definition. Plainly it is not much use asking 'what is *the* definition of Democracy?', for straight away one is presented with a wealth
of theories and doctrines about what should be done or how things
should be done. We don't abandon such questions entirely, both
the language and popular expectation hardly allow us to, but
the only rational way to hold such discussions is by attempting to
gain some prior agreement about the meaning of the other concepts
involved if we were to unpack the complex concept. Perhaps for
advanced-level pupils or students it is sensible to begin with complex, compound concepts like Democracy and to 'unpack' them, to
work backwards to their component elements; but with earlier ages

and lesser ability levels, it is surely better to begin at the
beginning.

Again, it may not only be the schools who need to realize the
advantages of beginning with an explicitly conceptual approach.
Consider both the tendency of political thought to degenerate into
a kind of strange 'facts plus learned definitions' history of
political thought, and of institutions to be studied 'purely
descriptively' in almost complete innocence that horrendous assumptions are being made by the very naming of parts right at the
beginning. Are we 'a system of *parliamentary government*' indeed?
We cannot perceive and think other than in concepts. Concepts
are, as it were, the building blocks with which we construct a
picture of the external world, including imaginary or hopeful
worlds. The concepts are not true or false, they simply help us
to perceive and to communicate.[18]

By a 'conceptual approach' I do not necessarily mean that the
concepts themselves should be taught directly. By a conceptual
approach I mean only to accentuate the obvious, that we think and
perceive in concepts, and to eliminate the negative, that we do
not directly perceive 'institutions' or 'rules' - these are
imposed upon us, taught to us, or gradually become clear to us as
patterns of behaviour, as specific structurings of relational concepts. Any cluster of concepts that we may suggest should not
constitute the skeleton of a curriculum, unless for some advanced
level indeed, but are rather for the teacher to have in mind and to
elaborate upon when the occasion arises, whatever kind of materials
or syllabus he is using. The teacher will be better able to help
the pupil or relate the disparate problems and issues of the political world if he or she has some sketch map, at least, of basic
concepts. Even a false one might be *almost* better than none at
all. I think it is possible to find a basic family of concepts
of a kind that occur in everyday language that could lead on and
in to, if the occasion arises, the more special vocabularies of
political science and political philosophy. But I am very sceptical that there is sufficient agreement as to what constitutes the
core of political studies as a discipline for it to be possible,
as it were, to miniaturize it for schools[19], to follow the
celebrated dictum of J.S. Bruner (which is the basic presupposition
of 'Nuffield Science') that 'any subject can be taught effectively
in some intellectually honest form to any child at any stage of
development'[20]. Perhaps the two rival international consortia
for political science will take up the challenge (at a half-
price entrance fee); but I doubt if it would be worth the effort -
or rather it would be doing something strange for political
science without doing much for political education. Political
science itself might even be better off for a greater underpinning
of political education. I recently suggested to some teachers
involved in curriculum development a diagram such as this and elaborated it in a working paper.(* p.191) May I thus expose my
naivete, or panic others to try to do better? But some such things

should be offered, observed and discussed.

Perhaps all I am really doing on this 25th Anniversary occasion
is making a rather awful personal confession that I am a bit fed
up with *political science* and am more interested in political
education - in my rather common sense sense of it. Since we are
not a discipline but a problem-area parasitic upon other disciplines, mainly History and Philosophy, we might as well try to act
like a parasite rather than an elephant: give up the claim for
an exclusive domain, our own palace graveyard, but buzz and sting
promiscuously everywhere, searching out the political implications
of (and within) so many other subjects, particularly in the
schools. I had though of writing a kind of characterization and
vindication of the 'British school of political studies' as against
the American: the awkwardness of our traditional 'institutions' and
(considered separately) 'ideas' approach; but our greater scepticism about general explanations and our commonsense assumptions
that, of course, theory and practice are related, hence our
ability to move easily between 'evidence' and 'relevance' and to
refuse the procrustean alternatives of value-free Science or
total commitment: understanding not explanation, relevance but not
commitment. But access to Whitehall and Town Halls is, in the
long run, pretty superficial compared with the importance of access
to political education in the schools. Here we in Great Britain
are the backward ones, despite the fact that we are now learning
a grim national lesson in the folly of our old beliefs that if the
elites are tolerant, beneficent and 'get it right', the education
of the masses, and our university concern in it, can be minimal.
Is politics only for *elites* and political education only, if at
all, for the universities? This should not be so and we can no
longer afford to let it be so. We should follow the example of
the new West German universities and make political education a
part of the curriculum. This is, of course, no dull or small proposal. It is an important - or dangerous, some will feel - proposition about the entailments for practice of a certain kind of theory.

---

* Then followed the diagram of concepts and definitions already
   reproduced above at the end of my second essay in section two,
   and that essay is the working paper referred to here. See p.111.

NOTES

1. Very little, if anything, has been written recently on this
subject in Great Britain compared with the United States and
Western Germany. W.A. Robson's interesting section of Great
Britain in his *The University Teaching of the Social Sciences:
Political Science*, (UNESCO), 1954) is now, of course, dated. But
mainly at the school level there is D.B. Heater *The Teaching of
Politics* (Methuen Educational, 1969) - which began the new interest in the subject; also his 'Politics as a University Discipline
and Political Education in Schools', in this book; H. Entwistle,
Political Education in a Democracy, (Routledge and Kegan Paul,
1972); and T. Brennan, *A Handbook for Teachers of Politics*
(Longmans, 1974). Also the journal, *Teaching Politics*, edited by
D.B. Heater (Longmans), is now in its third year. Our four or
five university journals of politics rarely, if ever, have articles on curricula and teaching methods. Perhaps R.A. Chapman's
Teaching Public Administration (R.I.P.A., 1973) is an interesting
exception.

2. The irrelevance of most political socialization research to
education is shown in H. Entwistle (1974); and in R.W. Connell
(1971) especially pages 228-235.

3. See Chapter 2, 'Citizenship and national expansion' in my
The American Science of Politics, (1959).

4. See H.G. Assel (1970).

5. Their set book G. Lewis and D.P. Potter (1974) is an excellent
example.

6. Although the interpretations that follow are my own, they arise
from the work of the new Programme for Political Education, jointly
sponsored by the Hansard Society and the Politics Association, with
support from the Nuffield Foundation.

7. See G. Moodie (1973). But perhaps 'politeracy' does immediately convey, better than 'political literacy', the connotation
of 'able to act politically'. Only at York can Politics and
Education be combined as a first degree.

8. Document No. 2 of the Programme for Political Education, paragraphs 2 and 3.

9. J.P. White (1973) shows another alternative: less compulsory
education, more voluntary, but more unity in the smaller compulsory component.

10. See M. Whitebrook (1974).

11. This has been characteristic, alas, both of the General Studies
Project (for Sixth Forms) materials, published by Longman from the
Resources Unit, York, and the famous Humanities Project kits
sponsored by the Schools Council.

12. But L.J. Macfarlane's *Issues in British Politics Since 1945*
(part of a new A-level series) goes further than anything else I
know in specifying how and why he picks the problems that he does;
and Paper 5 of the Programme for Political Education by Alex
Porter and Robert Stradling provides general guidelines.

13. See generally on bias I.A. Snook (1972a), and his own short
book for teachers (1972b). Two important essays could not be included in the smyposium, J. Wilson (1964) and R.M. Hare (1964).

14. Taken from Document No. 2 of the Programme for Political
Education.

15. Jean Piaget's classic, *Six Psychological Studies* is a perfectly
sensible and accessible book. See especially L. Kohlberg, 'State
and sequence: the cognitive developmental approach to socialization' in D.A. Goslin (Ed), *Handbook of Socialization Theory and
Research* (Rand McNally, 1969); J.L. Tapp and L. Kohlberg, 'Developing senses of law and legal justice', *The Journal of Social Issues*,
27:2 (1971), p.69; J. Adelson and R.P. O'Neil, 'Growth of political
ideas in adolescence: the sense of community', *Journal of Personality and Social Psychology*, 4:3 (1966); J. Adelson, 'The political
imagination of the young adolescent', *Daedalus*, 100:4 (1971);
J. Gallatin and J. Adelson, 'Legal guarantees of individual freedom: a cross-national study of the development of political
thought', *The Journal of Social Issues*, 27:2 (1971); and R.W.
Connell op. cit., the first full-length study to have emancipated
itself from structural-functionalist assumptions of political
socialization research and to have looked more to social and
educational psychology.

16. A recent A-level book that does this admirably is W.N. Coxall,
(1973).

17. See R.W. Connell (1971). I think generally of the kind of
approach that Ernest Gellner would have us adopt. See Gellner
(1973) Chapter 2, 'Concepts and society'.

18. See I.C. Jarvie (1972), but also Sir Karl Popper's (1969)
powerful warning or reminder that concepts are only concepts, they
are not theories, they are not themselves knowledge.

19. Derek Heater (1973) has tried very plausibly to read 'the
mainstream' of the discipline back into school levels.

20. J.S. Bruner (1960) page 33.

REFERENCES

ASSEL, H.G. (1970), *Ideologie und Ordnung als Probleme politischer
Bildung*, Ehrenwirth Verlag.

BRENNAN, T. (1974), *A Handbook for Teachers of Politics*, London:
Longman.

BRUNER, J.S. (1960), *The Process of Education*, Harvard: Harvard University Press.

CHAPMAN, R.A. (1973), *Teaching Public Administration*, R.I.P.A.

COXALL, W.N. (1973), *Politics: Compromise and Conflict in a Liberal Democracy*, London: Pergamon Press.

CRICK, B. (1959), *The American Science of Politics*, London: Routledge and Kegan Paul.

ENTWISTLE, H. (1972),*Political Education in a Democracy*, London: Routledge and Kegan Paul.

GELLNER, E. (1973), 'Concepts and society' in E. Gellner, *Cause and Meaning in the Social Sciences*, London: Routledge and Kegan Paul.

HARE, R.M. (1964), 'Adolescents into adults', in H.B. Hollins (Ed), *Aims in Education: The Philosophic Approach*, Manchester: Manchester University Press.

HEATER, D.B. (1969), *The Teaching of Politics*, London: Methuen Educational.

JARVIE, I.C. (1972), *Concepts and Society*, London: Routledge and Kegan Paul.

LEWIS, G. and POTTER, D.C. (Eds) (1974), *The Practice of Comparative Politics*, London: Longman.

MacFARLANE, L.J. (1975), *Issues in British Politics Since 1945*, London: Longman.

MOODIE, G. (1973), Some problems of political education, *Teaching Politics*, May

POPPER, Sir. K. (1969), *Conjectures and Refutations* (Third Edition) London: Routledge and Kegan Paul.

ROBSON, W.A. (1954), *The University Teaching of the Social Sciences: Political Science*, Paris: UNESCO.

SNOOK, I.A. (1972a), *Concepts of Indoctrination: Philosophical Essays*, London: Routledge and Kegan Paul.

SNOOK, I.A. (1972b), *Indoctrination and Education*, London: Routledge and Kegan Paul.

WHITE, J.P. (1973), *Towards a Compulsory Curriculum*, London: Routledge and Kegan Paul.

WHITEBROOK, M. (1974), Literature and the teaching of politics, *Teaching Politics*, May and September.

WILSON, J. (1964),'Education and indoctrination', in H.B. Hollins (Ed), *Aims in Education: The Philosophic Approach*, Manchester: Manchester University Press.

The Authors

BERNARD CRICK is Professor of Politics and Head of the Department
of Politics and Sociology at Birkbeck College, London University.
He obtained a first-class honours degree in Economics from
University College London in 1950; then his Ph.D. at LSE. He did
postgraduate work at LSE and Harvard, lectured at LSE from 1957 to
1966, and was Professor of Politics at Sheffield from 1966 to 1972.
Professor Crick was President of the Politics Association from
1969 to 1976 and is Chairman of the Programme for Political Education. He is joint editor of *Political Quarterly* and his previous
publications include *The American Science of Politics* (1959),
In Defence of Politics (1962), *The Reform of Parliament* (1964 and
Political Theory and Practice (1973).

DEREK HEATER read History at University College, London and taught
in the RAF, in schools and at Brighton College of Education. He
is now Head of the Humanities Department and Dean of the Faculty of
Social and Cultural Studies at Brighton Polytechnic. He has been
particularly active in promoting political education: he was the
Founder-Chairman of the Politics Association and is now the editor
of its journal, *Teaching Politics*. He has written numerous articles
on the teaching of contemporary affairs, the most recent and substantial of which are reprinted in this volume. He has also
published the following books: *Political Ideas in the Modern World*
(1960), *Order and Rebellion: A History of Europe in the Eighteenth
Century* (1964), *The Cold War* (1965), (Editor) *The Teaching of
Politics* (1969), (with Gwyneth Owen) *World Affairs* (1973), *Contemporary Political Ideas* (1974), and *Britain and the Outside World*
(1976).

INDEX
Author Index

Subject Index